The Cowboy Hero and Its Audience

The Cowboy Hero and Its Audience:
Popular Culture as Market Derived Art

by

Alf H. Walle

Bowling Green State University Popular Press
Bowling Green, OH 43403

Library of Congress Cataloging-in-Publication Data

Walle, Alf H.
    The cowboy hero and its audience : popular culture as market derived art
/ by Alf H. Walle.
        p. cm.
    ISBN 0-87972-811-6 (cloth) -- ISBN 0-87972-812-4 (pbk.)
        1. Western stories--History and criticism. 2. Cowboys in literature.
    3. Books and reading--United States--History--20th century. 4. Popular
    literature--United States--History and criticism. 5. Popular culture--
    United States--History--20th century. 6. American fiction--20th century
    --History and criticism. 7. American fiction--West (U.S.)--History and
    criticism. 8. Frontier and pioneer life in literature. 9. Western films--
    History and criticism. 10. West (U.S.)--In literature. I. Title.

    PS374.W4 W25 2000
    813'.087409-dc21

                                                        99-051870

Cover design by Dumm Art

CONTENTS

This book is dedicated to the English Department of the University at Buffalo, the professional home of many valued friends and colleagues.

ACKNOWLEDGMENTS

This book came about because I have traveled in diverse intellectual circles. When evaluating a writer whose work falls within one scholarly tradition, it is fairly easy for the reader to understand how and why a specific chain of thought has developed. During my career, in contrast, I have worked within several disciplines and, therefore, my peculiar weaving of eclectic concepts could easily confuse the reader. As a result, the primary purpose of this acknowledgment is to clearly state my background. Doing so both acknowledges debts and helps the reader to understand how I combine various chains of thought.

I began my intellectual life as an anthropology student majoring in archaeology at the University of Arizona in the 1960s. While there, I took courses in archaeological theory from Raymond Thompson, whose teaching combined a vast knowledge of archaeology with insights regarding the nature of the intellectual world. Thompson's "signature" idiosyncrasy was his insistence that students use the spelling "archaeology" instead of "archeology." Although both spellings are correct, Thompson observed that those who used the "archeology" version of the word tended to be the "new archeologists" who, he polemically asserted, had little respect for the intellectual traditions of the past. In Thompson's mind, the "archaeology" spelling represented an appreciation for one's intellectual ancestors and, therefore, he embraced the "*ae* form" as a badge of honor.

Although I do not use a specific spelling of a "pet" word as a symbol of intellectual correctness, Thompson did teach me that rival academic traditions emphasize different things and, therefore, their embrace or rejection has far-reaching implications. The attitude symbolized by Thompson's quirk is clearly reflected throughout my book.

As a graduate student, at the State University of New York at Binghamton and the University at Buffalo, I continued to work in archaeology notably with Nickolas van der Merve, Bill Lipe, and Marion White. From Lipe, I developed an interest in analyzing artifacts in order to understand the complex social and economic forces underlying them. From Marion White (and her colleague Louise Sweet with whom I took several seminars), I developed an interest in social and economic determinism. These ideas, reworked and put to new uses, have a significant role to play in the present work.

As my career developed, I began to apply the tools of economic and social determinism to living cultures, not merely to the archaeological record. The avenue by which I made this transition was through folklore, a discipline that bridges anthropology and literary criticism. Studying folklore at the University at Buffalo with Bruce Jackson, I began to merge anthropological ideas of economic determinism with the critical analysis of artifacts created by "traditional people" or "folk." Just as folklore is aligned with anthropology, it also intersects with literary criticism; these parallels eventually led to my work analyzing American literature, film, and popular culture. During this phase of my development, Leslie Fiedler was a major influence upon my thought. Ultimately, both Jackson and Fiedler were on my dissertation committee; that early document, incidentally, forms part of the intellectual foundation for this book.

After completing my training in the humanities, I earned a post-doctoral MBA in marketing and I have taught marketing on and off for the last 20 years as well as developing a publishing record in both business and the humanities. Along the way, I have received the help of numerous individuals. My first mentor within marketing is Mike d'Amico. For the most part, marketing has not been concerned with humanistic perspectives; d'Amico, however, introduced me to the work of Wroe Alderson, an eclectic scholar who, while firmly niched within the field of marketing, had a freewheeling style that meshed with my interests.

Due to my attraction to Alderson, I became friends with Donald Dixon, who introduced me to the discipline of macromarketing. Macromarketing (and related sub-disciplines such as marketing history) seeks to expand beyond the usual "customer orientation" of mainstream marketing scholarship in order to deal with the broader dimensions of the field. The paradigms and foci of these sub-disciplines have provided the avenue by which I have entered marketing as a contributing scholar. In the field of macromarketing, I am especially indebted to Chuck Goeldner, George Fisk, and Bob Nason. Without the tireless work of Stanley Hollander, it is doubtful that marketing history would have developed into the provocative sub-discipline it has become.

Still, my work needed to be connected with some of the mainstream concepts of marketing in vital and productive ways. John Ryans, an eclectic marketing scholar whose work is closely attuned to the needs of practitioners, provided a means of connecting my work with the marketing profession in ways which transcend the ivory tower.

From the sub-disciplines of marketing mentioned above (albeit viewed through the lens which Ryans provided) I developed my own idiosyncratic means of combining marketing scholarship with the humanistic disciplines. While in recent years various scholars have come to embrace aspects of the humanities within marketing and consumer research, my background stems from my work in macromarketing and marketing history coupled with my pre-existing background in the humanities. Without the leadership provided by my marketing colleagues represented by those specifically recognized above (and the thinking they represent), it is unlikely that I would have been able to achieve what I have accomplished here. Thus, although my work intersects in important ways with the current humanistic research agenda within consumer research and while much of that work is very useful, I come to the same phenomena from another intellectual tradition: merging macromarketing and marketing history with anthropology, folklore, and literary criticism.

During the 1997-98 academic year, I was able to return to the University at Buffalo English department, where I had earned my doctorate many years before. I had been away from the humanities for a long time and, as a result, my thinking was "rusty" and dated. Under these circumstances, I did not have the intellectual toolkit required to complete a book which synthesized literary criticism, popular culture scholarship, and marketing thought. Due to my year back at Buffalo, however, I was able to regain my intellectual groundings in the humanities and, thereby, successfully complete this project.

I am especially grateful to Buffalo's Bob Newman, who facilitated my being hired for the year, to Kenneth Dauber and Mark Shechner, the chairmen who administered the department during my time there, and to Milli Clark, my immediate supervisor. What could have been an interim period of thankless "adjuncting," became a year in which I was treated with the kind of unselfish camaraderie which can (and did) lead to significant intellectual achievements. While I am especially appreciative to the specific people I have singled out, I am indebted to the entire English department of the University at Buffalo for what turned out to be a most productive (and enjoyable) year. This book is my "thank you" to them all.

PREFACE

Deterministic paradigms (various theories that the world and those within it are predictably impacted by influences beyond their control) have a long and prestigious history which dates back thousands of years. The ancient Greeks and Romans, for example, were profoundly influenced by Stoic philosophy that envisions an all-powerful force (that is bigger and more powerful than the individual) and the notion that this force controls the universe and everything in it. Based on that premise, the Stoics argued that living in harmony with inevitable fate and destiny is the key to true happiness. From the time of Saint Augustine, furthermore, Christian tradition has emphasized the theory of predestination (another deterministic paradigm). During the Reformation, Protestant theologians, borrowing from Augustine, more fully developed this theory of determinism and embraced it as a keystone of their religious thought. Thus, deterministic theories have long been held in high esteem within the Western world. Besides the Western intellectual tradition, various Oriental philosophies also exhibit deterministic tendencies; thus, Taoism is based on a desire to follow the inevitable and predestined way of nature (the Tao) and to find happiness and fulfillment by accepting life and fate at face value and without blinking.

Once the impact of the industrial revolution began to be felt, new versions of determinism arose in order to deal with the implications of the socio-economic transformation being triggered by technology. The work of Karl Marx is a key example of such responses to changing circumstances. Often viewed as a controversial political figure, Marx's most far-reaching achievements are as a nonpartisan social theorist, not as a political activist. Marx theorized that influences interconnected with a society's economic system exert profound influences upon all aspects of humanity and society. As a result, the economic choices that people make inevitably transform them in profound ways.

Marx, of course, is not the only nineteenth-century advocate of economic determinism. American anthropologist Louis Henry Morgan immediately comes to mind as a parallel thinker. In Morgan's *Ancient Society* (1877), he argues that social customs (such as family structures and marriage patterns) had evolved through stages such as "promiscuity," "group marriage," "polygamy," and "monogamy." An economic determinist, Morgan theorized that economic pressures exerted influences that transformed society and its institutions.

Morgan posed his theories of economic determinism independently of Marx. Indeed, Morgan's publications on the subject predate and influenced Friedrich Engels' *Origin of the Family, Private Property, and the State* (1884, trans. 1902). This influential monograph dealt with the same subject matter as Morgan's *Ancient Society* and Engels developed an almost identical argument; Engels, furthermore, acknowledged an intellectual indebtedness to Morgan. The deterministic theories that Morgan developed, incidentally, went on to form the underpinning of Soviet anthropology; Morgan emerged as the father of Soviet anthropology because his beliefs regarding economic determinism closely parallel theories held by Marx.

As with other models which simplify reality in order to make it more easily understood, deterministic theories tend to focus on a few key variables, not all of reality. As a result, deterministic theories don't attempt to be robust and all encompassing; instead, they seek to be simple enough to be easily grasped. The process of simplification comes through a strategic process of elimination. As various of Marx's letters attest, however, he was well aware of the complexities of social life and he understood the multiple influences which impact society. Nonetheless, Marx chose to focus upon economic determinism because he felt it was a dominant force which deserved primary attention.

But this observation raises a key issue: at what point do the benefits of simplification (legitimately focusing on key variables) fall into the trap of becoming simplistic (eliminating so many variables that the model, while seductive, loses its explanatory value)? Dealing with the costs and benefits of simplification is essential when evaluating deterministic theories, such as those posed by Marx, Engels, and Morgan.

Over the years, infusing deterministic analysis with other models and variables in order to balance them has occupied much scholarly activity. Devising methods to broaden the deterministic model, revisionists attempt to more accurately depict primary causes and their impacts. These model builders often introduce additional variables into their models in order to overcome the limitations of a naive determinism. The ultimate goal is to account for all significant influences that impact the phenomena being investigated.

Strict determinists are like house-cleaners who do not have a sense of how people actually live. They want everything to be completely predictable and "in its place"; as a result, a high value is given to structure, order, and recurring patterns. The entire investigation is orchestrated around predictability and, in the process, reality gets lost.

Those who rebut determinism argue that in real life people don't really live their lives in totally predictable, structured, and predetermined ways. By analogy, the house-cleaner may complain that a client leaves a pile of books scattered around his or her easy chair. This "mess," however, is actually an artifact of life as it is actually lived; nonetheless, the unyielding house-cleaner is unable to accept people the way they really are; when deterministic theories are relaxed to acknowledge people and how they actually live, the model becomes more credible.

The flaw in the thinking of naive determinists is parallel to those of the housekeeper. Strict and unyielding laws of social and economic determinism fail to acknowledge that people do not always function in a completely orderly and predictable way; nonetheless, strict determinists prefer to theorize that they do. Thus, although deterministic models (such as that of Marx) have many contributions to make, detractors point to their tendency to oversimplify reality by not taking all of human nature (and the potentials of human response) into account.

Various scholars, of course, seek to adjust their models in order to acknowledge a range of human choice that transcends determinism. In doing so, these scholars attempt to compensate for the limitations of the model. In dealing with this dilemma, two alternatives exist. One group starts with deterministic models and then "fleshes" out the paradigm by working other influences into it. The Frankfurt school of Marxist analysis can be offered as a theory and method that strives to transcend the limitations of determinism by embracing a wider range of influences and responses.

As an alternative, some thinkers have consciously sought to transcend deterministic models, not to refine them. Modern French philosophy (existentialism, poststructuralism, and deconstructionist analysis, etc.) are examples of this initiative. The scholars who pursue these options focus on individuals and their unique responses; on occasion, furthermore, a circumscribed group, not the society at large, is investigated. When doing so, scholars argue that individual responses to the influences of the mass culture are not inevitable, predictable, or completely predetermined. Just as strict determinism is overly simplistic and needs to be tempered, those who center their investigations around the individual, in turn, needed to add deterministic perspectives in order for their method to adequately reflect reality. Thus, strict determinists typically need to concentrate more upon the individual while scholars who center upon the individual, can benefit from taking theories of social determinism into account. In both cases, the full potential of human beings as independent, thinking creatures is better and more completely acknowledged.

This monograph is a part of the longstanding intellectual tradition of "fine tuning" determinism in order to make it more useful. Like the Frankfurt school and contemporary French philosophy (and its off-shoots), my goal is to enhance a theory of social and economic determinism by making it more robust.

While earlier embellishments of determinist theory typically involve contributions from the humanities, the new materials added here were originally developed within the "applied arts." To be specific, this monograph melds aspects of social/economic determinism with concepts from the business disciplines of marketing and consumer research.

To those who look at Marx as primarily a political animal, business theory and Marxist analysis will appear to be strange bedfellows. After all, Marx was an avowed and impassioned enemy of business. When looking at the theoretic underpinnings of Marxism and business thought, however, profound similarities emerge. Business theory is, in its own way, essentially deterministic. Modern business thought (especially that stemming from marketing and consumer research) attempts to predict human response using social and economic theories. Thus, business scholars use social and economic theories to predict human response. In doing so, marketing scholars and consumer researchers meld aspects of the social and psychological sciences with their own strategically oriented research perspectives. These are deterministic models that can be usefully integrated with parallel perspectives deriving from the humanistic tradition. Since business thinkers have already found ways to merge determinism and individualism, these techniques can be readily applied to the study of popular culture.

By linking the determinist focus of business thought with classic deterministic models from the humanities, it becomes possible to employ a wealth of focused theories from consumer research that predicts how and why people behave the way they do when they embrace goods and services. And since services such as art and entertainment can be viewed as products, these business theories can be usefully applied to types of critical analysis such as that typified by popular culture scholarship. Indeed, these two research streams (one coming from the humanities, the other from strategic thought) are mutually reinforcing and together they benefit from the effects of synergism.

The fact that modern marketing and consumer research have actively broadened beyond business and the profit-making sphere (in order to widen their range of application) helps facilitate this transition. Thus, modern marketers increasingly deal with phenomena such as popular culture and they actively borrow concepts and methods from the humanities when doing so.

The specific topic of this monograph will be the history of the cowboy story from approximately 1820 until approximately 1970. Being a synthesis of popular culture scholarship, literary criticism, and consumer research, this work provides a test case of combining these different disciplines in mutually beneficial ways. The text is divided into three sections: a theoretical introduction, a cluster of substantive chapters, followed by a more general, overarching analysis. Here, I will provide a brief overview of my goals and methods in order to orient the reader to what will follow.

The first four chapters constitute a theoretical introduction. The first chapter, "The Cowboy Hero: A Suggestive Overview," distills in abstract what will follow. The second chapter, "Consumer Response, Qualitative Methods and Critical Analysis," provides a general overview of the current trend towards the use of humanistic techniques within consumer research. This is followed by "Criticism, Collective Response, and Popular Culture," which demonstrates that the current humanistic research stream in consumer research is strongly weighed towards individualistic research. The theoretic section concludes with "Relevant Tools from Marketing and Consumer Research"; it deals with a number of theories from consumer research which are relevant for popular culture scholarship.

After the theoretic superstructure has been presented, a cluster of substantive chapters deal with specific Western American authors and/or varieties of the cowboy story. The first substantive chapter considers the career of James Feminore Cooper and depicts Cooper as an innovator who was able to crystalize a number of key issues related to individualism and morality; Cooper's vision established a foundation that has been transformed by later authors. In marketing terms, Cooper is depicted as the innovator who "invented" a product and started it on its original life cycle.

The discussion of Cooper is followed by "Owen Wister's All Conquering Hero: The Turner Thesis Restarts the Product Life Cycle," which details how Cooper's plot formula was updated in the early twentieth century. By Wister's time, Cooper's innovation had become passé and the product-type he innovated was in decline. By merging Cooper's plot formula with Frederick Jackson Turner's frontier thesis of American history, however, Wister renewed the genre. In specific, Wister transformed Cooper's hero (a loner who must retreat to the desert) into an archetypical symbol of America who is able to use the skills and temperament he gains on the frontier in order to transform society and succeed within it. Wister's innovation gave the cowboy story a new lease on life and made it a staple of American popular culture. In marketing terms, by adjusting the product, Wister restarted its life cycle.

While Wister's reformulation was highly successful, some writers sought to transcend his vision by de-emphasizing the power of the individual and by focusing on the coercive forces of society. Zane Grey, in specific, reworked Wister's formula by depicting the lone individual as defeated by society. This alternative, however, did not mesh with the worldview held by most Americans, who continued to embrace individualism as their basic worldview. As a result, the public rejected Grey's vision and it had little impact upon the popular culture of the era.

While Grey portrayed the defeat and death of the individualistic hero, Walter Clark depicted the cowboy as an antihero who does what he has to do in order to survive. Like Grey's ill-timed prototype, Clark's work is an excellent example of Western American fiction, but it did not impact the evolution of the genre because it conflicted with cherished views that were reflected by Wister's formula. Neither of the precedents presented by Grey and Clark had any sustained impact upon the evolution of the genre.

Although the innovations of Grey and Clark could not become established in the pre World War II era, as social conditions and world views changed these same formulas were able to emerge as staples of the genre. This potential is discussed in two chapters that deal with (1) the fatalistic Western where the hero dies, and (2) the antiheroic Western where the hero compromises himself in order to survive or succeed. "The Fatalistic Western: Alienation and Cultural Evolution" discusses how in the post World War II era, the worldview of the public changed, which allowed Grey's fatalistic plot formula, which had been unacceptable to earlier generations, to emerge as a highly lucrative product. This transformation occurred because changing worldviews rendered Wister's all- achieving hero passé and unbelievable; this change in the popular worldview created a niche for the fatalistic Western of the era.

By the same token, in "The Modern Antiheroic Cowboy: Survivor in an Amoral Desert," the changing worldwiew of the public is used to explain how Clark's antiheroic plot formula, which had been unacceptable in the 1940s, emerged as a popular product in the 1960s. As with the fatalistic Western, the same shift in worldviews which rendered Wister's plot formula passé and unbelievable created a niche for the antiheroic Western. Both the antiheroic and the fatalistic variants of the cowboy story are adjustments that restarted the genre on new life cycles.

In the substantive chapters, the reader is provided with a rather truncated and selective discussion of the critical traditions involving Western American literature, and no attempt is made to provide any kind of exhaustive review of previous research. The reason for this editorial choice results from my desire both to save space and to provide a cross-disciplinary account that will interest scholars from both popular culture and consumer research. If the topic of Western American literature was one that was seldom considered by scholars, I would have had a greater responsibility to provide some kind of well-organized grounding in the critical literature; the existing wealth of materials on the subject, however, allows me to limit my discussions in this area. I hope that my doing so will not inconvenience the reader.

Having chronicled the history of the cowboy story in a number of freestanding essays, a culminating chapter combines and integrates the analysis: "The Cowboy Story, 1820-1970: A Composite Analysis." Although various uses of marketing theory and methods have been intertwined within earlier chapters, this was done in ad hoc ways. In this synthesizing essay, a number of classic marketing theories (such as the product life cycle and the adoption curve) are fully integrated into an analysis of the history of the genre over a period of 150 years. As a result, marketing theory and practice participates as a full partner in an analysis of popular culture.

Works Cited

Morgan, Louis Henry. 1877. *Ancient Society.* New York: Holt & Company.

Schein, Harry. 1955. "The Olympian Cowboy." *American Scholar* 24: 309-20.

Walle, Alf H. 1973. "The Frontier Hero: A Static Figure in an Evolving World." *Keystone Folklore* 19: 207-24.

——. 1996. "Hack Writers and Belle Letters: The Strategic Implications of Literary Achievement." *Journal of Popular Culture* 30.3: 185-96.

——. 1998. "Evolving Structures and Consumer Response: Dynamic Transformation of *The Fugitive* and *Mission Impossible.*" *Management Decision* 36.6: 399-406.

Warshow, Robert. 1954. "The Westerner." *Partisan Review* March-April 21.2: 190-203.

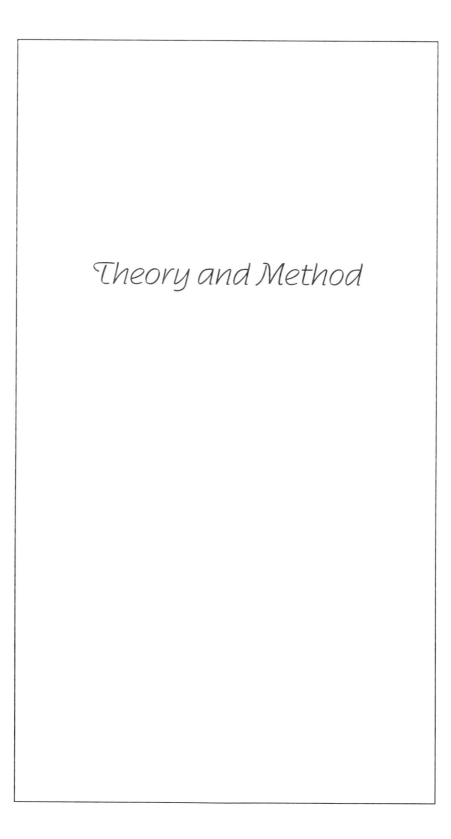

Theory and Method

1

THE COWBOY HERO:
A SUGGESTIVE OVERVIEW

Popular culture scholars are humanists who study the art, literature, and the mass media of a society in order to gain a greater understanding of those who create and consume these cultural artifacts. A tactic commonly employed by popular culture scholars is to use the creative arts as convenient empirical evidence and to extrapolate or "tease out" cultural and social phenomena that are revealed by analyzing them.

Central to the methodology used in this monograph is a focusing upon specific plot motifs and/or characterizations that could (or, in contrast, could not) be successfully marketed to the members of an evolving society. Popular culture scholars clearly recognize how the mass media industry reflects the ethos of a society and aspects of life which are relevant to it. By focusing upon phenomena that the public chooses to consume, scholars gain insights regarding the population being studied. Nonetheless, popular culture scholarship has primarily evolved from humanistic scholarly traditions, not those of the applied, strategic and/or professional disciplines. As a result, most popular culture scholarship has not formally incorporated research tools that have been developed by business scholars (such as marketers and consumer researchers). Nonetheless, there is a general recognition that studying the success or failure of specific examples of popular culture in the marketplace has a significant contribution to make when analyzing an audience.

A Merging of Consumer Research and Popular Culture Scholarship

Strategic disciplines deriving from business (such as marketing and consumer research) are consciously and vitally concerned with why people embrace certain products while rejecting others. The underlying principle of marketing and related disciplines is "the marketing concept," which states that the only reason for an organization (and/or its products) to exist is serving and satisfying their customers and clients. Due to this focus, marketers are primarily interested in assessing the needs, wants, and preferences of their markets (or potential markets).

Historically, marketers have tended to rely upon "formal" techniques largely inspired by the methods of the hard sciences; under such circumstances researchers have gone on to apply these tools to problems involving the marketplace. Contemporary marketers and consumer researchers, however, have sought to expand their array of methodologies by embracing qualitative techniques that derive from the humanities and the social sciences. As a result, consumer researchers are embracing the techniques of humanistic disciplines (such as the critical analysis of popular culture) in order to better understand consumers, their desires, and what influences them.

Broadening the research options available to consumer researchers has resulted in the merging of their discipline with cultural criticism and analysis. In doing so, the insights of the psychological and social sciences, as well as those of critical analysis, are becoming focused around the marketplace. Doing so is currently a popular strategy within marketing scholarship and consumer research. Because of this trend, cross-disciplinary strategies have become increasingly common within business scholarship.

Certainly, there has been a recognition by some popular culture scholars that merging the techniques of marketing/consumer research is potentially to the benefit of both disciplines. In this regard, I (publishing in the *Journal of Popular Culture*) observed:

Literary figures have long employed strategies, tactics, and methods that are remarkably similar to modern business disciplines such as marketing . . . in large measure, the field of consumer behavior parallels the discipline of popular culture since both seek to predict and explain how and why people either embrace certain aspects of culture or, in contrast, reject them. (1996, 185)

Starting from this basic premise, I point out that at least two different research strategies can be used in this regard. One considers the artists who create popular culture to be strategically oriented individuals who consciously craft products so they will be attractive to a specific market (audience). Where this is true, the artist performs ad hoc "marketing research" and "strategic market analysis" (intuitive though it may be) and then crafts specific products of popular culture according to the perceived demands of the market (audience). By evaluating successful examples of popular culture that were able to satisfy their market, consumer researchers and popular culture scholars can gain insights regarding the audience and why it chooses to consume specific motifs, plotlines, and characterizations.

The second approach does not deal with popular art as a strategic responding to consumer demand; in contrast, it considers popular art to be the product of the unconscious mind of the artist. In such cases, scholars assume that the unconscious feelings, desires, fears, etc. felt and experienced by artists are inadvertently reflected in popular art and, thereby, by extrapolating these influences, the scholar gains a better understanding of the audience. In this kind of research, suggestive clues (which are unintentionally incorporated into the work of art by the artist) are used as evidence for better understanding the audience (which is investigated using the author's mind and its products as surrogate measures of the larger society). The artists who provide these clues, however, are viewed as being unaware of the true importance and significance of the motifs and characterizations they employ; as a result, the researchers do not consider the artists to be strategically oriented. Naturally, in some circumstances both conscious and unconscious influences may be intertwined in the same work of art.

I continue by arguing that although the interests of (1) marketing scholarship/consumer research and (2) criticism/popular culture scholarship largely coincide, they come from different intellectual traditions and, therefore, they have not been usefully melded. I conclude:

The study of popular culture provides long term historical evidence regarding how a range of consumer goods (entertainment) have been marketed for thousands of years . . . Today the fields of marketing/consumer behavior and popular culture are converging. These disciplines come from different roots, but increasingly focus upon the same phenomena. For both disciplines to grow to their maximum stature, they need to join forces, not stand alone. (Walle 1996, 195)

Just as popular culture scholars, such as myself, have recently begun to overtly advocate merging their discipline with consumer research, consumer researchers have begun to propose a similar synthesis. Although these trends will be discussed in some detail in later chapters, at this time I will present one particularly illustrative example that portrays significant parallels between the initiatives of the two fields. This example demonstrates that by studying shifts in the plotlines of popular culture over time, changing aspects of the audience and what influences it can be revealed; these phenomena are of interest to both consumer researchers and popular culture scholars.

Evolving Plots Through Time: A Test Case

Today, consumer researchers are becoming increasingly involved in analyzing popular culture in order to understand how and why people embrace certain artistic products. In "Evolving Structures and Consumer Response: Dynamic Transformations of *The Fugitive* and *Mission Impossible*," for example, I (writing in the marketing/consumer research literature) examine parallels in the evolution of two TV series of the 1960s that were remade as feature films in the 1990s. According to my analysis, both TV series involve noble and moralistic protagonists; both films, however, center on betrayal by a supposed friend. In *The Fugitive* movie, Dr. Richard Kimble is framed for murdering his wife in order for a ruthless, supposed friend to successfully market a dangerous drug (which Kimble can inadvertently prove has negative side-effects). In *Mission Impossible*, Jim Phelps, the leader of the MI team, sells out his friends and colleagues for personal profit only to have a survivor (played by Tom Cruise) eventually unravel the scheme.

Having presented this empirical evidence, I suggest that the contemporary emphasis upon betrayal reflects changes in the evolving view of the world held by many people. While audiences of the 1960s may have tended to believe in heroic and noble people, I theorize that by the 1990s a sizeable market segment had come to expect the worst from others. This shift in the audience's worldview made a plotline focused on betrayal attractive and believable; this trend towards plotlines that emphasize betrayal, furthermore, is continued in TV series that aired at the turn of the twenty-first century, such as *La Femme Nikita*. I conclude that:

If researchers conclude that transformations in the plotlines reflect the evolving worldview of society, it can be argued that TV series/films, such as *The Fugitive* and *Mission Impossible* respond to structural changes in society; this type of analysis and the insights it provides is of practitioner value to marketing management. (1998, 405)

Significantly, this article demonstrates how the tools and analytic methods of popular culture scholarship can be employed by consumer researchers who seek to explain how and why the demand for certain types of artistic/creative products varies through time. Aside from an occasional impressionistic article, however, this goal of merging consumer research and popular culture has not been systematically pursued.

Currently, the existing research stream that seeks to synthesize marketing/consumer research with the humanities/popular culture scholarship has been suggestive and impressionistic, not rigorous and sustained. The aforementioned article about *The Fugitive* and *Mission Impossible*, for example, can be critiqued in these terms. Although that article points to situations where popular culture scholarship and business research can be usefully intertwined, the example does not go beyond an anecdotal level of analysis. In addition, the time range considered in that article is fairly short and the transitions discussed are cut and dry. This kind of pioneering research has a legitimate role to play in conceptualizing ways in which both popular culture scholarship and consumer research can and should evolve; such analysis, however, cannot stand as an end in itself. The limitations inherent in the existing research stream must be overcome in order to transcend pure theory.

More Substantial Examples Needed

This monograph presents a sustained, rigorous, and tightly focused melding of popular culture scholarship and marketing/consumer research. It accomplishes this goal by closely examining a specific genre of popular literature (the cowboy story) through the use of a hybrid analysis that combines relevant aspects of both popular culture scholarship and consumer research. In doing so, the analysis is able to more accurately analyze the evolution of the genre over a period of 150 years (from roughly 1820 to 1970) in a way which more accurately transcends and contributes to our current understanding of the subject.

This particular topic is especially viable because the cowboy story has been widely discussed in literary criticism, film criticism, and popular culture scholarship. By combining popular culture scholarship with consumer research, this monograph is able to offer an innovative interpretation of the cowboy story that has not been previously available. Because of the enhanced explanatory potential of the cross-disciplinary model, suggestions are made regarding how the research options presented here can be usefully deployed in other situations.

Before presenting the general chain of thought to be introduced here, it is useful to present key components of the methodology to be employed. They include:

This monograph seeks a greater knowledge of American national character and/or the belief structure typically held by a major segment of American society.

It is assumed that a propensity to consume examples of popular culture that embrace specific plot motifs and characterizations is, to some degree, influenced by the dominant belief structure and/or "national character" of a culture or society.

Since it is possible to examine the popular culture of earlier generations and how the public responded to it, popular culture scholars and consumer researchers can chart long-term changes in national character and/or belief structures and how these changes have impacted the consumption of popular culture.

By examining the success and failure of certain artistic products and by interpreting them with reference to both popular culture and consumer theory, a more robust analysis results.

This cross-disciplinary methodology, furthermore, can simultaneously serve the interests of both disciplines. Because popular culture scholars have always been consciously concerned with the marketability of certain artifacts and because their models seek to explain the success or failure of these products in terms of the characteristics/needs of specific target markets, popular culture scholars share a universe of discourse with consumer researchers. Because popular culture scholarship has largely evolved out of intellectual traditions from the humanities, however, it has not taken full advantage of the theories and perspectives offered by modern business thought. Joining forces as partners will clearly benefit both fields.

A Multidimensional Interpretation of the Cowboy Story

A discussion of the modus operandi of the techniques to be used here lays the groundwork for the basic chain of thought of this monograph. As discussed, the public's changing response to popular art through time is viewed as empirical evidence that can be used when identifying concomitant changes in society. In doing so, the project will:

Employ consumer theory to interpret the audience's response to popular culture, and

Examine examples of popular culture in order to analyze consumer response.

As indicated above, this study will focus these tactics around a historical analysis of the cowboy story.

In order to simplify the analysis which follows, key aspects of the argument to be presented can be outlined as follows:[1]

1. Artists have typically held the personality of the cowboy hero as an unchanging constant.

2. The fate of the hero has emerged as a variable that has been altered in order to respond to changing conditions/evolving public opinion.

3. As the belief structures of large segments of the American population have shifted, the popularity of specific plot formulas has evolved accordingly. Thus, the static, unchanging hero has been subjected to varying fates which

reflect the changing worldview of the audience. This evolution is viewed as a response to social and environmental pressures.

4. By studying these variations though time and by considering them with reference to transformations within the culture and the world view of society, popular culture scholars and consumer researchers can better understand those who embrace various products. By examining how consumer demand for certain kinds of literary products evolves in concert with (a) transformations in national character and (b) the world-view of the public, both popular culture scholarship and consumer research can more effectively achieve their goals.

The theory that the personality of the hero remains constant while the fate of the hero changes in tandem with changes in society is the unique contribution of this monograph from a popular culture point of view. These tendencies can be usefully analyzed by merging the methods of popular culture scholarship with those of consumer research. Using this overview as a touchstone, I will analyze a number of noted Western American novels and an array of important cowboy movies.

Employing this general model, the monograph embraces a variant of the myth and symbol method (an established technique of literary criticism, American studies, and popular culture scholarship that focuses upon aspects of culture shared by large segments of the population). In doing so, the analysis is able to link relevant theories from consumer research with those of popular culture scholarship. The goal is to predict when and why certain products of popular culture rise or fall in popularity. In doing so, this work merges methods, orientations, and interests of popular culture scholarship with those of consumer research in order to present a hybrid analysis that more adequately serves the interests of both fields. In doing so, this monograph provides a test case regarding how to integrate existing research techniques and theories from both fields into a holistic, broader, and more robust analysis.

As indicated above, this monograph combines a variant of popular culture scholarship and critical analysis with relevant theories from marketing and consumer research. In doing so, a resulting hybrid method provides a stronger and more powerful analysis than would exist if consumer research or popular culture scholarship was employed independently of each other. By presenting this example, the value of a specific cross-disciplinary melding is demonstrated. And since the analysis centers on the analysis of popular culture, it is particularly useful to popular culture scholars.

The monograph will first analyze a number of important phases/authors in the history of Western American literature. I will analyze these both critically and with reference to concepts from consumer research (such as the product life cycle and theories regarding how consumers come to embrace new products). After the various phases/authors have been analyzed separately, all will be simultaneously interpreted in a culminating chapter that considers each author/phase in relation to the others.

The first phase in the history of Western American literature to be considered is James Fenimore Cooper's Leatherstocking Tales. Cooper crystallized the character of the noble frontiersman as an archetypal symbol of America and he established the basic conflict of pitting this hero against an amoral and effete civilized world. Although Cooper created a dramatic dilemma that has often been copied and embellished by later artists, certain aspects of his vision were destined to become obsolete and dated. As a result, Cooper's basic plot formula (which centered around the displacement of the heroic figure to a desert where civilization cannot follow) eventually became passé because it no longer coincided with the worldview held by the American public.

Writing in the early twentieth century, however, Owen Wister was able to restart the frontier story on a new product life cycle while preserving both the character of the hero and his conflict against an amoral/effete civilization. Wister wrote in the era of Frederick Jackson Turner's "frontier thesis of American history," which argued that the frontier experience made Americans inherently superior to other people and civilizations. Wister, incorporating aspects of Turner's popular "origin myth" of American society, transformed Cooper's noble, but outcast, hero into an all-conquering superman from the frontier who is more effective than the products of the civilized Eastern United States (as well as those who come from a long-sedentary Europe). By merging the frontier story inspired by Cooper with Turner's frontier thesis in ways that corresponded to the popular tastes and beliefs of his era, Wister established a formula which was to dominate the genre of the cowboy story for over 50 years.

Even though Wister's portrayal of the frontiersman/cowboy as a moralistic and all-achieving superman dominated the genre for decades, some insightful authors, such as Walter Clark and Zane Grey, rejected this vision. Both attempted to transform the Western in ways that reflect the notion that the noble individualist from the frontier is actually trapped in a social context that is beyond his control. Although both Grey and Clark wrote excellent novels that parallel the modern anti-heroic and fatalistic Westerns, their work could not dislodge the frontier thesis that had been codified within Wister's formula. From around 1900 until about 1960, the power of the frontier thesis as a popular American "origin myth" was so strong that plotlines which conflicted with it could not become established as more than random, atypical, or "offbeat" products.

By the post World War II era, however, the myth of the frontier thesis began to be tempered by the vision that society is more powerful than the individual and that people must adjust themselves to circumstance if they are to prosper (or even merely to survive). Due to this emerging worldview, plotlines featuring a hero who dies (and/or where his survival is contingent upon adjusting to circumstance) became plausible. When such beliefs and worldviews became powerful conventional wisdoms for a large segment of the population, the fatalistic and anti-heroic plotlines (reflective of beliefs that could not establish themselves in the era of Clark and Grey) were able to become popular formulas for the cowboy story.

The analysis of this phenomena is best accomplished by merging humanistic scholarship (that deals with the collective response of large segments of the population) with theories of marketing and consumer response (that explore how and why certain products tend to be embraced by specific groups). The myth and symbol method is particularly useful in this regard. This monograph will explore the evolution of the cowboy story (as outlined above) through a joint use of popular culture and consumer theory.

Initially, a cluster of three chapters will provide an overview of the theories, concepts, and techniques of analysis to be employed. Each of these chapters provides a theoretic discussion that is relevant to the arguments that follow. Probably each reader will be familiar with parts of these chapters and, as a result, they will find parts of my discussion to be rather elementary. The reason why I stick to the basics is that, since this is a cross-disciplinary analysis, most readers, while well versed with parts of my discussion, will be covering new ground in other areas. This is true for both consumer researchers and for popular culture scholars. As a result, I have provided elementary overviews for both fields so all readers can come to the later chapters with the tools needed to appreciate the viability and significance of the cross-disciplinary analysis being proposed.

These theoretical chapters will be followed by separate discussions of specific authors/phases of the cowboy story. While each chapter can be read as straight social criticism, each also benefits from a combining of popular culture and consumer theory. A synthesis chapter that deals with the cowboy story as a genre that has evolved from 1820 to 1970 provides a culmination to the analysis. These examples demonstrate how the methods used here that combine the humanities and consumer research can be used in other contexts to the benefit of both consumer research and popular culture scholarship.

Note

1. For readability, the narrative of the presentation will contain minimal citations. Readers who seek a more fully developed presentation of the ideas contained herein are referred to the author's research which presents this basic chain of thought (Walle 1974; 1996; 1998). For an early presentation of these ideas in terms of the marketing profession see Walle 1991. Of these works, Walle 1974 presents a quick and useful overview as related to the folklore literature.

Works Cited

Schein, Harry. 1955. "The Olympian Cowboy." *American Scholar* 24: 309-20.

Walle, Alf H. 1974. "The Frontier Hero: A Static Figure in an Evolving World." *Keystone Folklore* 19: 207-24.

——. 1996. "Hack Writers and Belle Letters: The Strategic Implications of Literary Achievement." *Journal of Popular Culture* 30.3: 185-96.

——. 1998. "Evolving Structures and Consumer Response: Dynamic Transformation of *The Fugitive* and *Mission Impossible*." *Management Decision* 36.6: 399-406.

Warshow, Robert. 1954. "The Westerner." *Partisan Review* 21.2 (March-April): 190-203.

2

CONSUMER RESPONSE, QUALITATIVE METHODS, AND CRITICAL ANALYSIS

The purpose of this chapter is two fold. Primarily, I seek to provide an overview of current trends in consumer research that involve the use of qualitative research methods. Realizing that many readers will come to this book with backgrounds in the humanities, it is necessary for me to provide a thumbnail (although idiosyncratic) orientation towards consumer research so the reader can more easily grasp what I seek to accomplish. By using this background material as a guide, the reader will be able to more easily appreciate the chains of thought in the chapters that follow and to recognize exactly how, why, and where the interests of consumer researchers and popular culture scholars coincide.

A second audience for this chapter consists of scholars who come from consumer research and are interested in studying popular culture and/or utilizing its methodology. These readers may find my discussions regarding consumer research to be elementary. It is hoped, however, that my reviewing of the history of consumer research (and how it has divided into camps which focus upon either social or individual response) will prove useful.

Consumer research, an applied social/psychological science often involved with business/marketing scholarship, has increasingly embraced tools and methods which stem from the humanities. A prestigious research stream (which has emerged in the last 15 years), it seeks to merge the techniques of literary/cultural criticism with the methods and goals of consumer research. The resulting cross-disciplinary innovation has two distinct potentials: (1) using the perspectives of consumer research to broaden and enhance the humanities and (2) vice versa.

This research stream in consumer research can be roughly broken down into two component parts. One applies qualitative methods deriving from disciplines, such as social anthropology, to the marketplace. In this regard, consumer researchers such as Russell Belk, John Sherry and Melanie Wallendorf have demonstrated how qualitative fieldwork techniques can be profitably employed by consumer researchers. The second research stream involves embracing the techniques of literary criticism and mythology to mesh with consumer research; Sidney Levy, Elizabeth Hirschman, Morris Holbrook, and Barbara Stern are important members of this research stream. The present project is clearly linked to the second initiative.

The options presented by critical analysis are particularly attractive to consumer researchers in an era in which business-oriented scholars seek ways to transcend their traditional reliance upon quantitative methods. Here, an overview of this qualitative research tradition is presented. In addition, I will demonstrate that the present qualitative research stream of consumer researchers has, understandably, concentrated upon applying the critical tools of the humanities to their needs. While the potential of using the techniques of consumer research to enhance humanistic scholarship is clearly recognized by these scholars, doing so is seldom pursued in actual practice.

Humanists, in turn, have independently concerned themselves with issues that are interconnected with consumer response. Because humanists have done so without the aid of business scholars, however, they have typically failed to benefit from insights that could have been embraced; as a result, consumer research (as a specialized discipline) has had a minimal impact upon humanists, such as popular culture scholars. Consumer researchers, furthermore, have been quite selective in their borrowing, preferring methods that center around the unique response of specific individuals and circumscribed groups. These consumer researchers have not been as interested in analyzing parallel and homogeneous responses by large segments of the population.

Expanding the Critical Focus

Humanists, such as popular culture scholars, have long been concerned with the public's response to artistic and cultural products. Why a particular plotline proves to be popular (marketable) at a specific point in time is of obvious interest to those who study popular culture. Changes in the popularity of specific plotlines and/or heroic types, furthermore, have long constituted an important form of empirical evidence that has routinely been examined by popular culture scholars. The use of this basic technique can be traced back to the critical methods of the ancient world. Aristotle, for example, based his theories of literature upon empirical evidence (i.e., literature with a track record of being either effective or ineffective). As a result, Aristotle was very concerned with what was popular in the "marketplace" and he interpreted literature accordingly. Due to this emphasis, Aristotle (in his *Poetics*) can be seen as anticipating the techniques of popular culture scholars who are also concerned with analyzing why certain products are popular with the public while others are rejected. Hardly a historic footnote, Aristotle continues to be highly regarded and his work has greatly influenced twentieth-century American literary critics such as Irving Babbitt, T. S. Eliot, and W. H. Auden. Thus, a market-related critical method existed long before the establishment of marketing and consumer research and the rise of specialized humanistic disciplines, such as popular culture scholarship, as free-standing intellectual pursuits. The focus of criticism immediately after World War II, however, concentrated primarily upon the techniques of excellent writing, and it did not center upon the social or cultural context of literature. During the 1950s, the new criticism, which avoided examining the content of literature in order to concentrate upon the nature of "fine writing," was in vogue.

In the 1960s, however, culturally oriented criticism, which focused on content and socio-economic considerations, gained a dominant position and, coupled with the growth of popular culture as a field of study, this analytic tradition greatly expanded. Although a broad and multi-faceted research stream evolved, I will analyze this movement with reference to one particularly important critic, Leslie Fiedler. Due to the long development of Fiedler's thought and its wide-ranging impact, Fiedler is a perfect mirror of socio-cultural criticism and its influences.

The foundation of Fiedler's intellectual paradigm is nested around a reworking of what is best described as "myth criticism": the premise that certain myths and symbols that appear and reappear in a canon of literature can be usefully analyzed by the critic or popular culture scholar. Fiedler reads American literature in order to identify certain mythic themes which dominate the literary heritage of popular culture of American society; by doing so, he merges social and literary criticism with popular culture scholarship. Fiedler has likened this technique to the anthropological method and he has even described his work as a sort of intuitive anthropological analysis.[1] Having isolated the mythic content of a canon of literature, Fiedler goes on to interpret society and literature according to his anthropologically-inspired model. Most representative of this phase of his career are his seminal *Love and Death in the American Novel* (1960) and the shorter, but more focused, *Waiting for the End* (1964) and *The Return of the Vanishing American* (1968).

By the 1960s when Fiedler became an internationally recognized critic, the impact of television was profoundly influencing American culture, art, and popular response. Fiedler responded by increasingly focusing upon popular culture, not high brow literature which was aimed at the elite. Particularly revealing in this regard is his *What Was Literature? Class Culture and Mass Society* (1982). Building upon and refining his mythic techniques, Fiedler suggested that certain cultural products respond to unconscious desires/needs which may be unarticulated even though they are profoundly influential. Fielder goes on to suggest that a particular literary work may possess a potential to influence and to become popular in spite of profound "flaws" which repel critics who concentrate primarily upon the craft of writing, not the functioning of literary art within the social or cultural milieu of the times.

In order to demonstrate these thematic perspectives, the second section of *What Was Literature?* consists of a number of case studies involving profoundly influential works of literature which, if evaluated according to standard critical criteria, emerge as profoundly flawed. Nonetheless, Fiedler demonstrates their value and significance as well as the legitimacy of seriously studying them. Thus, *What Was Literature?* can be read as a tour de force of popular culture scholarship.

Fiedler, without mentioning the term, has an obvious interest in "consumer behavior" and he affirms that analyzing consumer response is a crucial aspect of the critic's obligations. Fiedler insists that merely applying the yardsticks and evaluative criteria of "fine writing" is not enough. By transcending "elite" criteria of evaluation, Fiedler perfectly bridges traditional criticism and popular culture scholarship. And because the discipline of popular culture has an obvious relevance to consumer research, Fiedler's interests and strategies simultaneously demonstrate the importance of a collectively oriented critical analysis to consumer research.

As a result of these interests and research agendas, the theory and method of consumer research has an obvious contribution to make to popular culture scholarship and vice versa. Scholars such as Fiedler are overtly aware that consumer response is important and that by analyzing how people respond in the marketplace vital clues regarding them and their popular culture can be analyzed. Nonetheless, popular culture scholars tend to employ their own intuitive means of dealing with the way consumers behave and their scholarship has not benefitted from the contributions of consumer research (a coherent and established discipline with its own intellectual heritage). By embracing the scholarly tradition of consumer research, however, a fruitful relationship between popular culture scholarship and consumer response can be developed. By envisioning popular culture scholarship as paralleling consumer research, both fields can be better integrated into the broad cross-disciplinary arena of scholarly activity.

The classic demonstration of how the techniques of consumer research can contribute to popular culture scholarship is Morris Holbrook and Mark Grayson's "The Semiology of Cinematic Consumption:

Symbolic Consumer Behavior in *Out of Africa*" (1986). While most consumer researchers study popular culture (such as film and TV) in order to gain insights about the nature of consumption, Holbrook and Grayson observe:

> The present approach differs from these [previous] efforts in focusing not on the issue of what artworks tell us about consumer behavior or how art is consumed, but on the question of what consumption can tell us about works of art. (375)

Having completed their analysis, Holbrook and Grayson reaffirm that it is possible and legitimate to use consumer research to (1) understand popular culture as well as (2) exploring consumer response through an analysis of popular culture. While it is possible to accomplish either goal, the decision on which tack to take depends on the goals of the specific research project.

More recently (1996), I drew a parallel between consumer research and popular culture scholarship. I observe:

> The discipline of popular culture has not significantly embraced the field of marketing and consumer research. . . . Because the creation of popular art is largely a market related activity, cross-disciplinary research would benefit both disciplines . . . the fields of marketing/consumer behavior and popular culture are converging. These disciplines came from different roots, but increasingly they focus on the same phenomena. (194-95)

As a result, popular culture scholars have much to gain from embracing aspects of consumer research. For many years, popular culture scholars and critics have been using ad hoc and independently invented models for analyzing the audience and consumer response. Unfortunately, the discipline of popular culture has not benefitted from an array of useful techniques and orientations which have been developed in consumer research (a focused discipline dedicated to the investigation of how people respond to products). By creating linkages between these two fields, scholars will be better able to integrate the tools of both disciplines in mutually beneficial ways.

As demonstrated by the work of Holbrook and Grayson (1986) and myself (1996), consumer researchers and popular culture scholars clearly recognize that the tools and techniques of consumer research have a significant potential value to the analysis of popular culture. By working together in coordinated ways, these two disciplines can be usefully merged to their mutual benefit.

Qualitative Methods in Consumer Research: Two Different Options

Although scholars such as Holbrook and Grayson (1986) and myself (1996) have actively sought to introduce the techniques of consumer research to the needs of popular culture scholarship, most consumer researchers have, understandably, concentrated upon applying critical techniques primarily to serve their own needs and priorities. A key motivation for doing so is the desire to transcend the quantitative methods that long dominated marketing and consumer research. For many years, statistical analysis and the "scientific method" were the yardsticks by which marketing scholars evaluated the rigor of their research. As time wore on, however, consumer researchers increasingly complained that these techniques were inappropriate when investigating a wide range of issues involving human response. In order to expand their toolkits, these scholars began to experiment with an array of qualitative techniques. In the quest for new methodologies, consumer researchers visited the humanities and the social sciences and they began to link their research to the qualitative research techniques that were found there. The current interest of consumer researchers in critical methods is one aspect of the tendency to expand beyond quantitative/scientific methodologies by borrowing relevant and appropriate qualitative/humanistic research strategies.

In order to put this intellectual process in historic perspective, it is useful to show how qualitative research has evolved in two distinct directions in the last 150 years. It is equally important to remember that, to a large extent, the current paradigms being used by scholars are artifacts of modern life and economic history.

The industrial revolution and its recurring aftershocks have led to a profound intellectual transformation that has exerted significant influences upon qualitative research. One way of dealing with this transition is through a consideration of the writing of novelists such as James Fenimore Cooper (who chronicled the eclipse of the moral individual by an amoral society) and Charles Dickens (whose bleak portrayals of the industrial revolution have long been read as an indictment of the social-economic system that spawned it); both authors focus upon the massive forces of society and how they displace or undercut individual people. The self-conscious message of both Cooper and Dickens is that encroaching technologies (and social structures based on them) have shifted the balance of power towards society and away from the individual. Indeed, the dilemmas that accompanied the industrial revolution demanded a rethinking of perspectives in ways that juxtapose the role of society vs. that of the individual and/or the circumscribed group.

These emerging positions are complementary and each addresses its subject matter in a distinct way. One paradigm (typified here by Karl Marx) de-emphasizes the individual in order to concentrate upon massive and impersonal socio-economic forces which Marx felt were primary and paramount. The second option constitutes a re-embrace of the individual and/or the circumscribed group by suggesting that the impacts of the industrial revolution and mass society can be mitigated and transcended in a number of specific ways. As will be argued below, both intellectual traditions continue to be vital and provocative and each has evolved in concert with the needs and issues of the times. Before proceeding with these later developments, however, it is useful to provide a thumbnail overview of the frameworks of these two traditions.

According to Karl Marx:

The mode of production in material life determines the general character of the social, political, and spiritual processes of life. It is not the consciousness of men that determines their existence, but, on the contrary, their social existence determines their consciousness. (1859, Preface)

This assertion, stripped of all qualifying digressions, distills the essence of classic Marxist thought.

Indeed, as is commonly acknowledged, Marx's philosophy and his view of social evolution almost completely downplay the power of the individual as a force in history. Instead, individuals are viewed as being set in time and place and they are considered to be products of the socioeconomic situation in which they, by chance, are thrust.

Some detractors, of course, have argued that Marx is inconsistent since, on the one hand, he urges people to action while, on the other hand, he asserts that since people are products of their times, their responses are inevitable and need not be prompted by him. A classic solution to this dilemma, of course, is to point out that Marx simultaneously pursued a dual career path. On the one hand, Marx was a professional political activist and, as such, he attempted to sway public opinion and influence behavior; on the other hand, Marx is an important social theorist who presents a powerful model of social determinism.

As the social sciences developed in the nineteenth and twentieth centuries, socially deterministic models flourished, especially in social anthropology which was primarily concerned with the pervasive impact of culture and society, not the needs or actions of specific individuals. In a classic article, anthropologist Alfred Louis Kroeber depicted culture as a "superorganic" entity which was independent of actual people even though it lived through them. In this regard, Kroeber observes:

The reason why mental heredity has nothing to do with civilization is that civilization is not mental action, but a body or stream of products of mental exercise . . . the social or cultural is by its very essence non-individual. (1917, 192-93)

In British social anthropology, furthermore, a polemic raged in the 1930s between Bronislaw Malinowski, who suggested that anthropology should deal with the needs of individual people and A. R. Radcliffe-Brown who insisted the field should concentrate upon the priorities and needs of society. Ultimately Radcliffe-Brown and his collectively-oriented paradigm prevailed.

The British structural/functional tradition popularized by A. R. Radcliffe-Brown and Bronislaw Malinowski is very different from what evolved in France and is identified with Claude Lévi-Strauss. The British focused upon society, its needs, and behaviors. Although British social anthropology recognized that individuals existed, they were not specifically investigated, and the method dealt, instead, with culture-wide issues. Lévi-Strauss, in contrast, took the opposite position; his work can be envisioned as "mental structuralism" because he is primarily interested in the functioning of the human mind, not the needs of the social system. As a result of these different research traditions, my work is more in line with British structuralism/functionalism while the work of Lévi-Strauss more closely parallels the interests of many consumer researchers who are more interested in the individual.

Within popular culture scholarship, literary criticism, and American studies, a similar intellectual focus emerged which centered upon how the larger culture influences the tastes, beliefs, and priorities of many of its members. The myth and symbol method, for example, suggests that large segments of the population respond to literature and popular culture in parallel ways because they embrace a similar cultural heritage, world-view, etc.

While socially deterministic models (such as those represented by classic Marxism, British social anthropology, and the myth and symbol method) are defendable as useful paradigms, as time went on it became obvious that this orientation led to intellectual blind spots. And where blind spots emerge, scholars strive to compensate for them. Thus, Western Marxists (such as members of the Frankfurt school) sought to temper social/economic determinism by examining (1) the power of individual people/circumscribed groups, (2) how they can influence the greater social and economic spheres, and (3) the degree to which they make decisions and evaluations without a complete reliance upon the social superstructures to which they fall heir.

In anthropological sub-disciplines such as "culture and personality," refinements in British structural/functionalism, and borrowings from the French intellectual tradition make it increasingly possible to deal with how individuals interact within and influence the collective world. In popular culture scholarship, American studies, and literary criticism, furthermore, collectively oriented methods (such as the myth and symbol method) are augmented by more individual-centered paradigms and research agendas (such as those associated with deconstructionism and poststructuralism). These later methods are also useful in analyzing the uniqueness of specific circumscribed groups.

Thus, one way for scholars to respond to the industrial revolution and the massive social influences which it represented is to begin with a paradigm of social determinism. Useful in many ways, classic versions of this model tend to under-emphasize the autonomy of individual people and the power of individual thought and action. As a result, later scholars within this tradition have tended to flesh out the socially deterministic paradigm by adding an individualistic component.

The alternative paradigm, in contrast, begins by emphasizing that even in a collective and industrial world, individual differences and the distinctiveness of circumscribed groups continue to survive and, perhaps, even to dominate. While the nineteenth century was impacted by the industrial revolution (a collective influence), it also saw the rise of the Romantic movement which celebrated both the individual (the cult of the Romantic hero) and the viability of circumscribed groups (typified by the vogue of Romantic nationalism). And while Marx advocated models of economic determinism, other intellectuals such as Soren Kierkegaard and Friedrich Nietzsche celebrated and championed the individual.

Although influenced by the same pressures as Marx, Kierkegaard and Nietzsche became concerned with individual response and consciousness. Indeed, although they exhibit profound differences (Kierkegaard embraced religion while Nietzsche repudiated it) both rejected models (such as those represented by Marx) which did not adequately deal with the individual.

Living and writing "before his time," Kierkegaard insisted that individual people should embrace what they believe and what is right for them. This position is very different from the classic Marxist orientation which argues that culture provides people with modes of thinking and acting which they inevitably embrace.

As an example of Kierkegaard's tendency towards the individual it is useful to look, in passing, at his "The Present Age" (1846). Paralleling present-day observers, Kierkegaard complains about the influence of the mass media and he goes on to observe: "The man who has no opinion of an event at the actual moment accepts the opinion of the majority or, if he is quarrelsome, of the minority" (1846, 265). The issue, of course, is that Kierkegaard points out that individual people are apt to embrace the will or world-view of the collective society (or reject it) without adequate reflection. While Marx considers this to be inevitable, Kierkegaard fights against the tendency. Carried to its logical extreme, Kierkegaard complains:

The [current] generation has rid itself of the individual and of everything organic and concrete and put in its place "humanity" and the numerical equality of man and man . . . [nevertheless] every individual must work for himself, each for himself. (1846, 269)

Moving from Kierkegaard to Nietzsche, a further emphasis upon the individual is advocated. Somewhat influenced by the theory of evolution and the concept of the survival of the fittest, Nietzsche assumed that all individuals possess an innate desire to gain power. Given this inherent need and propensity, Nietzsche celebrated the hero as a "superior" individual who is able to achieve his goals through personal power and prowess. This individualistic vision, of course, is profoundly different from collective paradigms such as those held by Marx (that suggest that social and cultural circumstances, not the will or personal strength of the individual, lead to heroic action and/or status).

Indeed, Nietzsche criticizes social institutions (such as religion) which de-emphasize the individual. Suggesting that no moral system is universally appropriate in all circumstances and that variation can and should exist, Nietzsche points to personal strength and choice, not collective obedience, as the handmaiden of achievement; these, of course, are individualistic perspectives.

Exerting a profound influence during their own era, Kierkegaard and Nietzsche have had their greatest impact in the post World War II era because they significantly influenced existential philosophy and its offshoots. Studying the social milieu of Europe in the post World War I era, a significant transformation away from an optimistic belief in cultural "progress" provided by the collective society can be clearly discerned. It became painfully obvious to those living in those times that the industrial revolution had not eliminated human misery. Indeed, the mechanization of war had made suffering all the more horrible. And while the industrial revolution sometimes led to economic prosperity, it also made society vulnerable to economic collapse (such as the international economic depression of the 1930s). Facing these impacts, many intellectuals sought an alternative to paradigms which centered around society, technology, and the modern collective world. Because they advocated a clearly individualistic perspective, Kierkegaard and Nietzsche provided a key for dealing with these issues and, thereby, they exerted a profound influence upon the development of existentialism.

Although existentialism is a complicated and multi-faceted phenomena, in the final analysis it tends to focus upon the individual. It also suggests that society often assigns identities and roles to people which are arbitrary and, perhaps, inappropriate or exploitative. These, of course, are issues which center around the plight of the individual. Such orientations, furthermore, have great value to those who seek to emphasize or champion the self-determinism of specific circumscribed groups. Thus, research agendas such as women's studies, American Indian studies, and black studies, etc. benefit from paradigms which derive from existentialism since they can easily deal with social roles and statuses as arbitrary and possibly oppressive. And since existentialism and its offshoots suggest that it is useful and legitimate to go beyond arbitrary and socially defined identities, this method and those which derive from it provide a technique for centering upon individual response. This, no doubt, is a major reason why the existential research stream and its offshoots have proved to be so useful in an environment where scholars examine the situation faced by individuals and/or circumscribed groups. These methods are also useful to partisan observers, and professional activists. And, of course, the disciplines of popular culture scholarship, American studies, and literary criticism have benefitted from such models.

Although these orientations provide a useful avenue for considering a number of vital issues, they also suffer from the same limitations which bedevil classic Marxism: they are so centered around one perspective that other valuable viewpoints and qualifying considerations are ignored. Just as strictly deterministic models can overlook the individual, classic existentialism and perspectives which spring from it are not designed to deal with the overarching impact of social and cultural forces. Just as Western Marxists (such as the Frankfurt school) needed to introduce the individual into their deterministic model, existentialism and related paradigms needed to acknowledge social, cultural, and economic influences in a systematic way (even though they focus primarily on the individual).

Representative of this need, and the ultimate response to it, is the assertion by Jean-Paul Sartre in his *Critique of Dialectical Reason* (1960) that Marxism constituted the essential philosophy of his era. Tracing the philosophic chain of thought since Kant and Hegel, he concludes: "[Marxist] dialectical reason can assert certain totalising truths—

if not the whole truth" (1960, 23). Having made this shift towards Marxist thought, existential philosophy and later developments (such as deconstructionism) became free to embrace key aspects of a powerful collectively oriented paradigm represented by Marxism. Nonetheless, the existential vision and its individualist thrust was largely preserved. This fusion continues to represent the current transformations of these perspectives into deconstructionism and poststructuralism.

Thus, the industrial revolution and the collective orientation it fostered has influenced social and philosophical thought in at least two different ways. Socially/collectively oriented scholars (represented by Marx) viewed the individual as putty in the hands of the evolving culture and economy; nonetheless, Marxists had to flesh out this position by adding an individualistic component to their paradigm in order for it to accurately account for important aspects of empirical reality.

Existentialism and its analogues, in contrast, are individualistic in essence, but their advocates need to embrace a collective perspective in order to reflect reality. Sartre attempted to provide this when he linked existentialism with Marxism. Thus, both naive Marxism and vulgar existentialism have transcended their original one-sidedness and established sophisticated and multi-dimensional models which can account for all the key factors and influences that impact people and society. And yet, the two paradigms (and what they are primarily designed to accomplish) continue to be very different. Both deconstructionism and the myth and symbol method will be analyzed and critiqued in later sections; deconstructionism focuses on the individual/circumscribed group while the myth and symbol method deals with society as a holistic entity.

The modern industrial world has exerted a profound impact upon scholarship. Nonetheless, this impact has led to largely opposite models; one concentrates upon the impact of society, the other is primarily concerned with the realm of the individual and/or the circumscribed group. Nonetheless, each model, if left to its own priorities, is incomplete and hyperbolic; as a result, each has inevitably embraced key aspects of its rival in order to more accurately reflect reality.

The Individualist Focus in Consumer Research

At the current time, consumer research (which embraces humanistic theories) tends to embrace the individualist perspective as discussed above. As a result, this research stream is able to pursue one set of research options but it is ill equipped to deal with others. Due to this situation, the field has not benefitted from the full array of theoretical options which the humanities has to offer. That situation is discussed below.

In the 1980s, consumer researchers found structural criticism/ mythology to be a technique which could be used to analyze consumer response. The history of this intellectual tradition exhibits the following pattern:

1. Noted consumer researcher Sidney Levy provided a general and suggestive structural model in the early 1980s.

2. Scholars such as Hirschman and Holbrook and Grayson redefined structural analysis in circumscribed and static ways in the late 1980s.

3. In the 1990s, models such as poststructuralism came to transcend structuralism and some marketing scholars depict structuralism as dated and passé.

The classic article which began this research stream is Sidney Levy's "Interpreting Consumer Mythology: A Structural Approach to Consumer Behavior" (1981). There, Levy consciously borrows the structural model of Lévi-Strauss[2] and lists some of the beneficial features of the method including: (1) viewing phenomena in terms of their "essential structural characteristics," not the unique social situation and (2) analyzing "universal cognitive processes" (51). Levy then observes:

If we take the idea that myths [and consumer stories/memories which he deals with as myths] are ways of organizing perceptions of realities, of indirectly expressing paradoxical human concerns, they have consumer relevance because these realities and concerns affect people's daily lives. (52)

Having linked consumer research techniques with the structural method, Levy is able to pursue a research agenda involving stories that were recanted by a sample of informants. He then uses these stories to create a structural analysis of the "food ways"[3] traditions of the sample of consumers he is studying. Having done so, Levy admitted that his work was general and exploratory. He observes: "The broad brush strokes indicated above may encourage further study of how families develop their particular little myths; how common cultural little myths change over time; how facts of behavior are modified in the telling. . . ." (60).

One representative means of accomplishing this goal was provided by Robert Grafton-Small in his "Marketing, or the Anthropology of Consumption," where he observes:

Marketing is considered to be a socially located practice [which] . . . may be seen to reflect and to reinforce the social structures, customs, and outlook of an entire culture. . . . After it is accepted that all goods have meaning but no one item does by itself, it becomes clear that consumers' understanding of goods must lie in the relations among all the goods available to them. (1987, 66)

Grafton-Small then points to structural analysis as one method of portraying the meaning-giving social context in which goods are consumed. Marketing scholars, therefore, have long recognized that social and collectively-oriented methodologies (such as that explored by Levy) can meaningfully deal with consumer response and the context in which consumption takes place. These scholars have also embraced a view of an overarching society and culture that impacts large segments of the population in parallel ways.

Instead of following up and expanding upon Levy's initial work, however, various consumer researchers have developed parallel and largely independent analyzes which are based on their own specific research agendas. Thus, Hirschman (1988) employed a version of the structural method in order to analyze and compare the television series *Dallas* and *Dynasty*. She concluded, "These series serve a valuable projective function for consumers." While Hirschman is interested in social and structural phenomena (that somewhat parallels what I want to accomplish) she also began to smuggle the individual back into the analysis.

Holbrook and Grayson (1986) use a form of semiology (a formal technique closely akin to structural analysis) to analyze the symbolism in the film *Out of Africa*. They conclude: "These artworks represent life, and the artistic uses of symbolic consumer behavior may tell us something about humanity itself. This view of symbolic consumption may thereby advance our understanding of the human condition" (380). The research agenda represented by Holbrook and Grayson is largely concerned with subjective response. Thus, Levy, Hirschman, and Holbrook and Grayson can be viewed as representing research options that range from socially centered (Levy) to those focused around individual response (Holbrook and Grayson) with Hirschman representing a middle ground.

David Francis' work (1986) meshes well with this general research stream. He observes: "Structuralism offers a method by which advertisements can be examined as complex semiotic structures" (1986, 197). In more recent years, Barbara Stern (1991; 1993; 1996) has further shifted away from structural, socially deterministic analysis in order to focus upon various formal techniques of literary criticism such as poststructural analysis and deconstructionism that focus upon individual response. Stern's forte is the adaption of various "individualist" research tools that stem from existentialism and contemporary methods of French philosophy that derive from existentialism. At the current time, these methods have tended to emerge as leading consumer research. Most recently, Stern has argued that structural analysis possesses inherent flaws which make it an inevitable failure (1996, 137).

As the interest in structural analysis has declined, the involvement in poststructural analysis has increased. Firat and Venkatesh (1995) and Sherry (1991), discussing postmodernism, provide good reviews and excellent bibliographies which touch on the poststructural movement in consumer research. At the same time, various consumer researchers such as Stern (1993, 1996) deal with postmodern and poststructural analysis as a further evolution of critical methods that is more useful than other options. Thus, it appears to consumer researchers such as Stern, that the intellectual tradition associated with structural analysis has "run out of steam," been surpassed by further intellectual advances, and today it tends to be considered passé by many consumer research theorists.

Formal Criticism: Evolutionary Advance or Ad Hoc Technique?

As consumer researchers have come to borrow from criticism, a clear pattern has emerged. The vast majority of these consumer researchers have embraced methods that stem from the more "formal" critical traditions which are anti-structural and they tend to link themselves to modern French philosophy. These techniques, by their very nature, tend to concentrate upon individuals and circumscribed groups, not society in general. Before discussing this trend, it is perhaps useful to provide an overview of the history of formal methods in critical analysis.

As it has evolved, the deconstructionist method of literary criticism is, at least superficially, based on the work of French philosopher/critic Jacques Derrida. A professional philosopher by training, Derrida provided a close and formal reading of the texts he examined. Derrida's apologists suggest that his techniques are more rigorous and useful than subjective generalizations based upon other methods. Derrida's defenders insist that the approach he has inspired provides an advanced and inherently superior form of critical investigation, and they argue that it should form the basis of future methodological developments in the field.

There is, of course, an alternative position. In the 1950s, the new criticism, which advocated a rigorous focusing upon the text being analyzed, was the dominant method of critical analysis. Focusing on the text alone, however, this method did not easily deal with the historic and socio/economic milieu of literature and it did not adequately explore the feelings and experiences of the author. As time went on, many critics began to reject the limitations imposed by the new criticism and the field increasingly sought to examine personal, socio-economic, and psychological variables and how the impact they have on literary creation and the reader's response to it. The new criticism was severely undercut as these new research agendas gained popularity in the 1960s.

The more formally-oriented scholars, however, did not completely die out and in the 1970s they found that Derrida's philosophy provided a way for them to re-establish their basic method. Deconstructionism's formal methodologies largely parallel the orientation of the new criticism, coupled with its ability to deal with the distinctive response of specific groups; as a result of these methodological advances, it has emerged as an important part of the critical scene. Although my analysis of this intellectual transition is idiosyncratic, Frank Lentricchia's (1980) *After the New Criticism* (which provides a detailed analysis of this phenomena) may be consulted for a more detailed account of this academic response and counter-response.

Thus, while some deconstructionists consider their method to be a further evolution of literary criticism which should be universally embraced by all literary scholars, other critics merely view it as the current version of formal criticism: a separate branch of literary analysis which is not inherently superior to other methodologies. This monograph embraces the later evaluation and suggests that deconstructionism and parallel methods are merely specialized tools which, while useful in a number of contexts, are not benchmarks by which all criticism should be evaluated. In this spirit, I will provide an overview of the technique.

Deconstructionism deals with the fact that in many (if not all communications) there is a certain ambiguity in what is being transmitted. Derrida suggests that this is especially true in the case of the written word and in complex written works such as novels. After reminding the reader of these truisms, the method suggests a number of important research agendas that may be fruitfully pursued. As Fredric Jameson has so aptly observed, deconstructionist critics encounter texts which they: "decipher and interpret as distinguished from the older views of those objects as realities . . . which in one way or another [they] attempt to know" (Jameson 1976, 205).

Based on this premise, deconstructionists develop a methodology which is based, in large part, upon the rejection of structural analysis. In this way, the method is able to counter the theory that the work of art "means" a specific thing. This, of course, throws the analysis back towards the individual. In the United States, these ideas came to full flower among members of the "Yale School" of criticism which includes critics such as Harold Bloom, Paul de Man, and J. Hillis Miller among others. Positioned as an heir to the new criticism, deconstructionism has emerged as an important methodology and it has helped to revitalize formal criticism.

Although deconstructionism may be appropriate in a number of contexts, the model tends to center upon the response of individuals and circumscribed groups, not culture as a collective entity. Although this should not deter researchers who truly need to use the model, scholars should remember that other methods may be superior for research problems that are centered around collective response.

Poststructuralism and deconstructionism are useful in describing why and where systems break down and situations in which people are in conflict and/or are not united. When such situations are being researched, deconstructionist techniques might be usefully applied. Where the research centers on how structures work and/or how different people or groups are influenced in parallel ways by these structures, the method is likely to be counterproductive. As indicated above, choosing a methodology involves tradeoffs; significant "downsides" of using post-structural and deconstructionist models exist.[4] And this fact needs to be overtly accepted and acknowledged by consumer researchers and popular culture scholars alike.

Based on this analysis, it becomes obvious that neo-formal methods represented by deconstructionist analysis are merely specialized tools, not universal advances. And it is self-evident that many scholars may be concerned with how large segments of society respond to aspects of popular culture in parallel ways. Certainly, the embrace of any methodological option necessitates inherent tradeoffs which the researcher must accept in order to enjoy the benefits which the technique provides. And, as discussed above, both collective and individualist research strategies possess both benefits and deficits which must be considered.

Transcending Circumscribed Analysis

Humanistic models (such as those that stem from critical analysis) have contributed exciting and productive potentials to consumer research. Today, qualitative methodologies (long considered to be suspect and non-rigorous by business scholars) have assumed their rightful place within the tool kit of the field; as a result, contemporary consumer researchers are embracing a wider range of options. I applaud all those who have been involved in broadening the field in innovative ways.

Consumer researchers, however, have come to focus upon formal techniques of analysis that have largely evolved from the existential tradition. It is easy to understand why this has occurred. Consumer researchers initially came to embrace qualitative techniques in order to deal with individual response (which methods such as demographics and statistical analysis could not easily explore). It seems only natural that the analytic techniques these scholars embraced would focus upon the individual; indeed, these are the models that have most often been emphasized by contemporary consumer researchers.

The decision to do so is a strategic response. As discussed above, Sidney Levy's seminal analysis is clearly structural and social in nature. Nonetheless, other consumer researchers have concentrated upon more individualistic paradigms because doing so was the best way for them to advance their specific research agendas.

As a result of prevailing research rosters, consumer researchers have not adequately embraced other humanistic traditions (such as those which analyze culture as an overarching entity that affects many people in parallel ways). Now that consumer researchers have accepted the value of qualitative tools, it is important for them to transcend centering merely on the individual or circumscribed group in order to consider the value of tools that investigate the behavior of the larger society. Some of these tools are showcased in this monograph. In order to demonstrate their potential value, these collectively oriented techniques are introduced and applied to a historic analysis of the cowboy story. In doing so, I continue the process of adjusting relevant aspects of humanistic research to consumer research and vice versa.

Notes

1. Personal communication.

2. Many anthropologists view Lévi-Strauss' model to be "mental structuralism" which deals with the universal structure of the human mind, not "social structuralism" which deals with the structure of society.

3. The term "foodways" is commonly used in folklore research and in cultural presentation.

4. For a fuller description of these issues, see my "Global Behavior and Unique Response: Consumption within Global Perspectives" in the 1997 (34.10: 700-08) issue of *Management Decision*.

Works Cited

Fiedler, Leslie. 1960. *Love and Death in the American Novel.* New York: Stein & Day.

—— 1960. *Love and Death and the American Novel.* New York: Criterion.

——. 1964. *Waiting for the End.* New York: Stein & Day.

——. 1968. *The Return of the Vanishing American.* New York: Stein & Day.

——. 1982. *What Was Literature? Class Culture and Mass Society.* New York: Simon and Schuster.

Firat, A. Fuat, and Venkatesh. 1995. "Liberatory Postmodernism and the Reenchantment of Consumption." *Journal of Consumer Research* 22 Dec.: 239-65.

Francis, David. 1986. "Advertising and Structuralism: The Myth of Formality." *International Journal of Advertising* 5.3: 197-214.

Grafton-Small, Robert. 1987. "Marketing or the Anthropology of Consumption." *European Journal of Marketing* 21.9: 66-71.

Hirschman, Elizabeth. 1988. "The Ideology of Consumption: A Structural Syntactical Analysis of *Dallas* and *Dynasty*." *Journal of Consumer Research* 15.3: 344-60.

Holbrook, Morris, and Mark Grayson. 1986. "The Semiology of Cinematic Consumption: Symbolic Consumer Behavior in *Out of Africa*." *Journal of Consumer Research* 13: 374-80.

Jameson, F. 1975-76. "The Ideology of the Text." *Salamagundi* 31-32: 204-46.

Kierkegaard, Soren. 1946. "The Present Age." *A Kierkegaard Anthology.* Ed. Robert Betall. Princeton: Princeton UP. Originally published in 1846.

Kroeber, Alfred Louis. 1917. "The Superorganic." *American Anthropologist* 19.2 (April/June): 163-213.

Lentricchia, Frank. 1980. *After the New Criticism.* Chicago: U of Chicago P.

Levy, Sidney. 1981. "Interpreting Consumer Mythology: A Structural Approach to Consumer Behavior." *Journal of Marketing* 45 (Summer): 49-60.

Marx, Karl. 1964. *Contribution to the Critique of Political Economy.* New York: International Library Publishing Company. Originally published in 1859.

Sartre, Jean-Paul. 1960. *Critique of Dialectical Reason.* Trans. Alan Sheridan-Smith. London: NLB.

Sherry, John. 1991. "Postmodern Alternatives: The Interpretative Turn in Consumer Research." *Handbook in Consumer Research.* Ed. Harold Kassarjian and Thomas Robertson. Englewood Cliffs, NJ: Prentice-Hall.

Stern, Barbara. 1993. "Feminist Literary Criticism and the Deconstruction of Ads." *Journal of Consumer Research* 19: 556-66.

——. 1996. "Deconstructive Strategy and Consumer Research: Concepts and Illustrative Exemplar." *Journal of Consumer Research* 23.2 (Sept.): 139-48.

Walle, Alf H. 1996. "Hack Writing vs. Belle Letters: The Strategic Implications of Literary Achievement." *Journal of Popular Culture* 30.3 (Winter): 185-96.

3

CRITICISM, COLLECTIVE RESPONSE, AND POPULAR CULTURE

Evolving Critical Tastes

Since World War II, literary criticism and cultural analysis have seen the rise of a series of rival models, each of which has dominated in its own time and place. Immediately after the war and until approximately 1960, the new criticism dominated. The basic strategy of the new critics is to focus almost entirely upon the "form" of literary works and to underplay or ignore their actual content as well as the context in which they were created. The primary goal of this kind of analysis is to distill and analyze the essence of excellent and effective writing. The new critics have been very influential, and properly so. Because they focused attention upon the writer's craft they resisted the temptation to let other, extraneous, phenomena distract them from their mission. In doing so, the new critics have provided significant insights regarding the nature of high literary art.

Nonetheless, by concentrating purely on literary methods, tactics, and strategies, the new critics inevitably ignored other important aspects of literature and popular culture. As indicated above, new critics concentrated on the essence of the writer's craft and they largely ignored cultural and social influences. While doing so may be a legitimate strategic choice, the decision to pursue this agenda is also a tradeoff in which one series of questions is pursued by turning a blind eye to other considerations which are ignored.

Some observers have suggested that the decision to center solely on form was a ploy that some new critics consciously employed in order to avoid incurring the wrath of ultra-conservative forces (such Joe McCarthy) during the anticommunist witch-hunts of the 1950s. Before the vogue of the new criticism, social criticism (which analyzed literature in terms of its social, political, or economic roots) largely dominated the field. Many of the critics who employed this sort of content-oriented criticism, furthermore, had strong socialistic leanings. During the anticommunist hysteria of the 1950s, however, pursuing a content-oriented analysis could result in the critic being stigmatized if politically sensitive themes were analyzed and discussed. As a result of the professional risks inherent in content analysis, it became a safer strategy to pursue critical analysis which investigated form without actively considering the content of literature in any significant and sustained manner.

By the 1960s, however, the pendulum had swung back and content-oriented criticism that centered upon the meaning of literature (and its place within a specific social/economic milieu) returned to prominence. The popularity of this type of criticism was further encouraged by the counterculture of the 1960s and the ethic of social activism which went hand in hand with it. During that era, much exciting content-oriented criticism was written; many worthwhile studies were conducted (even if some of this work was flawed by its one-sidedness). The formal critics had lost ground in the 1960s; however, they did not completely die out. Ultimately, formally oriented scholars began to search for a new way to reestablish themselves. Their means of doing so lay in embracing aspects of the poststructural movement as articulated by French philosopher and critic Jacques Derrida. Through linking itself with poststructuralism and deconstructionism, formal criticism, as an institution, reestablished itself within the critical world as a respected method.

Having presented this overview, it becomes necessary to briefly focus on contemporary French philosophy and its impacts upon contemporary formal criticism and, indirectly, upon consumer research.

The Deconstructionist Model

As indicated above, after a brief dominance of content/social criticism in the 1960s and 1970s, the formal critics rebounded by linking themselves with the methods of critical analysis which stem from French philosophy of the post World War II era. As shown in the second chapter, it is this formal tradition of criticism which has had the most significant impact upon consumer researchers who seek to apply humanistic and literary theories to their work. These emerging traditions (in both the humanities and consumer research) are complex and no effort will be made to fully review them here. Instead, I will focus upon the deconstructionist method because of its high profile within both fields.

Chapter 2 discussed how the deconstructionist method within the humanities and literary criticism is largely inspired by the work of French philosopher/critic Jacques Derrida, a professional philosopher by training. A major breakthrough in Derrida's career was his assertion in the late 1960s that the structural method was dead. This pronouncement ultimately led to the development of deconstructionism and poststructuralism. These new methods and orientations fit in well with the research agendas of the formal critics who often insist that the approach

Derrida inspired provides an inherently superior form of critical analysis that should form the basis of future methodological developments in the field.

There is, of course, an alternative position to such partisan posturing. As discussed above, in the 1950s, the new criticism (which advocated a rigorous focusing upon the text being analyzed) was the dominant method of critical analysis. Focusing on the text alone did not evaluate the historic and socio/economic milieu of literature and it did not adequately explore the feelings, experiences, and goals of the author. As time went on, many critics began to reject the limitations imposed by the new criticism and critics increasingly sought to examine personal, socio-economic, and psychological variables and how they impact literary creation and the reader's response to it. New criticism was severely undercut as these new research agendas gained popularity in the 1960s.

The more formally oriented scholars, however, did not completely die out and in the 1970s, they found that Derrida's approach provided a way for them to re-establish themselves. Deconstructionism, as a methodology, unites the formal interests of the new criticism with an ability to deal with the distinctive response of specific, circumscribed groups. As a result of these methodological advances, it has emerged as an important part of the critical scene. Still, it is not designed to easily deal with aspects of the macro-culture and, being tailored for certain specific purposes, it does not constitute a universal advance. Nonetheless, various approaches loosely linked with deconstructionsim (such as the new historicism) have been developed in order to deal with macro issues of society.

While some deconstructionists consider their method to be a universal advance in literary criticism which should be embraced by all literary scholars, other critics view it merely as the current version of formal criticism: a specialized branch of literary analysis which is different, but not inherently superior to other methodologies. This monograph embraces the later perspective and suggests that deconstructionism and related tools are specialized techniques that, while useful in a number of contexts, are not benchmarks by which all criticism and cultural analysis should be evaluated.

As discussed above, deconstructionism deals with the fact that ambiguity often exists in human communication. This fact has created a number of circumstances where deconstructionism and poststructuralism are the preferred methods of analysis and where they are more effective than alternative analytic techniques. In addition, models such as those deriving from existentialism conveniently examine differences between people and groups. As a result, they are ideal for analyzing a range of research problems concerned with individuality and distinctiveness.

Embracing formal analysis, on the one hand, and the study of distinct groups, on the other, scholars such as members of the "Yale School" of criticism, including Harold Bloom, Paul de Man, and J. Hillis Miller among others (Hartman, Bloom, de Man et al. 1979) joined with those who sought to analyze the visions and perspectives of circumscribed populations (that are often defined in terms of sex, race, ethnic origins, economic class, sexual orientation, etc.). The result has been the development of a powerful and influential paradigm of analysis that has been embraced by different scholars for a variety of reasons.

Poststructuralism and deconstructionism are useful when a universal "structure" is not being examined and/or where various sub-populations that have their own distinct visions are being investigated. When such phenomena are being researched, deconstructionist techniques are particularly useful. When the scholar seeks to study recurring structures that impact large segments of society, however, the method is likely to be counterproductive.

Deconstructionist methods, furthermore, have always focused upon a close and tight analysis of the text (Derrida's "there is nothing outside of the text" dictum is the rallying cry of the method). Essentially, deconstructionism examines texts in order to discern their inconsistencies and/or multiple meanings and ambiguities. According to Michael Wood:

Derrida . . . doesn't deconstruct his texts, he asks them to help him in the deconstruction of the philosophy in which they are implicated. (1977, 27)

In layman's terms, Derrida suggests that language, as a distinct entity, creates meaning in its own right and that this meaning or communication can exist independent of the speaker (via the mental processes of the individual listener). As a result, communication involves more than the strategies of the communicator; deconstructionism focuses upon this latter phenomena.

When Derrida asserts "there is nothing but the text," however, he tends to de-emphasize the social and cultural contexts of literary art. While this tactic may be legitimate and useful in a number of circumstances, various critics (such as Terry Eagleton) have complained about limitations inherent in the ahistorical nature of deconstructionist analysis. And over the years, deconstructionism has become linked to formal criticism (which is also ahistoric). Focusing upon the ambiguity inherent in writing, for example, the Yale school emphasizes that literature and language are largely metaphorical and, as a result, their meaning varies and is not exact.

The present study agrees with critics such as Terry Eagleton who champion the use of an historical perspective. According to this basic method (which is embraced in this monograph) literature, popular culture, and the public's response to them are interpreted to be the result of social and cultural structures. By studying these artifacts of literature and popular culture, therefore, a greater understanding of the culture can be extrapolated.

This type of focus is profoundly important to consumer research. Situations may exist where poststructuralist or deconstructionist models are inherently superior, but as Eagleton suggests, they tend to skirt historical and socio/economic evaluations. Certainly, where doing so is useful and appropriate, those methods should be used; in situations where scholars primarily examine socio/economic influences, however, it may be more appropriate and useful to employ other, more social structurally oriented, models.

In the contemporary world, scholars are often concerned with the behavior of individuals and subgroups. As a result, formal methods have arisen that deal with this kind of phenomena. In the contemporary world, dealing with the perspectives of circumscribed groups has become fashionable. While much of this research is of high quality, we must not let these successes detract our attention from the significance of many collective, culture-wide questions and the models which are specifically designed to examine them.

The Case for Collective Analysis

In many circumstances, scholars (both in the humanities and in consumer research) are concerned with investigating people as members of a specific culture or society and how they respond in parallel or analogous ways. Even the most casual analysis of human behavior will include circumstances where collective response dominates. As such, research agendas based on the overarching influence of culture are legitimate and have a long and illustrious history.

The above observation, of course, does not deny that many circumstances exist where more individualist models are useful or even superior. I am merely observing that in many situations social or cultural analysis best achieves the goals of the scholar. Where this is true, individualistic research strategies are likely to be counterproductive.

A key means of pursuing collective cultural/social analysis is to analyze shared beliefs, behavior patterns, tastes, preferences, etc. Having identified common patterns that exist in the culture or society, it becomes possible to investigate the culture in a more systematic way. By doing so, the scholar can gain a better understanding of the culture and the social milieu in which consumption takes place. Changes over time, furthermore, can provide clues regarding the cultural evolution of the society and what triggers these changes.

Although members of a larger culture may simultaneously be part of one or more smaller circumscribed groups, they may also be members of the larger society/culture and respond as such. Much of my research, for example, stems from the discipline of folklore (which concentrates upon the distinctiveness of various cultural and social enclaves). Folklorists, however, clearly recognize that a specific person may simultaneously be a part of a "folk culture" and the larger society.

The key issue being advanced here is that, in many circumstances, people react and behave as members of a larger social entity. By studying this behavior, it becomes possible to explore aspects of culture and social response which could not be conveniently pursued if the scholar focused upon the individual or the distinctiveness of the circumscribed group.[1] There exist many situations both in popular culture scholarship and in consumer research where an analysis of the impact of the larger culture is useful and productive. And where this is true, collective analysis is the most appropriate analytic tool.

Perhaps, as suggested in Chapter 2, the collective/structural paradigm has sometimes been overused. As a result, the options represented by deconstructionism and poststructuralism often prove to be useful alternatives. Nonetheless, by rejecting structural analysis in toto and by depicting it as inherently flawed, the pendulum swings back too far. The myth and symbol method is a specific collective/structural model which has proved to be useful in analyzing literature and popular culture. As a result, it will be employed as the theoretical underpinning of this monograph.

The Myth and Symbol Method

Popular culture scholarship, literary criticism, and American studies often seek to understand the nature of North American civilization in general; they typically investigate this phenomena through an examination of its artistic products and the public's response to them. As with other areas of scholarship, the techniques used and the paradigms embraced by the myth and symbol method have been impacted by broad trends within the intellectual community. Nevertheless, these scholarly traditions provide a focused and well established research stream concerning society, culture, and behavior patterns that stem from them.

The myth and symbol method is a classic means of pursuing this type of research. The approach is based on the belief that an overarching entity (which is usually envisioned as "national character") exists and that it predisposes many, if not most, people in a society to respond in roughly parallel ways to certain examples of art, literature, and popular culture. A favorite technique of the myth and symbol method is to suggest that American literature and popular culture embody distinctively American themes (myths and symbols). As a result, a large number of Americans respond to these artifacts in parallel if not in identical ways. Those seeking an overview of the method may want to consult Smith (1957), Slotkin (1986), and Sklar (1975). In the minds of many critics (including the present writer), Leslie Fiedler is a grand master of this method and he and his classic books on American life and literature are highly regarded, even if Fiedler and his vision are sometimes accused of being eccentric.

Two classic examples of the myth and symbol school that focus on the American frontier experience are Henry Nash Smith's *Virgin Land* (1960) and Leo Marx's *The Machine in the Garden* (1964). Since Smith's work can be easily connected with later and more sophisticated versions of the myth and symbol school (i.e., the work of Richard Slotkin 1973, 1985, 1992), the present analysis will focus upon him. As the title suggests, *Virgin Land* is primarily concerned with the image of the frontier and its impact upon American self-identity. Smith forcefully argues that the image of the nineteenth-century West profoundly impacted American culture and the worldview which Americans embraced.

Essentially, Smith argues that the image of the West provides a number of myths and symbols which have been worked and reworked for generations. By examining these symbols (in artifacts such as literature), Smith argues that the essence of American society can be better understood. Thus, literature is a "secondary variable" which is impacted and influenced by a "primary variable" consisting of American national character. By examining the secondary variable, the primary variable (which is reflected therein) can be usefully analyzed.

Being primarily concerned with his substantive subject, not methodological issues, Smith has been attacked on the grounds that he lacked a systematic theory and a coherent methodology. Other scholars, however, have come to Smith's defense and extrapolated the methodology which is implicit in his work (Marks 1963; Trachtenberg 1977).

For a number of reasons, the myth and symbol method has fallen from fashion in recent years. This decline in popularity, however, is not due to a fatal flaw in the method, but has occurred because research tastes have changed. As mentioned above, many contemporary scholars are concerned with the vision of specific groups. These scholars tend to concentrate upon distinctive (defined by race, sex, social class, sexual orientation, etc.) subgroups and how they view the world in their own unique way. Given these research interests, the myth and symbol method (which is centered around investigating overarching aspects of culture that impact many people and groups in similar ways) is inappropriate; as a result, many contemporary scholars find models that are influenced by poststructuralism and deconstructionism to be more appropriate for their work. The new historicism is an example of such methods even though it largely parallels key aspects of the myth and symbol method. The decision of these scholars to abandon the myth and symbol method, however, is basically strategic in nature. The myth and symbol method is not inherently flawed; it is, however, designed to deal with a number of specific scholarly problems that are not the concern of many contemporary scholars.

Collective Analysis and the Cowboy Story

As indicated above, the myth and symbol method examines literature, film, and popular culture in order to document and analyze aspects of the larger culture and society. Various mainstream critics have included popular Western or cowboy stories[2] within the sample of works they analyze; by doing so, these critics gain a greater flexibility than if they had concentrated solely upon so-called "serious literature." Other critics, in contrast, have specialized in analyzing the cowboy story as a specific genre. This monograph examines the cowboy story as a distinct genre from the time of James Fenimore Cooper to approximately 1970. The reason for the cutoff date is purely practical; using a 150-year time frame, I am able to usefully chart a number of trends in society and demonstrate how they impacted the propensity of authors to use certain plotlines within a genre of popular literature. If the analysis were continued to the present, furthermore, the argument would have become overly complex because in recent years the cowboy story has become intertwined with issues involving themes including the plight of the American Indian, feminism, and ecology. As a result, the clean and crisp argument would have become blurred and nothing would be gained in the process.

While a number of general, mainstream critics examine the Western along with other genres of literature, film, and popular culture, an array of critics focus primarily upon the Western or cowboy story (see, for example, Cawelti 1998; French 1973; Wright 1975; McDonald 1987; Kites 1969; Parks 1982). Typically, the Western is investigated and various aspects of American culture are explored either by a close analysis of a few, carefully chosen examples or via a broad investigation of a large canon of work that examines the cowboy story in relation to other genres. This scholarly tradition often attempts to provide generalized theories about cultural trends, belief structures, and/or the national character of the United States.

Since the amount of critical materials on the Western is vast, even a superficial review of this scholarly tradition is impossible. It becomes necessary, therefore, to narrow the discussion down to one representative and particularly illustrious critic, Richard Slotkin (whose work will also be used to represent a modern application of the myth and symbol method). Slotkin presents an excellent literature review, and therefore, to save space, I will not duplicate his efforts here.[3]

Richard Slotkin is a native of the East; for him the West is a symbolic place, not a home. Over the last 25 years, Slotkin has written an impressive multi-volume review of Western American literature and popular culture (which he calls "mythology"). Slotkin's strategies and terminology make it easy to connect the myth and symbol method (which his work represents) with tactics which have long existed within consumer research. Noted marketing theorist Sidney Levy (1981), for example, explicitly employs concepts associated with mythology in order to examine consumer rersponse. In that article, Levy is primarily interested in using the techniques of mythology in order to understand micro social units, such as the family. In this regard he observes:

The broad brush strokes indicated above may encourage further studies on how families develop the particular little myths [which impact consumer behavior]: how consumer myths change over time; how facts of behavior are modified in the telling; what the facts or the modified tellings are being used to say. . . . (Levy 1981, 60)

Consequently, although Levy is concerned with the micro/family sphere while Slotkin and the research stream which he represents focus upon wide societal issues and trends, the essential techniques and goals are somewhat parallel: studying a popular "mythology" in order to understand broader belief structures and/or behavior patterns. Thus, a clear precedent[4] for employing techniques in ways analogous to Slotkin's use of the myth and symbol method has long existed within consumer research.

To a large extent, Slotkin's vision of the Western is a reaction against that of Henry Nash Smith, whose *Virgin Land: The American West As Myth and Symbol* (1950) was long acknowledged as the definitive treatment of the subject. Smith forcefully argues that the image of the nineteenth-century West profoundly impacted American culture and the view that Americans embraced. Smith argued that much of this symbolism was positive: a garden of Eden; heroic, bigger than life heroes;

the adventure of empire building; bountiful opportunities; etc. An eloquent writer, Smith's largely upbeat treatment of his subject (and the implications it had for interpreting American national character) was convincing to a generation of critics.

The 1960s and the era of protest which coincided with it, however, gave rise to a new generation of scholars who possessed a different vantage point. Slotkin represents this later tradition and over the years he has authored a multi-volume tour de force on the subject and has emerged as a major spokesman for the position which he represents. In the early 1970s, Slotkin reworked and published his doctoral dissertation under the title *Regeneration through Violence: The Mythology of the Frontier: 1600-1800* (1973). Slotkin's goal was to systematically undercut Nash's (then conventional) views; he agreed with Nash that the key to American history and national character lay in the West; he, however, focused upon traits such as violence and racism: the negative potential of the Western movement. Slotkin, incidently, was overtly influenced by phenomena such as the Vietnam War and a string of abuses which he suggested our country had committed, both domestically and internationally, over the years.

The second volume in the series, *The Fatal Environment: The Myth of the Frontier in the Age of Industrialization: 1800-1900* (1985), focuses upon the ruthless aspects of the settling of the West and how both the native peoples and immigrants who settled the West were harmed by this process. As in *Regeneration through Violence*, *Fatal Environment* transcends the more positive perspectives of earlier scholars (such as Nash) and concentrates upon the negative alter ego of the frontier. The last volume of the trilogy, *Gunfighter Nation: The Myth of the Frontier in the Twentieth Century* (1992), draws parallels between the classic "cowboy and Indian" movies and American foreign policy after World War II.

In *Gunfighter Nation*, Slotkin focuses upon the image of the Western gunfighter who has the power to dispense justice in a hostile world and he suggests that this icon has become a mythic archetype that became transformed into an ideology justifing America's post World War II role as "watchdog to the world." The reader might also be interested in Slotkin's "Buffalo Bill's Wild West and the Mythologization of the American Empire" (1993). In accordance with the myth and symbol method, Slotkin interprets American culture through a content analysis of a particular genre of literature. At the beginning of *Regeneration through Violence*, for example, Slotkin observes: "The mythology of a nation is an intelligible mask . . . of national character" (1973, 3). Having made this statement, he studies the "mythology" of the West and the frontier in order to understand American culture. Slotkin finds mythology to be a secondary variable which is impacted by national character, the primary variable. By examining and exploring this secondary variable, key aspects of the primary variable (the subject of interest to the scholar) can be better understood.

By looking at this technique, as demonstrated by Slotkin's work, it becomes possible to quickly grasp the methodology to be used here:

1. This monograph seeks a greater knowledge of American national character and/or the belief structure typically held by Americans.

2. It is assumed that the propensity to consume examples of popular culture that embrace specific myths and symbols is, to some degree, influenced by the prevailing belief structure and national character.

3. Since it is possible to examine the popular culture of earlier generations and how the public of those eras responded to it, popular culture scholars and consumer researchers can chart how changes in national character and/or belief structures have impacted changes in the consumption of certain types of popular culture.

Conclusion

Since World War II there have been a number of fads in research which have shifted from content/social analysis, on one hand, to focusing upon formal analysis that is centered upon individuals and circumscribed groups, on the other.

Currently, centering upon formal methods, the uniqueness of specific subgroups, and their distinctive perspectives is in vogue. As a result of these prominent research agendas, analyzing overarching aspects of culture shared by large segments of a culture or society has declined in popularity. This situation, however, merely reflects the current scholarly fashion, not the legitimacy of methods which attempt to analyze culture as a holistic entity.

In order to demonstrate the value of an overarching/holistic cultural analysis and how this method can be usefully linked to consumer research, the evolution of the cowboy story will be examined. In doing so, a method of studying the evolution of popular art is presented. It is hoped that by doing so, useful linkages between these fields can be more strongly established.

Notes

1. Here I am thinking in terms of certain intuitive concepts such as "mainstream society," "circumscribed groups," "folk enclaves," etc. I, of course, am aware that these are slippery terms and that the lines dividing them are blurred. And, as indicated above in my reference to folk cultures, a person may simultaneously have one foot in two worlds. Although using these terms may lead to a certain ambiguity, they have served well in the past in disciplines such as folklore and, therefore, will be employed here in an informed and guarded way.

2. In this paper I tend to equate the terms "cowboy story," "Western," or "frontier fiction" and use them interchangeably. Some readers may object and legitimately point to important distinctions. I equate the terms because they view the cowboy story as a specific component or subset of the Western genre. The strategy in this paper is to focus upon change and stability within a specific genre; the terminology chosen advances this research goal. The author, further-more, has done so in refereed scholarly journals (1973; 1995), thus, professional critics acknowledge the method as legitimate.

3. Although not specifically discussed here, I find the work of Warshow (1954) and Schein (1955) to be two readable and insightful overviews of the Western as a genre. They, in specific, are recommended to the reader who has an interest in the subject.

4. Although I applaud Levy's insights regarding the value of literary theories such as those which derive from mythology, the current paper does not make explicit use of Levy's model (which derives from the work of anthropologist Claude Lévi-Strauss). On other occasions, however, I have employed a Lévi-Strauss type of analysis (Walle 1996). Although this paper does not build upon Levy's model, it does follow Levy's precedent of using mythological theory in consumer research.

Works Cited

Cawelti, John G. 1972. *The Six Gun Mystique*. Bowling Green, OH: Bowling Green State University Popular Press.

——. 1998. *The Six-Gun Mystique Sequel*. Bowling Green, OH: Bowling Green State University Popular Press.

de Man, Paul. 1979. *Allegories of Reading: Figural Language in Rousseau, Rilke, and Proust*. New Haven: Yale UP.

French, Phillip. 1973. *Westerns: Aspects of a Genre*. New York: Viking.

Hartman, Geoffrey, Harold Bloom, Paul de Man, et al. 1979. *Deconstruction and Criticism*. London: Routledge and Kegan Paul.

Jameson, Fredric. 1975-76. "The Ideology of the Text." *Salamagundi* 31-32: 204-46.

Kites, Jim. 1969. *Horizons West*. Bloomington: Indiana UP.

Lentricchia, Frank. 1980. *After the New Criticism*. Chicago: U of Chicago P.

Levy, Sidney. 1981. "Interpreting Consumer Mythology: A Structural Approach to Consumer Behavior." *Journal of Marketing* 45.3: 49-61.

Marks, Barry. 1963. "A Concept of Myth in *Virgin Land.*" *American Quarterly* 15: 71-76.

Marx, Leo. 1964. *The Machine in the Garden*. New York: Oxford UP.

McDonald, Archie. 1987. *Shooting Stars: Heroes and Heroines of the Western Films*. Bloomington: Indiana UP.

Miller, J. Hillis. 1982. *Fiction and Repetition: Seven English Novelists*. Oxford: Basil Blackwell.

Parks, Rita. 1982. *The Western Hero in Film and TV*. Ann Arbor, MI: U of Michigan P.

Schein, Harry. 1955. "The Olympian Cowboy." *American Scholar* 24: 309-20.

Sklar, Robert. 1975. "The Problem of American Studies 'Philosophy': A Bibliography of New Directions." *American Quarterly* 27: 245-62.

Slotkin, Richard. 1973. *Regeneration through Violence: The Mythology of the American Frontier 1600-1800*. Middleton, CT: Wesleyan UP.

——. 1985. *The Fatal Environment: The Myth of the Frontier in the Age of Industrialization*. New York: Atheneum.

——. 1986. "Myth and the Production of History." *Ideology and Classic American Literature*. Ed. Sacvan Bercovitsch and Myra Jehlen. New York: Cambridge UP. 70-90.

——. 1992. *Gunfighter Nation: The Myth of the Frontier in Twentieth Century America*. New York: Atheneum.

Smith, Henry Nash. 1950. *Virgin Land: The American Land as Myth and Symbol*. Cambridge: Harvard UP.

——. 1957. "Can American Studies Develop a Method?" *American Quarterly* 9: 197-208.

Trachtenberg, Alan. 1977. "Myth, History, and Literature in *Virgin Land.*" *Prospects* 3: 127-29.

Walle, Alf H. 1972. "The Western Hero: A Static Figure in an Evolving World." Presented at the Annual Meetings of the American Folklore Society, Nashville, Tennessee.

——. 1973. "The Frontier Hero: A Static Figure in an Evolving World." *Keystone Folklore* 19: 207-24.

——. 1976. "The Cowboy Hero: A Static Figure in an Evolving World." Diss., SUNY Buffalo.

Warshow, Robert. 1954. "The Westerner." *Partisan Review* 21.2 (March-April): 190-203.

Wood, Michael. 1977. "Deconstructing Derrida." *New York Review of Books*. 3 March: 27-30.

Wright, Will. 1975. *Six Guns and Society*. Berkeley: U of California P.

4

RELEVANT TOOLS
FROM MARKETING AND CONSUMER RESEARCH

As demonstrated in Chapter 3, a lively and productive cross-disciplinary movement exists that concerns itself with adjusting the theory and method of the humanities to serve the needs of consumer researchers. Thus far, however, marketers and consumer researchers have benefitted from a rather one-sided process of borrowing. The humanities have not systematically embraced the techniques derived from marketing and consumer research.

As discussed in Chapter 1, however, both consumer researchers and popular culture scholars have recognized that the business disciplines have much to contribute to the humanities, in general, and popular culture scholarship, in specific. This chapter will introduce a number of key concepts from marketing which have a significant relevance to this specific monograph and to popular culture scholarship as a discipline. It is hoped that the discussion of how these concepts can be integrated into the humanities will prove useful in both ad hoc ways and in more fully integrating humanistic scholarship with the business disciplines.

It should be emphasized in this regard that the tools being discussed here derive primarily from the practitioner realm of business, not from the ivory tower of pure scholarship. This practitioner orientation, however, should not keep these models from being usefully employed by scholars who seek to merge consumer research with popular culture scholarship. Indeed, while the models borrowed may not be "state of the art" from the point of view of business scholars, they are commonly used by practitioners and they form a key part of the conventional wisdom of marketing and consumer research. The reason for the pervasiveness of these models lies in the fact that although they may not be academically "correct," they do parallel reality well enough to be useful. In addition, these models are easily articulated to others and their essence can be readily grasped by a wide ranging audience. As a result, they have emerged as part of the bedrock of modern strategic thought in business. Just as other deterministic models, they attempt to usefully simplify reality by accepting certain distortions in order to better analyze and discuss the processes being investigated.

A basic and recurring theme of this monograph is that the tactics of business and the humanities can and should be usefully intertwined. As a result, it is essential for humanists (such as popular culture scholars) to systematically borrow relevant theories from marketing and consumer research and vice versa. In order to portray the potential of applying marketing theory and methods to popular culture scholarship, I will analyze two interrelated concepts: the *product life cycle* and the *diffusion of innovations* model. These theories have been extremely influential within marketing and consumer research for many years. As a result of their proven value and their potential relevance to the analysis of art, literature, and popular culture, each will be discussed and adjusted to the needs of the humanities. Relevant discussions of these theories will be presented both as an end in themselves and as an illustration of all other marketing theories which may be usefully employed by humanists. By being aware of these specific examples and the vitality of practitioner thought in marketing which they represent, scholars will better able to perceive the potential of merging marketing and the humanities as equal partners in areas where their interests coincide.

The Product Life Cycle

The product life cycle is one of the most influential theories of modern marketing thought. Popular among practitioners, teachers, and scholars because of its intuitive appeal, the product life cycle orients marketers/consumer researchers around a number of important strategic and tactical options which have a profound explanatory potential. Since coming to prominence in the 1960s, the product life cycle has emerged as one of the cornerstone concepts of business strategy; for that reason (coupled with its potential relevance to the humanities), it deserves a thoughtful consideration here.

The product life cycle draws an analogy between the career of a product and the life cycle of a living organism. Thus, products are viewed as being "born," growing, reaching maturity, declining, and "dying." In addition, marketing theory has devised a number of generalized tactics and strategies which can be used when products are at various phases of their life cycle. As a result, the model is not merely a useful didactic device; it also provides specific advice to marketers and strategic planners at distinct phases in the life of the product.

According to the product life cycle, when products are introduced, they have few sales and can be viewed as "helpless," although they might have a future potential. As a result, these products need to be nurtured and encouraged. After this "infancy" products begin to grow and sales increase. These products and their marketing are continually fine tuned in order to mesh with consumer demand. Eventually, products reach maturity and become freestanding and profitable. Sales peak. As time goes on, however, most products begin to grow old and decline. In some situations, sales fall off, but the product remains viable; in other cases, the product "dies."

A graphic portrayal of the product life cycle model is usually presented as

Stages of the Product Life Cycle

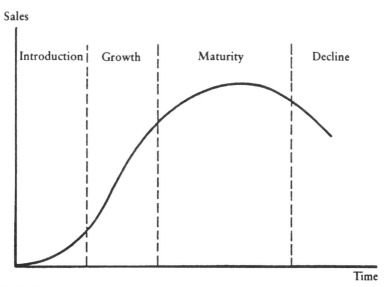

Fig. 1. From Walle 1998, 159. Based on general use of the model.

Marketing theorists, of course, are aware that variations in this process can exist and that the product life cycle is not identical for all products. Thus, in a fad, the rise and fall of a product's sales is very rapid and there is no distinct or lengthy "maturity" phase. In some cases, furthermore, a product which seems to have entered the decline stage will experience a rebirth. Typical variations in the product life cycle are portrayed in Figure 2.

On various occasions, furthermore, marketers have posed any number of variations and refinements in the product life cycle. Nonetheless, all these re-formulations presuppose that the product life cycle does exist (in some form) and that marketers can usefully employ it when forging strategies and tactics.

Although this general model (and its variants) has proved to be an effective heuristic device, significant variants are often observed. Thus,

Product Life Cycle Variations

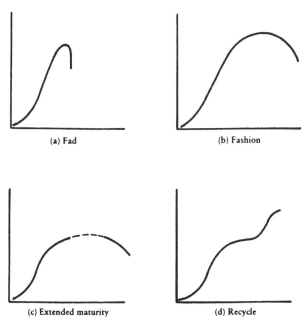

Fig. 2. From Walle 1998, 160. Based on general use of the model.

some theorists insist that the maturity stage can be subdivided into an initial period of intense competition which is followed by a phase of stability (Wasson 1974). Others have pointed to the fact that during the decline phase a low level of sales might be maintained for a long time. This period, dubbed petrification (Michael 1971), can remain profitable for many years even though the product shows all the symptoms of being in decline. Although pure scholars may debate the credibility of the Product Life Cycle model, the traditional model presented in Figure 1 continues to be its most popular conceptualization and it is routinely taught (often with little attention to refinements) in many marketing courses taught in business schools.

A Detailed Look at the Product Life Cycle

As outlined above, the product life cycle draws an analogy between the career of a product and the typical life history of an animal. As a result, the model has considerable intuitive appeal and it emerges as a helpful heuristic device when used to depict emerging marketing strategies and tactics. More than merely an analogy, however, the product life cycle has become identified with a wide array of concepts and conventional wisdoms regarding each specific phase of existence. For this reason, each stage will be discussed individually in some detail:

INTRODUCTION:

Description: During the introduction (birth), the product is unknown and/or consumers may be resistant to the innovation it represents. In addition, since the product is new, the production capacity (the amount of the product which can be brought to market) tends to be small. As a result, sales are low, while the price is high. By initially charging a high price, however, the firm may be able to recoup its initial investment through a relatively small number of sales.

Strategies: The first organizations to market a new type of product need to build consumer demand for the product type. These innovative firms, however, know that if their pioneering work is successful other organizations will choose to compete. As a result, innovative firms should introduce the product type to consumers, on the one hand, while attempting to build consumer loyalty for their specific product, on the other.

GROWTH:

Description: During the growth phase, sales and profits rapidly expand. Initially, various brands may compete for dominance. Advertising and promotion are often of particular importance. As competition increases, prices are lowered to win new customers from the competition. Often product variants will be marketed to distinct segments which have specific wants or needs. As sales increase, total marketing costs and efforts probably increase, but since these expenses are spread out over a higher sales volume, the marketing cost per item typically declines. Eventually, the growth rate slacks off and the market begins to be saturated.

Strategies: As competition increases, enhanced promotional activity and an expanded distribution network can be important to success. Often the product will be offered in forms such as prestige and economy models. Attempts should be made to build customer loyalty. Still sales can be gained by catering to unserved segments, not merely by taking sales from competitors.

MATURITY:

Description: The market becomes saturated. The growth rate declines. A period of "competitive turbulence," in which various weaker firms are forced to withdraw from the market, may exist. If this is true, non-dominant firms may be fighting for their place in the market. Dominant firms, in turn, strive to maintain their position. Although in the growth phase, it had been possible to gain sales by catering to those who had not previously used the product, in the maturity stage, marketers are often forced to win sales by taking market share away from their competitors. Since many people already have the product (or have experienced it), the total number of potential new customers declines. The maturity stage is usually a period of intense competition and a period when the customer, not the producer, is in a strong bargaining position.

Strategies: In the early stages of maturity, there may be a period of intense competition (competitive turbulence) and firms will need to decide if they are to remain in the market or withdraw. If they decide to remain, they must deal with the fact that the market is becoming saturated and that competition is increasing. Dominant firms tend to remain in the business because they anticipate that other firms will eventually withdraw and leave the market to them. With the market saturated, it becomes necessary to take customers from competitors in order to boost sales (or even to maintain sales levels).

DECLINE:

Description: As sales fall off drastically, various producers and marketers abandon the product. During this phase, the product may require an increased amount of managerial effort if it is to remain competitive, especially since sales and industry-wide profits are both declining. In addition, such "obsolete" products may make the company appear to be unprogressive or old fashioned. Products that survive, however, may be in an enviable position since they will face minimal competition.

Strategies: Often firms must decide if they are to withdraw a product immediately or slowly phase it out over time. If the product seems to be entering a "petrification" stage, competitive firms can "settle in" for the "long haul." Since a loyal market niche might remain, surviving firms find themselves in a dominant position and profits will rise.

The product life cycle, therefore, is a patterned and predictable process that (marketers and consumer researchers assume) products inevitably experience. As a result, all products are believed to experience some version of this life cycle which is depicted as analogous to the mortal existence of a living being. Using this analogy, marketers and consumer researchers have generalized and standardized strategies and tactics which can be employed at specific times during the product life cycle. The value of universal or generic responses is considered to be one of the major benefits of the product life cycle model. A table which presents an overview of the Product Life Cycle model is presented below:

The Product Life Cycle: An Overview

Factors	Introduction	Growth	Maturity	Decline
Sales Level	Slow Growth.	Rapid Growth.	Slows/stabilizes.	Falls.
Competitors	Few.	Increasing.	Many until shakehout.	Decline.
Basic Strategy	Build consumer awareness and acceptance of product type.	Penetrate the Market. Develop consumer loyalty.	Maintain market loyalty or withdraw from competition.	Phase out product or cater to specific niche.
Product	Basic model.	Variations.	Cater to specific market. Maximum variation.	Cull out all but a few basic products.
Price	High.	Falling as costs decline.	Falls further to meet competition.	(1) Falls to low level or (2) Rises if remaining niche will pay premium.

Fig. 3.

Although this discussion of the product life cycle is far from complete, it does demonstrate aspects of the model which popular culture scholars can profitably consider. First, the product life cycle draws an analogy between the career of a product and the life of a living being; although the model is actually a heuristic device, marketers often deal with it in, more or less, literal terms. Marketers and consumer researchers, in addition, use the product life cycle in order to choose the most appropriate tactics to apply to a product at various times during its life. Since products of popular culture rise and fall in popularity in ways which are reflective of the product life cycle, the method provides a useful set of tools of potential value to popular culture scholars.

Such an overview of the product life cycle is useful to popular culture scholars since it demonstrates important aspects of the mindset of the marketing profession and because it codifies key theories which can be applied to the analysis of popular culture. Popular culture scholars, however, need to remember that this heuristic device has often gained the status of a conventional wisdom which tends to be applied in uncritical ways and, as a result, marketing scholars may not question the validity of the model on all occasions. A significant value of the product life cycle, however, is that it usefully outlines how the market for products tends to evolve through time. Popular culture scholars can profit by being aware of these theories and by applying them to cultural analysis when and where appropriate.

The Product Life Cycle and Portfolio Analysis

In order to fully appreciate the implications of the Product Life Cycle, it is useful to consider another key method of business strategy known as "portfolio analysis" that is usually associated with the Boston Consulting Group. According to portfolio analysis, commodities should be viewed as distinct "strategic business units" that are usually envisioned as specific products or product lines. In such an analysis, a specific genre of popular culture (such as the cowboy story) might be considered as one such product or strategic business unit. In addition to merely listing the available products, portfolio analysis analyzes specific products in order to determine their current and future roles in the marketplace. Some products, for example, might currently be popular/profitable while others may not, as yet, have reached this potential, but constitute the wave of the future. Another group of products may have faded to such an extent that they should be discontinued. By understanding the current role of specific products or product types, it becomes possible to consider each in relationship to other alternatives and to evaluate them accordingly.

To facilitate such an evaluation of products, for example, the Boston Consulting Group recommends focusing upon two separate factors; (a) the growth rate of the product, in general, and (b) the total market share of the particular firm. Using these criteria, products can be divided into four categories which are defined below:

Stars: The product category is rapidly growing and the individual firm is a strong competitor with a significant market share.

Cash Cows: The product's growth rate is low, but the firm is a strong competitor within that industry.

Question Mark: The product category is high growth, but the firm is a fairly weak competitor.

Dogs: The industry is low growth and the firm is a weak competitor.

Based upon this depiction of products and the formal analysis which proceeds from it, each product is evaluated in terms of the long term goals of the firm. Graphically the analysis appears as:

Product Portfolio Model

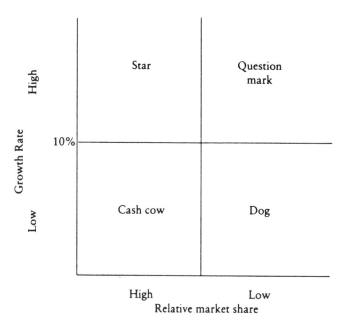

Fig. 4. From Walle 1998, 168. Based on general use of the model.

What is most important here is that the analysis suggests specific strategic orientations regarding each product/product type. Cash cows are mature products that are currently profitable, but may be on the brink of decline. Stars are high growth products that, although not highly profitable yet, should be groomed as the wave of the future, because (if they successfully mature) stars may evolve into lucrative cash cows. Question mark products are weak competitors but the product category is rapidly growing; as a result, they, too, might be transformed into popular and lucrative cash cows.

Dogs, in contrast, are weak, low growth products and are likely candidates for elimination. The key principle of the product life cycle and parallel models is that products are viewed as having a specific role at a specific time in history and it is assumed that this role continues to evolve through time. Analysts need to be concerned with both the present and the future.

In addition to the Boston Consulting Group model, the General Electric "strategic business planning grid" provides a similar, but somewhat more qualitative analysis. Both techniques consider products in terms of the total environment and how the role of the product evolves.

And both methods chart the progress of products in relation to other alternatives. The GE model, however, tends to be more subjective.

What is crucial for popular culture scholars to remember is that marketing scholars and consumer researchers tend to look at products and their "place in the world" as evolving and ever changing. In addition, strategic planners believe that products tend to eventually fade from the marketplace. It must be acknowledged, of course, that the product life cycle model is a useful concept, but one which can be misused. Even within mainstream business circles it has often received severe criticism. Thus, the product life cycle has been accused of influencing marketers to withdraw products while they were still viable (Harrell and Taylor 1981). Indeed, Nariman Dhalla and Sonia Yuspeh urge marketers to "forget the product life cycle concept" (1976). Nonetheless, the product life cycle is a key concept of marketing and consumer research that has served the profession well.

Many influential marketers continue to embrace the product life cycle even though some scholars point to limitations in the model. Many years ago, noted marketing theorist Philip Kotler complained that declining products tend to be more trouble than they are worth and that the product life cycle provides one rational means of dealing with them and the problems they potentially cause (Kotler 1965). Today, many marketers continue to agree with that assessment. Thus, even though scholars are aware of theoretical problems with the product life cycle, the business community is often willing to accept these limitations in order to reap the benefits which are offered.

Portfolio analysis is a convenient means of using concepts inherent in the product life cycle when evaluating product lines and their evolving role in the marketplace. Like the product life cycle model, portfolio analysis and similar models can be intuitively understood by the nonspecialist. The model, furthermore, employs various analogies which are potentially useful to popular culture scholars. Although portfolio analysis has been criticized on various theoretical grounds, the method is useful and respected.

The Diffusion of Innovations

The product life cycle and related theories deal with products in generalized ways but they do not consider what particular sorts of people will embrace a product at specific times during its life cycle. Knowing the characteristics of those who are likely to buy merchandise at specific periods, however, is invaluable strategic information; this sort of projection can assist management when appropriate strategies and tactics are being planned. It can also help popular culture scholars to perceive how patterns of consumer response can impact the popularity of cultural products. Because of the implications of this information, a major focus of marketing thought has concentrated on determining precisely when specific types of people are on the verge of becoming customers and, therefore, when they should be targeted with appropriate marketing efforts.

The most prominent tool for dealing with such issues is the diffusion of innovations model. Originally posed by Everett Rogers in the 1960s (Rogers 1962, 1983), the diffusion of innovations model has emerged as a powerful and ubiquitous perspective of modern marketing thought. Combined with the product life cycle, a powerful combination of theory and technique results which has significant strategic implications. Essentially, the diffusion of innovations model predicts that certain well defined and easily identifiable types of people tend to adopt products at precise and predictable times. Using such predictions, management is able to foresee when specific target markets are ready to adopt a product and, as a result, the product can be more effectively marketed.

By focusing the firm's attention around people who are likely candidates to purchase the product and by grooming other segments of society so they will acquire the product at a future and predictable period, optimal strategies can be created. In view of the fact that the diffusion of innovations model channels managerial action in productive directions, it is not surprising that the theory has found a significant place among marketing's strategic toolkit.

According to the classic diffusion of innovations model as advanced by Rogers, the consuming public is comprised of five separate groups. The first is the Innovator class which, according to the model, comprise approximately 2 1/2% of the population. Innovators are followed, in order, by the Early Adopters (13 1/3%), Early Majority (34%), Late Majority (34%) and Laggards (16%). It is useful to briefly describe each category as well as the strategies that are recommended when selling products to each group:

INNOVATORS:
Description: Innovators are upscale, young, and educated people who are willing to take risks. Although their numbers are small, they are the first group to adopt the product and they are viewed as the opinion leaders who influence "early adopters," the first large market segment to embrace the product.

Strategy: Since they are small in number it may be necessary to price the product at a high level in order to get an acceptable return on investment. Doing so is usually possible because innovators are affluent. Since the product may initially be unknown, considerable attention must be devoted to educating the innovators about the product. The product and its promotion, however, must reflect the tastes of the young, affluent, and educated.

EARLY ADOPTERS

Description: Although early adopters are the opinion leaders of those who adopt the product after them, they are influenced by the innovator class. Early adopters tend to buy products early in the life cycle, but they do so with caution; unlike innovators, early adopters are not risk takers. Although relatively young, affluent, and educated, early adopters do not quite match the innovators in these criteria.

Strategy: Since innovators are the opinion leaders of early adopters, winning the initial patronage of innovators is crucial for the continued success of the product. Since early adopters are not risk takers, risks must be reduced or mitigated. This can be done by providing information on the product (in advertising and public relations, for example) and in making early adopters feel confident that they will be successful in using the product and/or be satisfied with it.

EARLY MAJORITY

Description: Early Majority consumers buy before most people, but they do so with great care and they are willing to take even fewer risks than Early Adopters. They tend to be skilled blue-collar workers or white-collar workers who do not supervise others. They have less education and money than innovators or early adopters.

Strategy: Market the product to this group after it becomes firmly established with the Early Adopter. Lower price. Make the purchase seem increasingly safe and/or conventional.

LATE MAJORITY

Description: Late Majority consumers buy the product fairly late in the product life cycle. The product is well established before the Late Majority considers adopting it. They tend to be blue collar, uneducated, and older. They have little money and cannot usually purchase the product until the price goes down.

Strategy: Late in the product life cycle it is often possible to sell a cheaper version of the product which will not compete against the expensive versions which more upscale people have already purchased. It might be possible to "unload" unsold merchandise to Late Majority consumers late in the product life cycle.

LAGGARDS

Description: Very poor, backward, and tradition bound. Probably will never buy the product or will not do so until it becomes a virtual tradition in its own right.

Strategy: Catering to this segment is throwing money away since laggards don't have money for the product and probably wouldn't buy it even if they did.

Graphically, these categories and their behavior can be depicted as:

The Diffusion of Innovations Process

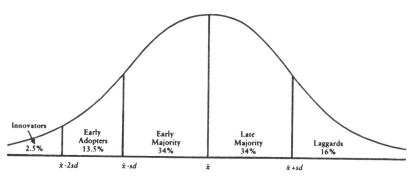

Fig. 5. From Walle 1998, 172. Based on general use of the model.

Besides listing and defining certain types of consumers and their differences, the diffusion of innovations model can be linked to the product life cycle. Since the product life cycle is assumed, furthermore, marketers tend to feel that the product merely provides a short term opportunity and, therefore, they have nothing to lose by constantly abandoning one segment of consumer in order to adjust the product to more effectively cater to new markets.

When marketers embrace the implications inherent in the product life cycle and the diffusion of innovations model, they assume the product has a limited life and that it must be constantly altered to respond to different classes of customers that emerge at different times. In addition, marketers typically assume that when products are embraced by those further down the cycle of adoption, the product will become tainted, passé, or old-fashioned; as a result, it will no longer be acceptable to the more progressive or upscale classes who initially bought and consumed it.

Portrayed graphically: the categories of consumers presupposed by the diffusion of innovations model can be portrayed as:

Diffusion of Innovations

Category	Innovator	Early Adopter	Early Majority	Late Majority	Laggards
Description	Young, risk takers, affluent educated.	Resembles the innovator, but doesn't take risks. Innovators are role models.	Older, less educated. Good, low status jobs. Careful about new products.	Even older and less education. Little money for new products.	Old, poor, uneducated.
When they buy	Introduction.	Growth.	Early maturity.	Late maturity.	Last to buy. May not buy.
Strategies	Introduce the product in way that appeals to segment.	Use innovators as opinion leaders. Make product safe.	Use early adopters as opinion leaders.	Lower price and quality. Portray product as generally acceptable.	Since they will probably not buy, do not waste effort on them.

Fig. 6.

This scheme has emerged as common sense to most mainstream marketers. And it can be applied to popular culture scholarship in useful ways.

As we have seen, the product life cycle model assumes that the career of a product is analogous to the life of an organism and that its popularity can be predicted accordingly. The diffusion of innovations model, furthermore, suggests the optimum benefits to the organization will result if the product (and its marketing) is constantly adjusted to cater to new classes of customers. A basic mechanism of marketing is to cheapen the product as it proceeds through the diffusion of innovations cycle since it must constantly be sold to increasingly less affluent customers.

Besides cheapening the price of the product, its quality may need to simultaneously be adjusted downward; although the initial innovators and early adopters tend to be picky about quality, the later customers who are poorer and less sophisticated will accept lower quality. Eventually, all but the laggards have bought the product; when this occurs, the product has proceeded through its life cycle and it hits a decline.

The diffusion of innovations model assumes that products may be abandoned by innovators as others come to embrace it. As a result, strategists urge the marketer to attempt to sell to each segment during only one phase of the product life cycle. Expanding a product's range to new target markets is a basic tool that marketers use to stimulate sales. Although doing so may involve reducing price or quality, these tactics are not perceived as having any negative potential since the product has already been bought by more affluent and sophisticated consumers (who are not predicted to make a large number of repeat purchases).

Conclusion

This chapter has dealt with a number of theories from marketing and consumer research that focus upon the popularity of products and how consumer demand evolves through time. Although the "correctness" of these theories has been challenged by some scholars, they have a long track record of useful service and for that reason they remain in vogue. This chapter has considered, in a more or less generic form, a number of models that marketers and consumer researchers routinely employ to explain patterns of consumer response. A key focus of this discussion, furthermore, is that these generic theories (when adequately adjusted to circumstances) may be of value in understanding artistic and literary products that constitute part of the popular culture of a society.

The first concept discussed involves the product life cycle; by embracing this paradigm, it becomes possible to envision a product as having a career which parallels the transitions from birth, to growth, to maturity, to decline, and eventually death. Marketers and consumer researchers have usefully applied the product life cycle to a wide range of goods and services. By linking these ideas to popular culture scholarship, it becomes possible to tap this useful metaphor.

Closely related to the product life cycle are portfolio analysis and the adoption curve which can be viewed as specialized applications of concepts which parallel and merge with the product life cycle. By thinking of literature and popular culture in ways which embody these concepts of marketing and consumer research, it becomes possible to (1) benefit from the intellectual traditions of marketing and consumer research and (2) present humanistic perspectives in ways which better mesh with the business disciplines. By doing so, the business disciplines and the humanities can be more fully and usefully integrated. Popular culture scholarship, in specific, has much to gain from this sort of cross-disciplinary endeavor.

Works Cited

Dhalla, Nariman K., and Sonia Yuspeh. 1976. "Forget the Product Life Cycle." *Harvard Business Review* Jan./Feb.: 102-10.

Hamermesh, Richard. 1986. "Making Planning Strategic." *Harvard Business Review* July/Aug.: 15-20.

Harrell, Stephen G., and Elmer J. I. Taylor. 1981. "Modeling and Product Life Cycle of Consumer Durables." *Journal of Marketing* 45.4 (Fall): 75.

Kotler, Philip. 1965. "Phasing Out Weak Products." *Harvard Business Review* March/April: 107-18.

Michael, G. C. 1971. "Product Petrification: A New State in the Life Cycle Theory." *California Management Review* 14.1: 88-91.

Rogers, Everett. 1983. *The Diffusion of Innovations*. New York: Macmillan.

Sproles, George B. 1981. "Analyzing Fashion Life Cycles: Principles and Perspectives." *Journal of Marketing* 45.4: 116-24.

Walle, Alf H. 1998. *Cultural Tourism: A Strategic Focus*. Boulder, CO: Westview P.

Wasson, Chester R. 1983. *Dynamic Competitive Strategy and Product Life Cycle*. Dayton, OH: Challenge.

Literary/Film Traditions

5

JAMES FENIMORE COOPER AND HIS INNOVATION:
A NOBLE BUT VULNERABLE PRODUCT OF THE FRONTIER

James Fenimore Cooper is a central, if not the pivotal, figure in the development of American literature. In his frontier fiction, Cooper crystallized two complementary themes which are crucial to American literature in general, and Western American literature in specific. First, Cooper viewed society as amoral and, although perhaps a necessary evil, essentially negative. He asserts that society seduces people into abandoning their personal morality; doing so leads to injustice and the dominance of amoral forces. Portraying this bleak perspective, Cooper depicts a heroic individualist who makes his own decisions and rejects the dictates of the amoral majority. This moral force, however, is inevitably crushed by the weight of culture and society.

Cooper was an innovator since he overtly crystalized and was the first writer to systemically market this seminal plotline and successfully introduce it to the American public. The Leatherstocking Tales quickly emerged as the popular culture of its era and it forms the foundation of several waves of popular Western stories which have been written since his time. Due to the impact of Cooper's vision, he is regarded as one of the classic authors of American literature.

Cooper and His Times
Both Cooper's environment and his own personal temperament influenced his classic theme in which an effete and amoral society is in conflict with the strong and moral individual. Raised in Cooperstown, New York, Cooper was the son of a major landholder and in his youth he had actually known aging frontiersmen who were to become the prototypes for his heroic figure. Cooper originally portrays Natty Bumppo, the heroic frontiersman, in old age. Thus, the character resembles frontiersmen as Cooper has actually known them. Decades later, Cooper depicted Bumppo's early years since an eager public demanded the stories and because Cooper needed the money they would earn. These characterizations, however, are shallow compared to the stature of the aged frontiersman of *The Pioneers* (1823) and *The Prairie* (1827), two of his

early frontier novels; literary critics routinely consider these novels to be classics.

As is often the case, Cooper's work is respected because it makes an original statement and, in the process, turned American literature on a new path. In terms of marketing and consumer research, Cooper started the life cycle of a new "product," the frontier story. Earlier writers, of course, had dealt with the frontier, but Cooper's writing was different because he depicted the frontiersman as inherently superior and noble while society, in contrast, emerges as effete and amoral. And Cooper's dramatic scenario, in which the individual and society are in conflict with one another, has become a recurring theme in Western American fiction.

Although Cooper consciously sought the approval of the social elite, especially when he was living in Europe, he, nonetheless, showed strong tendencies of being hostile to culture and society. These tendencies can be traced to Cooper's early childhood; his elementary school teacher, for example, was a pompous pro-English intellectual whom Cooper despised. Cooper's disapproval of his academic superiors was later displayed when he was at Harvard; in one revealing prank he trained a donkey to sit in an instructor's chair and imitate the professor. He was eventually expelled from Harvard because of such irreverent behavior.

Cooper's literary career, furthermore, began as a direct result of his tendency to downgrade his literary superiors; his first novel was written after he insisted he could write better than the popular novelist he had just read. Challenged to make good on his boast, he began his literary career. Combining his experience on the raw frontier with a covert (and sometimes overt) disdain for society, Cooper created a formula which grew to epic stature and, in later permutations, survives to this day: The hero is a lone and moral individual who confronts an amoral world characterized by blind conformity. As will be argued, after Cooper established his product, it has been revised continually in order for it to adjust to popular beliefs and tastes. Thus, although Cooper established the product life cycle of the frontier or cowboy story, other writers kept the product in vogue by tailoring it to the needs and demands of later markets. But before dealing with these revisions, it is necessary to look at Cooper and his innovation.

In Cooper's mind, the evolution of American society is a vicious circle. In the series of novels which make up the Leatherstocking Tales, a complex form of social control (government and law) causes the displacement of Natty Bumppo, a strong product of the frontier whose personality is at odds with a culture of mindless conformity. As we shall see, Bumppo is typical neither of civilized society nor the frontier; he represents the truly moral person—a rarity in any environment. Bumppo's morality manifests itself in two ways. First, he makes personal judgments which are based upon a compassionate humanity and a sense of justice, not upon abstract laws or rules. Second, Bumppo is a cultural relativist. He does possess a personal morality, but he judges others by their own particular code. As long as people remain true to their ideals, Bumppo respects them. Because of Bumppo's attitudes, however, he is exiled: a fate Cooper depicts as inevitable for moral man in an amoral world. Elsewhere, in the Littlepage novels, for example, Cooper predicts the fate of a society where morality and strong-mindedness are thwarted; the Littlepages, a noble family of landholders, are nearly destroyed by the greed of their amoral tenants. In the Leatherstocking saga, the storyline is just the reverse and the landlord (Judge Temple) eliminates Natty Bumppo, a noble and moral force, from society.

There is an obvious similarity between Cooper's life and the themes of oppression about which he wrote. Vernon Parrington (1930, 222) put it well when he said Cooper's "outspoken individualism was a constant irritant to a sensitive majority . . . the right of the individual to question the herd pronouncements was a right not acknowledged by the herd." Nonetheless, his frontier stories caught the public imagination and they have emerged as examples of classic American literature.

A weakness of Cooper's writing is that the ultimate fate of his heroes is seldom developed in a realistic way. First, Cooper often ended his novels on a positive note which often results in artificial and stilted resolutions. The ending of the Littlepage trilogy is a case in point. Throughout three Littlepage novels, Cooper depicts a family which is increasingly exploited and persecuted; they are threatened, their church pew is desecrated, and their assets are destroyed by arsonists. In the climax, the Littlepage home is actually attacked by a mob, but, at the last possible moment, a band of Indians friendly to the Littlepages arrives to save the day, and the Littlepages live happily every after. This pointless and gratuitous finale undercuts the message of the entire series and leaves the fate of the Littlepages unresolved in any realistic manner. It is easy to see why Cooper ends the series the way he does; these novels are a commentary on an actual historic event, the anti-rent strikes, and Cooper was actively attempting to sway public opinion. Partisan motivations, however, often lead to awkward and banal endings in Cooper's fiction; politics and literature do not usually mix well.

A second reason that Cooper routinely ends his novels in a contrived and unrealistic manner is his belief that the wilderness was the final refuge for the truly heroic person and a skilled woodsman, like Natty Bumppo, could successfully escape the confines of civilization by retreating to where society cannot follow. Although many of Cooper's heroes would like to leave society, only Natty, the skilled frontiersman, is able to survive without its help. Cooper's other protagonists are the products of society, and for better or worse, they must remain there. In *The Pioneers*, for example, Cooper juxtaposed Natty Bumppo, the frontiersman, with Ben Pump, a former sailor living in Templeton. Both Bumppo and Pump incur the wrath of society, but only Bumppo can escape civilization. Towards the end of *The Pioneers* Pump expresses a desire to go west with Bumppo. Pump, unfortunately, is not skilled in the ways of the frontier and when Bumppo leaves, he and his dog go alone.

Cooper's works abound with heroic personalities who are somewhat similar to Bumppo, but, nevertheless, who are unable to abandon society. Harvey Birch of *The Spy*, for example, is a peddler: both the product and the agent of society and civilization. Nevertheless, he is a strong individualist and possesses an internalized morality similar to that of Bumppo. During the Revolution, Birch becomes a double agent for the American cause and he is forced to pose as a traitor. Although Birch is despised by all (except for George Washington, who shares the secret that he is really a hero), he is far superior to the people who hate him; he alone is motivated by a moral purpose and not the chance of personal gain. In *The Redskins*, furthermore, Hugh Littlepage refuses to give in to the wishes of the greedy tenants not so much for personal gain (which admittedly is a consideration), but more as a matter of principle: he feels that a stand has to be made against the amoral forces of society. Hugh, however, is a cultured gentleman, not a rugged frontiersman. The central and recurring message in all these novels is that society tends to oppress or destroy the truly moral individual; Cooper's heroes come from different backgrounds, not merely the frontier, but all typically end up in a struggle against an amoral society. It remained for historian Frederick Jackson Turner to popularize the notion that the frontier experience itself created heroic people. Although Cooper seems to foreshadow Turner in some ways, Cooper was less concerned with the origin of individualism than with its inherent worth and its vulnerability within society. As we shall see in the discussion of Owen Wister, however, it was Turner's frontier thesis of American history which helped to recast Cooper's plot formula in ways which restarted the product life cycle.

Contrary to superficial appearances, Natty Bumppo is primarily an archetypal individualist and not merely a "noble savage." Even if Cooper sometimes utilizes rhetoric reminiscent of Jean-Jacques Rousseau, he does not dwell on Bumppo's origin; Natty is not representative of a "devolved humanity." As early as 1927, Lucy Hazard (106) noted that Cooper was not merely aping the Romantic tradition, observing:

The cardinal doctrines of Rousseau's philosophy are, first, the essential good-ness of human nature. Second, the essential badness of human institutions. On both of these counts *Deerslayer* is heretical. . . . Leatherstocking, then cannot be regarded as an adequate embodiment of the Rousseau philosophy of back to nature.

In his *Notions of the Americans* (1839), Cooper stated his position as follows: "The red man [savage] disappears before the superior moral and physical influence of the whites" (1839, 17-18). This is hardly a Rousseauistic sentiment and smacks of the same chauvinism which 50 years later was expressed through Social Darwinism. Thus, in many ways Cooper was a product of his times. Nonetheless, he developed the dramatic scenario of a noble and moral product of the frontier who is in conflict with civilized Easterners. And it was this characterization and the accompanying dramatic tension that transformed Cooper's vision into a recognizable, duplicate-able, and readily accepted product of pop-ular culture.

The Leatherstocking Tales

A consideration of Cooper's Leatherstocking saga is essential to a study of Cooper because only there does he present a full vision of the frontier and its individualist hero. Of the five novels in the series, only *The Pioneers* and *The Prairie* need to be considered in detail here. In *The Pioneers*, the first in the series to be written, Cooper argues that society, through abstract and unyielding regulations, undermines moralistic indi-vidualism. In *The Prairie*, Cooper draws the individualist epic to a con-clusion by showing Bumppo transcending society in the Great American Desert, a place where civilization and society cannot intercede. The remaining three novels, *The Last of the Mohicans* (1826), *The Pathfinder* (1840), and *The Deerslayer* (1841), expand Bumppo's character, give the schism between the individual and society a greater historical perspec-tive, and develop ancillary sub-plots. Although these three novels some-what sketch out Cooper's broader vision, *The Pioneers* and *The Prairie* are the definitive stories which define Cooper's innovation.

A clue to *The Pioneers* can be found in a short book entitled *A Guide to the Wilderness* (1809), written by Cooper's father, William, a year before he died. The last heading in this pamphlet was entitled "absurdities," and the last item under that heading is as follows:

As to those Western counties of New York which I have been describing, they are chiefly peopled from the New England states, where the people are civil, well-informed, and very sagacious; so that a wise stranger would be much apter to conform at once to their usages than to begin by teaching them better. (1809, 49)

Much of the plot of *The Pioneers* is an amplification of this statement. Natty Bumppo, a stranger, would teach the settlers through his personal example. He possesses a knowledge of conservation and a theory of social control and law which depends upon his personal moral and ecological judgments, not arbitrary rules applied by rote. Although it would be "apter" for Bumppo to "conform at once," he doesn't and as a result he is eventually banished to the wilds.

Bumppo, according to Cooper, is: "unlike most of those who live a border life, he united the better instead of the worst of the . . . [Whites and Indians]. . . . He was a man endowed with the choicest and perhaps rarest gift of nature; that of distinguishing good from bad" (1892b, 103).

There are two distinctive qualities to Bumppo's morality and personality. He is truly moral; he can distinguish the good from the bad, and he acts in accordance with such judgments. Second, he is a cultural relativist and he judges people on their own terms, not by abstract standards set up by himself or by his culture. Bumppo realizes that no action can be judged as moral or immoral unless the personal code of the actor is taken into account.

Acting in accordance with his internalized morality is seldom easy for Bumppo. An extreme example of this tension appears in *The Deerslayer*, when the captive Bumppo is given temporary freedom on a promise that he would return and submit himself to his captors. He keeps his word even though doing so means almost certain death by torture. On many occasions Bumppo inconveniences himself for moral reasons. This is one of the more dramatic examples of this tendency.

Other less dramatic examples of Bumppo's strong, internalized morality can easily be found. Bumppo is often placed in danger because of his conscience. In *The Last of the Mohicans*, Bumppo decides to divulge the location of a secret cave, "the harboring place," in order to protect an endangered party which includes women. They hide the women in the cave after Bumppo observes, "it would not be the act of men to leave such harmless things to their fate, even though it breaks up the harboring place forever" (1892, 23). Because of this decision, Bumppo and his companions are drawn into a fight which is not their own and one of them, Uncas, is killed.

Bumppo doesn't impose his private beliefs or his moral standards upon others. He realizes that good and bad must be interpreted with reference to the personal morality of the actor. He observes, for example, "It would be a great offense for a white man to scalp the dead; whereas it's a signal virtue for an Indian. Then ag'in, a white man cannot ambush women and children in war, while a redskin may. 'Tis cruel work, I'll allow; but for them it's lawful work; while for us it would be grevious work" (1892a, 23). Bumppo is a true individualist; he does things his own way and he judges others with reference to their own morality. In the twentieth century, especially in the era of Nazi Germany, intellectuals found that a cultural relativistic view, if carried to an extreme, can thwart meaningful moral evaluations. In the nineteenth century, however, the world tended to be so ethnocentric that relativistic visions such as Cooper's are refreshing. Even though Cooper had some ethnocentric orientations, he did realize that merely focusing on his own moral edicts when evaluating others was inappropriate. Cooper makes this point by contrasting Bumppo with two common social types. One is essentially moralistic, but is not relativistic, and possesses only half of Bumppo's desirable qualities. The second is neither moralistic nor relativistic.

Judge Marmaduke Temple is representative of the first type; he is honest, but lacks the ability to judge people on their own terms; although obviously moral, he is inflexible in his evaluation of others. For Temple, the law must be impersonal and abstract. When the foolish settlers shamelessly and needlessly slaughter the game around the Templeton area, for example, Temple outlaws hunting. The edict affects all people, even Bumppo, the professional hunter. Since Temple's law can't distinguish between a legitimate and an illegitimate hunter, Bumppo is prosecuted for killing a deer; this is just one of many examples throughout the story where the judge and his appointees make rulings which, evaluated from a humane or even a rational perspective, are obviously both counterproductive and unjust.

It should be added that treating Bumppo in this manner is not an easy and pleasant task for Judge Temple, who is greatly indebted to the aging hunter. Natty helped Judge Temple to settle the region and he had recently saved the life of the judge's daughter, Elizabeth. But Temple believes the law must be applied impersonally to all people equally. During Bumppo's trial, for example, the judge emphasizes "my private feelings must not enter into the judgment" (1892b, 409).

While Judge Temple is a moral man, his agent, Hiram Doolittle, exploits the law in a self-serving manner. Although Temple is merely overly abstract, Doolittle is amoral and exploitative: the complete opposite of Natty Bumppo. Incorrectly believing Bumppo is secretly smelting valuable metals in his cabin, Doolittle uses his office for self-serving reasons in an attempt to get the treasure for himself. When Doolittle's scheme is foiled, he has Bumppo arrested and imprisoned.

Even though Cooper depicts Bumppo as the moral force and champion of justice, he is constantly oppressed and ultimately banished. A prologue of this oppression occurs during a turkey shoot where Bumppo competes. Bumppo's flintlock rifle fails to fire properly and only the powder in the pan of his rifle ignites. (This occasionally happens to any flintlock and is not necessarily the result of carelessness or an unskilled marksman.) Due to this unavoidable misfire, Bumppo has not been able to demonstrate his skill and, in actuality, he has not fired his gun since the slug was still in the barrel. Nevertheless, an official declares that a flash in the pan constituted a shot and demands that Bumppo pay a second entrance fee in order to participate. Since Bumppo has no more money, he is denied an opportunity to demonstrate his skills. Happily, Elizabeth Temple pays the second fee and Bumppo is able to defeat all the contestants, even though the prize Bumppo wins goes to Elizabeth.

Later in the novel, Cooper depicts the amoral nature of society in overt terms when Bumppo commits the unpardonable sin of showing disregard for the laws of society when he refuses to allow Hiram Doolittle to search his property. To make the situation even more black and white, we are told that Doolittle has a history of inappropriately interfering with Bumppo's private affairs. Bumppo, understandably, rejects Doolittle's unreasonable demands, pushes Doolittle off the cabin steps, and points his gun at Doolittle's assistant, Bill Kirby, warning him not to serve the warrant.

At Bumppo's trial, it is proven that Doolittle was acting for personal gain and not for the benefit of society. As a result, Bumppo is cleared of charges that he wrongly attacked Doolittle. He is, however, found guilty of opposing and threatening Bill Kirby, Doolittle's assistant. Bumppo is punished because he opposes the law even though it is proven that the law was being used to deprive him of his rights. For this crime Bumppo is placed in the pillory, sentenced to 30 days in jail, and fined $100.00, which has to be paid before he can go free. This is more money than Bumppo has, and except for the generosity of an old friend, he would have been subject to imprisonment. It is this kind of scenario in which the moral individual is pitted against an amoral (or even immoral) society that made Cooper's work distinctive as a recognizable product which was later reworked by others.

Ironically, Judge Temple, himself, has no right to make the law since he doesn't actually own the land in and around Templeton. Temple had bought the land with money entrusted to him by a Major Effingham many years before. Believing Effingham to be dead, the Judge had used the money for his own purposes. The contradiction becomes complete when

Bumppo is prosecuted because he wouldn't let Doolittle into his home precisely because Effingham (who is still very much alive) is hiding there. Bumppo has been secretive around his home because he believes Effingham is in potential danger. Thus, Bumppo has been harassed by the false authority of Judge Temple while protecting Major Effingham, the actual and legitimate landlord. Effingham dies soon after it is disclosed that he is the legitimate owner of the land and on his tombstone it is written that Bumppo was a "faithful and upright friend and attendant" (1892b, 449). With legitimate authority dead and buried, Bumppo must move on and leave the amoral society which ultimately exiles him.

Portraying various types of authority, Cooper depicts people who, at various times, had been the legitimate authority of the Templeton area. The first is the now-alcoholic Chingachgook, who represents the remains of pre-white authority. The second is Natty, the first white to know the area and the man who educated the white settlers to the ways of the frontier. The third is Major Effingham, a member of society who has the legal claim to the land. These three legitimate authorities are bound together for their mutual benefit and protection; this pact, however, does not allow them to prevail over the illegitimate, but de facto authority of Judge Temple. Chingachgook and Effingham die, and Natty is banished.

At the end of *The Pioneers*, Cooper sets the stage for Bumppo's last conflict. Hiram Doolittle, the immoral opportunist, leaves for the west at about the same time Bumppo begins his last trek to the frontier. Doolittle hopes to scatter "his professional science and legal learning throughout the land" (1892b, 49), which of course, is the same law which had oppressed Bumppo in the first place.

If Natty Bumppo is to find a haven from Doolittle and his breed, Cooper has to discover an environment where society can never intercede and replace him. Cooper was aware that the flow of American history had moved ever Westward and that previous frontiers had ultimately been swallowed up by civilization. If Bumppo is to receive more than a brief reprieve, he needs a place where society can never usurp him. During the 1820s, the concept of the Great American Desert was in vogue, and this image provided Cooper with a sanctuary for his hero. "The notion of a continuous desert began to be widely accepted after 1820 and . . . it was soon to appear on most maps of the United States" (Malcom 1966, 6). This desert was a large area located primarily in the plains or prairie region: "It has an average width of between five and six hundred miles, extending along the base of the Rocky Mountains from north to south, as far as we have any acquaintance with that range" (James 1823). In a report to the Secretary of State, Stephen H. Long concluded that this region was: "almost wholly unfit for civilization and, of course, uninhabitable by a people depending on agriculture for their subsistence. Although tracts of fertile land, considerably extensive, are occasionally to be met with, yet the scarcity of wood and water . . . will prove an insuperable obstacle" (Muszynska-Wallace 1949, 194). Cooper had read Long's work and as E. Muszynska-Wallace has pointed out, Long's treatises cannot be overlooked as a source for *The Prairie*: "Numerous details are drawn by Cooper from its pages. And so specific are some of these materials, transferred from the narrative to the novel, that no uncertainty as to the source whence they came can exist" (1949, 103). Entire anecdotes from Long's *Expedition to the Rocky Mountains* were borrowed and worked into *The Prairie*.

Cooper really believed these descriptions were accurate: "Cooper shared the mistaken notion of his day that a kind of American Sahara, unfit for all types of agriculture stretched almost to the foothills of the Rockies" (Flanagan 1941, 103). In the opening paragraph of *The Prairie*, for example, Cooper tells the reader that "nature had placed a barrier of desert to the extension of our population to the West." This hypothesized desert provides a haven for Bumppo, because Cooper believed civilization can't follow his hero into the desert. Critics who do not emphasize Cooper's belief in a Great American Desert can easily interpret the landscape of *The Prairie* as primarily symbolic. Henry Nash Smith, for example, believes *The Prairie*'s setting is an "idealized neutral territory or testing ground for heroes" (Smith 1950). Another critic, Merrill Lewis, has suggested "the landscape is essentially meta-phorical, a part of a dramatic situation and a reflection of a moral condition . . . " (Lewis 1970-71, 196). Such interpretations assert that Cooper is using poetic license to mold symbolic environments. In reality, Cooper attempted to paint a realistic picture of the Great American Desert and he utilized recently published descriptions of the prairie to make his portrayal credible. The landscape of *The Prairie* is unrealistic because Cooper relied upon false accounts. Contemporary reviews of *The Prairie*, such as Timothy Flint's, point to Cooper's unrealistic treatment of the plains and noted that Cooper had never actually visited the place.

The plot of *The Prairie* can be quickly summarized: Natty Bumppo has retreated from civilization; his new home is the Great American Desert. Members of society also begin to invade this sanctuary. In the end, the environment proves inhospitable to society, which must eventually and inevitably retreat back to the East. Bumppo is given the option of returning to civilization, but he refuses; he has finally found an environment where society cannot displace him.

In *The Prairie*, Cooper develops three characters in considerable detail: the aged Natty Bumppo, the squatter Ishmael Bush, and Dr. Obed

Battius, the scientist. Bumppo represents the truly moral individualist who is constantly thwarted by an amoral society. Bush is symbolic of authority. Dr. Battius embodies the amoral scientific point of view which Cooper disapproved of and feared.

The character of Natty Bumppo is primarily the same as he appeared in *The Pioneers*. He is older, wiser, and has lost some of his physical prowess. Vestigial remains of his former strength survive, however: "his form had withered, but it was not wasted. The sinews and muscles which had once denoted great strength, though shrunken, were still visible" (1892b, 15). Because his body is old and weak, Bumppo has become a professional trapper, which he considers to be an unmanly vocation.

Although in *The Pioneers*, Natty had been inept in his dealings with society, in *The Prairie*, he demonstrates considerable sophistication in his encounters with society and, as Donald Ringe has observed, "the trapper is able to answer every argument that Dr. Bat attempts against him" (Ringe 1961). Cooper transformed Bumppo into an eloquent spokesman primarily because he wanted a protagonist whose mental facilities could surpass those of the trained thinker. Bumppo's essential character, however, remained the same as it had been in *The Pioneers*.

Bumppo understands that the codes of arbitrary law, which caused his alienation from the East, are valid and meaningful in certain contexts; he believes the law is evil, but in some circumstances, he acknowledges it is necessary. Speaking to Ellen Wade, Natty observes, "The law—'tis bad to have it, but, I sometimes think, it is worse, where it is never to be found" (1964, 25).

As the book progresses, Natty aids the microcosm of society which is marooned on the desert. Bumppo, Ellen Wade, and Paul Hover, for example, are captured by a band of Sioux Indians but are saved by Bumppo's quick wit. In this situation a herd of stolen horses is brought into camp and,

the trapper caught the knife from the hands of the inattentive keeper with a power that his age would seem to contradict, and at a single blow severed the thong of hide which connected the whole of the drove. The wild animals snorted with joy and terror and tearing the earth with their heels, they dashed away into the broad prairie in a dozen different directions. (1964, 51)

In the confusion which follows, the captives make a successful escape.

After reuniting with the Bush party, Bumppo meets Captain Middleton, whose metaphoric name underscores that he represents the middle path between the individual and society. Through Middleton, we learn that the Bush clan has been holding Middleton's wife captive and that he has come to rescue her. Discovering this, Bumppo helps Middleton escape. They are all eventually recaptured by the Indians, but only because an unexpected snowstorm makes it impossible for them to travel without leaving easily followed tracks in the newly fallen snow. Again the party escapes and again it is Bumppo who makes an escape possible.

Throughout all this, Bumppo's quick thinking and decisive action are vital; he has adapted to the desert, and is superior to the intrusive society which cannot adjust. Bumppo's savvy in the desert resembles his youth in upstate New York; in the desert, however, society cannot displace him; he has found a home from which he cannot be banished.

At story's end, Paul, Ellen, Inez, and Captain Middleton ask Bumppo to return to the East and a comfortable life. Instead, Bumppo decides to stay in the desert so that he can die away from civilization. Although Bumppo has been oppressed by society even while he served it, the forces of society relentlessly ask more of the tired old trapper. Dr. Battius, the scientist, urges Natty to return to the East and divulge his lore. He states: "there are obligations which every man owes to society and to human nature. It is time that you should return to your country-men, to deliver us one of those stores of experimental knowledge."

Bumppo is not swayed by Battius' plea. He has paid his dues in full and now he owes himself something: freedom from the cares of the civilized world. Instead of returning to society, Bumppo joins a band of Indians. When he dies a year later, he is looking to the West. Just before death, he rises and firmly says one last word: "Here" (1964, 345). Bumppo knows that beyond the Rockies the land is fertile and will eventually be exploited by society. He also knows that the East has already been largely raped and wantonly destroyed. Bumppo can't tolerate or survive in either place; but "Here," between the areas of established and future culture, there exists a middle ground where society cannot compete. This middle ground is the Great American Desert. Bumppo represents the moral individualist who finds his refuge in the desert which society cannot use and does not want.

The second major character is Ishmael Bush, a man whose name is obviously metaphorical. In the Bible, Ishmael was cast out of society and forced to wander in the desert. This is essentially the fate of Ishmael Bush: he is a squatter who is thrown off his land when the legal owner takes possession. The biblical Ishmael gained wisdom during his desert exile and eventually returned to society. In *The Prairie*, Ishmael's fate is similar. His last name Bush reminds the reader that Cooper's Ishmael wanders through the prairie (an environment of bushes, not trees).

Ishmael and his party represent a microcosm of society and metaphorically depict civilization in the unyielding desert. The numerous members of the party represent various social types and include an intellectual elitist (Dr. Obed Battius), a small-business man (Paul Hover), an orphan (Ellen Wade), a criminal (Abiram White), and a leader and authority figure (Ishmael). The various age groups of society are also represented; Ishmael and his wife are middle aged; Paul, Ellen, and some of the sons of Ishmael are in their earlier phases of adulthood; and some children are occasionally mentioned. The party, therefore, resembles a typical cross section of Eastern society.

Chapter 2 of *The Prairie* demonstrates how society, as represented by the Bush clan, can quickly exhaust the sparse resources of the prairie. Wanting firewood for one evening's camp, the party destroys a grove of trees which on the prairie is a rare and valuable resource. This destruction, Cooper suggests, is typical of both the techniques and the needs of society. Bumppo, aware of the implications of this waste and destruction, asks:

what will the Yankee choppers say when they have cut their path from the Eastern to the Western waters. . . . They will turn on their tracks like a fox that doubles, and then the rank smell of their own footsteps will show them the madness of their waste. (1964, 65)

Although, in a plentiful land (such as the virgin forests of the East), society might have the luxury of being wasteful, in the desert resources are scarce and cannot be wasted. Ironically, although Bumppo hates such wanton destruction, these very habits of society protect him since they prevent the desert from being settled.

As the book progresses, trouble befalls the Bush camp. Their horses and cattle are stolen by the Indians. Bush's eldest son is killed, seemingly by Natty Bumppo. Various members of the party desert Bush; Captain Middleton and Natty join the deserters. The trials and sufferings which Bush faces ultimately result in his voluntary return to the East, a retreat which underscores Cooper's premise that society cannot conquer the Great American Desert.

Ishmael Bush, however, is not a stock character; he is able to make judgments based upon circumstances, he does not merely apply the letter of the law as Judge Temple had done. When, at the end of the story, he wields authority, he is compassionate, and, therefore, superior to Judge Temple, who can only apply the law to the letter.

The trial of Captain Middleton is a case in point. Middleton has clearly committed violent crimes against society (as represented by the Bush clan), since the captain had "broken into my encampment, aiding and abetting, as they have called many an honester bargain in destroying my property" (1964, 309). Although this is true, Bush realizes that Middleton did these things in an attempt to rescue his wife. As a result, Bush declares, "The matter is settled between us . . . you and your wife are free" (1964, 309). Such flexibility and compassion are superior to Judge Temple's court, where disobedience cannot be tolerated even for just cause.

Bush's ultimate test occurs when Bumppo is tried on the charge of murdering Bush's son. Natty's fate looks bleak since Ishmael has "previously made up his mind" (1964, 307) regarding the fate of his prisoners. Nevertheless, Bush reconsiders when Bumppo reveals that he not only isn't guilty, but he witnessed Bush's brother-in-law, Abiram White, commit the crime. When the report is proven to be true, Bumppo is set free.

The final crescendo comes when Bush must decide the fate of Abiram White, his friend, his wife's brother, and the killer of his eldest son. This is a hard decision for Bush and he doesn't immediately render a verdict. Finally, after a day of traveling, Bush, his wife, and the murderer retire to a distant hill to hear the decision.

Bush admits the difficulty in making his decision: "Ay therein lies the hardship of the case. I had brought my mind to the punishment of that houseless trapper, without great strivings, for the man had done me few favors" (1964, 319-20). When she realizes what the verdict will be, Bush's wife desperately tries to save her brother's life, first through the use of biblical authority and then, adopting a purely emotional argument, pleading, "my blood, and the blood of my children is in his veins, cannot mercy be shown" (1964, 321). Although Bush believes in mercy and compassion (as demonstrated in the earlier trials), he also believes all defendants should have parity. He reminds his wife that "when we believed that miserable old trapper had done this deed, nothing was said of mercy" (1964, 321). Bush thus renders his verdict: "you have slain my first born and according to the laws of God and man, you must die."

After rendering the various rulings, judgments which are far superior to those of Judge Temple, Bush leads his party back to the East. They are, after all, symbolic of Eastern society which, according to Cooper, could not survive in the prairie. Bush and his followers are last seen "pursuing their course towards the settlements." As they approached the confines of society, "the train was blended among a thousand others. Though some of the numerous descendants of this particular pair were reclaimed from their lawless and semi-barbarous lives, the principles of the family, themselves, were never heard of more" (1964, 326). Cooper is not optimistic enough to make his analogy to the biblical Ishmael complete. In the Bible, Ishmael returns to society with wisdom and he becomes the ancestor of a great nation. The lessons of the desert, however, fail to make Bush a founding father. Instead, he, like Bumppo, fades into oblivion.

The last major character in *The Prairie* is Dr. Obed Battius; like Ishmael Bush, his name is metaphorical. As Ringe has pointed out, the name Battius implies an intellectual blindness (1961, 319). He is literally "as blind as a bat" when it comes to certain ethical and intellectual considerations. His first name, Obed, is the first four letters of obedient and, in due course we find that his blindness is largely due to the fact that he obediently adheres to the conventional wisdom of the intellectual community.

Dr. Battius, like certain eighteenth- and nineteenth-century social philosophers typified by the Enlightenment, believes that if people have a proper education they will act morally, and "education might eradicate the evil principle" (1964, 215). Battius disagrees with Natty Bumppo, who believes that man is "the same, be he born in the wilderness or in the town" (1964, 215). Most people, Natty believes, are essentially evil; at least their motives are suspect. As a result, education won't eliminate a person's selfish and evil tendencies. This is underscored when we find that Dr. Battius, himself, for all his pious talk, is primarily motivated by desire for fame and recognition. He, for example, wistfully states that if people knew what he and his fellow naturalists had gone through, "pillars of silver, and statues of Brass would be reared as the everlasting monuments of their glory" (1964, 212).

Dr. Battius' theory that knowledge and education make people moral receives an empirical test when the court of Ishmael Bush tries the people who had transgressed his unsophisticated law. According to Battius, Bush would be a poor judge because he lacks a formal education and he is not an intellectual. As we have seen, however, Bush's law is compassionate and is not constrained by an overly codified legal structure.

When Battius himself comes to trial, he learns that the Bush party has turned against him and his elitist beliefs. All the defendants except Dr. Battius are treated with a certain of degree of dignity. They are considered capable of standing trial and of knowing the difference between right and wrong. Dr. Battius, however, is considered unfit to stand trial. In the words of Esther Bush, Ishmael's wife: "make no words with a man who can break your bones as easily as set them, and let the poisoning devil go. He's a cheat from box to phial" (1964, 310). Battius is released without the dignity of being tried as a responsible person. Although Battius believes his education makes him morally superior, others find him to be merely corrupt. This decision foreshadows Clarence Darrow's speech in the Leopold-Loeb trial, which argues that since society had not provided his seemingly sophisticated clients with a moral basis for their actions, society cannot judge them guilty. Because they lack a moral code, Leopold, Loeb, and Dr. Battius are spared. There is some indication that Dr. Battius realizes the error of his ways and comprehends the wisdom of Bumppo's views. He urges Bumppo to return to the East and give the world his "stores of experimental knowledge" (1964, 332). This completes Cooper's discussion of the amoral nature of modern society.

The Pioneers and *The Prairie* established a formula for the frontier story and for American literature which survives to this day. The hero is superior to the society which usurps him. Nevertheless, he is constantly displaced by the encroachment of civilization. For Bumppo, however, the Great American Desert provides an escape where he can retreat. In the desert, he ceases to be the spearhead of civilization and he lives without the fear of eviction.

The cult of the individualist hero survived and transcended Cooper, but the concept of the Great American Desert died within his own lifetime. "During the 1840s the explorations of Fremont, the political activities of Thomas Hart Benton, the annexation of Texas, the cession by Mexico of the lands from New Mexico to California and the Westward movement . . . paved the way for a new concept" (Malcom 1966, 9).

This new concept appears in Cooper's later frontier fiction. In the preface to *The Oak Openings* (1848), his last romance of the wilderness, Cooper observed: "there is nothing imaginary in the fertility of the West. Personal observation has satisfied us that it must surpass anything that exists in the Atlantic states" (1982, 14). Such sentiments, of course, contradict *The Prairie*: the myth of the desert was gone. Instead of using the desert for a sanctuary for the heroic figure, Cooper fell back upon religion and observed "the main course is onward; and the day, in the sense of time, is not distant when the whole earth is to be filled with the knowledge of the Lord." In his own lifetime, Cooper repudiated the saga of the Leatherstocking Tales. Even so, it remains the high point of Cooper's writings and a keystone of our literary heritage. Although Cooper's prose style has sometimes been criticized, the scenario of the moral individual of the frontier confronting civilization has had a profound effect on American literature. The "acid test" of literature is the impact it has upon future generations. So judged, Cooper's vision deserves a high rating.

A Distinctive Formula
Defined and envisioned in the 1820s and reflective of sentiments which became identified with "Manifest Destiny" a few years later (which suggested that the culture of the East was inevitably destined to

transform the entire North American continent in its own image), Cooper's plot formula bears the imprint of the era. In general, Cooper depicts culture and civilization as irresistible. Nonetheless, Cooper also accepted the prevailing belief that certain regions were unsuitable for civilization and would serve as a refuge for the frontier spirit which was being displaced from other, more fertile, regions. As a result, the Leatherstocking Tales form a commentary on contemporary events as Cooper viewed them.

Beyond this, Cooper created an immortal character who is a moral and inherently superior product of the frontier. Cooper also codified a basic conflict between this memorable character and the forces of an effete and amoral civilization. Cooper depicts his hero as a vestigial remain who can only survive in a hinterland which society and civilization did not want. These themes eventually emerged as passé.

In creating Bumppo and his conflict against civilization, however, Cooper crystalized the first generation of what eventually emerged as the cowboy story. In doing so, Cooper created a genre of popular literature which, in a series of appropriate reworkings, has had a long and influential life.

Works Cited

Cooper, James Fenimore. 1839. *Notions of the Americans*. Philadelphia.

——. 1892. *The Last of the Mohicans*. New York: P. F. Collier. Originally published in 1826.

——. 1892a. *The Deerslayer*. New York: P. F. Collier. Originally published in 1841.

——. 1892b. *The Pioneers*. New York: Appleton. Originally published in 1823.

——. 1964. *The Prairie*. New York: Airmount. Originally published in 1827.

——. 1982. *The Oak Openings*. New York: Appleton. Originally published in 1848.

Cooper, William. 1897. *A Guide to the Wilderness*. Rochester, NY: George Humphrey. Originally published in 1809.

Ferrell, Robert H. 1994. "Manifest Destiny." *American Academic Encyclopedia* 13. Danbury, CT: Grolier. 117.

Flanagan, John T. 1941. "The Authenticity of Cooper's *The Prairie*." *Modern Language Quarterly* 2: 103.

Hazard, Lucy. 1927. *The Frontier in American Literature*. New York: Thomas Crowell.

James, Edwin. 1823. *Account of an Expedition from Pittsburgh to the Rocky Mountains Performed in the Years 1819-20. . . . From the Notes of Major*

Long, Mr. T. Say, and Other Gentlemen of the Exploring Party. Philadelphia: H. C. Carey and I. Lea.

Lewis, Merrill. 1970-71. "Lost and Found in the Wilderness: The Desert Metaphor in Cooper's *The Prairie*." *Western American Literature* 3.3: 196.

Malcom, C. G. 1966. "Early American Exploration and Cis-Rocky Mountain Desert." *Great Plains Journal* 5.2 (March).

Muszynska-Wallace, E. Soteris. 1949. "The Sources of *The Prairie*." *American Literature* 21: 191-200.

Parrington, Vernon. 1930. *Main Currents in American Thought.* New York: Harcourt Brace.

Ringe, Donald A. 1961. "Man and Nature in Cooper's *The Prairie*." *Nineteenth Century Fiction.* 16: 145.

Smith, Henry Nash. 1950. Introduction. *The Prairie* by James Fenimore Cooper. New York: Holt Rinehart and Winston.

6

OWEN WISTER'S ALL CONQUERING HERO: THE TURNER THESIS RESTARTS THE LIFE CYCLE

In depicting Natty Bumppo as a noble frontiersman in conflict with an effete and amoral society, James Fenimore Cooper created a dramatic tension that, in one form or another, has continued as a mainstay of American literature and popular culture. As a result of its long term impact on these themes, the life cycle of the cowboy story can be viewed as beginning with Cooper's work. Although Cooper's scenario of the noble hero confronting society has continued to impact the popular imagination, crucial aspects of Cooper's vision became dated. This situation caused a general decline in Cooper's popularity in the later part of the nineteenth century.

Cooper's forceful portrayal of the "great American desert" as a hinterland where society could not establish itself, for example, proved to be in error, and by the 1890s everyone was aware of his inaccuracies. Cooper clearly believed that almost the entire West (certainly the great plains region as an entity) was completely unsuited for civilization. In the post Civil War era, however, vast stretches of the plains were successfully settled and transformed into fertile farmland. And the completion of the transcontinental railroad effectively connected the frontier to both the East and the West coasts: a situation that led to rapid growth and economic development. The massive influx of European immigrants in the post Civil War era, furthermore, resulted in the rapid settling of the West: a situation unanticipated by Cooper and those of his generation. While Cooper based his Leatherstocking saga on a premise that the great American desert would always stand as a barrier to civilization and as a haven for the noble frontiersman (who is displaced from the East by an encroaching civilization), the plains emerged as just another resource to be harvested, and by the 1890s it had become rather thickly settled. The people who lived there, furthermore, experienced civilized lives as a result of the railroads, which, by that time, crisscrossed the entire country. Due to these developments, Cooper's vision of history was viewed as grossly inaccurate.

Not only did the current events of the post Civil War era disprove Cooper's vision, Americans increasingly became aware of their own distinctive identity as a unique people. An early statement of this emerging orientation, of course, is Ralph Waldo Emerson's "The American Scholar," which urges readers to embrace their own indigenous intellectual traditions and not to merely model themselves after European prototypes. In a well-crafted sentence, Emerson observes: "We have listened too long to the courtly muses of Europe" and he goes on to celebrate the distinctiveness of the New World and the thinking that should spring from it. While Cooper tended to depict a European-styled culture inevitably establishing itself in the New World and displacing distinctively American people (such as Bumppo and the Indians), by the late nineteenth century, the public was focusing upon American civilization as a distinct and unique phenomena and as a cause for pride and respect. Cooper's Leatherstocking Tales did not conform to this emerging ideal, and actually contradicted it; not surprisingly, the tales became dated and passé.

Closely related to the prevailing view that Americans possessed a positive and productive uniqueness is the fact that American intellectuals and the social elite were actively fighting for parity with their European cousins. Chauvinistic Europeans often dismissed American civilization as a weak reflection of the cultural traditions of Europe and Americans as cultural and intellectual second-class citizens. In this environment, Americans sought a means of asserting their equality or superiority.

Cooper's plotline in the Leatherstocking Tales undercut the goals of progressive Americans to raise their status within European circles; Natty Bumppo, the frontiersman (the true product of America), is depicted as being incapable of effectively interacting with society and is shown being inevitably displaced by it. This message, of course, reinforces the assertion by Europeans that they and their societies were superior to those of the New World. For Americans to portray their equality or superiority, they needed to transcend Cooper's vision of the true American as a rather pathetic vestigial remain being pushed aside by the advance of civilization.

Thus, although Cooper presented an attractive heroic figure in Natty Bumppo and an exciting conflict between the Western hero and Eastern civilization, the frontier story, as developed by Cooper, fell into decline because it conflicted with the emerging worldview of the American public. The original Cooper formula survived in low quality "penny dreadful" novels marketed to the lower classes, but the product was in a clear decline. The sophisticated reading public, in contrast, read novelists such as Henry James, who focused upon the interplay between sophisticated Americans and Europeans. Given this environment, the future of Cooper's innovation looked bleak. This situation, however, was destined to change due to a significant shift in American intellectual history and a restart of the product life cycle of the frontier story which capitalized on these changes.

The last third of the nineteenth century was an era of profound change and adjustments for the citizens of the United States of America. Mark Twain dubbed the era "the gilded age" (1873); thus, he suggested it was not a golden age, although it appeared to be so, at first glance. In the 1860s, the destructions of the Civil War redirected the nation's economy increasingly towards industrialization. The rampant immigration of the 1870s through the 1890s, furthermore, rapidly settled the West, which until that time had largely been a wilderness. In spite of changing demographics, Americans continued to define themselves and their nation with reference to the wild frontier and the freedom and self reliance which went hand in hand with life away from civilization.[1] Quickly and unexpectedly, however, the frontier era of American history proved to be coming to a close.

The classic analysis of this transition, of course, is Frederick Jackson Turner's "frontier thesis of American history." Responding to the facts as he saw them in 1893, Turner observed that the frontier had closed around 1890 and that, thereafter, the future of American history would revolve around urban and civilized life. Thus, he asserted, the first phase of American history had ended. Nonetheless, Turner insisted that the 400-year frontier experience was destined to exert a long-term impact upon American culture and society; in specific, he believed that the frontier had profoundly influenced the American psyche and that the resulting national character and spirit would continue to reap dividends throughout the foreseeable future.

According to such a vision, Americans, although of European descent, had interacted with a rugged wilderness in ways which allowed them to slough off a veneer of weakness which, Turner suggested, was an artifact of life in Europe. Although Turner is celebrated as a seminal thinker, other writers (such as Mark Twain) stated similar ideas and did so at an earlier time. In his *Innocents Abroad*, for example, Twain suggests that due to the massiveness of St. Peter's in Rome (an artifact of civilization), people "were insects . . . [the vastness of the building] has a diminishing effect on them" (1869, 271-72). Suggesting, by extension, that the frontier allowed the traits of self-reliance, personal strength, and individualism which had atrophied in Europe to reassert themselves in the New World, Twain, as Turner, implied that Americans (as a people, society, and nation) had emerged as stronger and more resourceful than overly civilized Europeans. Turner's thesis, presented by him in 1893 at a conference of professional historians, immediately caught the imagination of American intellectuals and, for all practical purposes, it was embraced as an origin myth regarding American character and civilization.

This theory was especially welcomed by the American elite who were attempting to raise their status in the circles of high society. For decades, the European upper crust had snobbishly dismissed America as an intellectual backwater, a mere shadow of the cultural heritage which stemmed from Europe. As a result, Americans (especially the American elites who sought social position on a par with their European rivals) were forced to endure the stigma of intellectual and cultural second-class citizenship.

The frontier thesis proved to be a perfect means by which Americans could assert their parity; and, by turning the tables on European chauvinism, they could claim a superiority of their own. In essence, the frontier thesis argued that Europeans were effete and that due to the crushing weight of overpowering cultural traditions, they had lost their prowess. In America, in contrast, culture was weaker and, as a result, people had become stronger and more vital. Thus, the frontier thesis presented a rationale for Americans to portray themselves as being on a par with (if not actually superior to) Europeans. Still, this theory (which is actually an origin myth regarding the American people and its spirit presented as historical analysis) had not been articulated in a dramatic or fictional manner that was capable of catching the general public's imagination.

By combining the frontier thesis with relevant aspects of Cooper's characterization, and by purging elements of Cooper's vision which were no longer relevant, an updated variant of Cooper's innovation could start the frontier story on a new life cycle. Owen Wister is the writer who accomplished this achievement.

Wister's Early Influences

Although an apologist for the rough, frontier individualist, Wister came from upper-class stock; he parallels Theodore Roosevelt since both sprang from the cultured East while gaining fame and influence as champions of the frontier spirit. Wister's grandmother, Fanny Kemble, furthermore, was an important Shakespearian actress who was at home with Victorian elites such as Robert Browning, William Prescott, John Motley, Ralph Waldo Emerson, Oliver Wendell Holmes, James Russell Lowell, Henry Wadsworth Longfellow, and Franz Liszt. Wister's mother, also culturally oriented, often entertained literary figures such as Henry James in the family home.

Wister studied abroad before entering Harvard in 1878, where he knew William Dean Howells, Theodore Roosevelt, and others destined for greatness. Upon graduation in 1882, Wister toured Europe and impressed Franz Liszt with his musical talents. Wister was a cultured blue blood, well connected, and he was comfortable interacting with the elites of both Europe and America.

Wister's vision of the West, however, was forged by a different set of influences. First, numerous Western trips to the plains gave Wister a personal relationship with the frontier and real-life models for his fiction. Second, Frederick Jackson Turner's frontier thesis (which asserted the frontier profoundly affected American civilization) gave focus and purpose to Wister's prose.

Looking at the journal of Wister's first Western trip (1885), it becomes obvious that his vision of the frontier and the frontiersman is already apparent. First, Wister believed that progress was cumulative and occurred within a social context. Once social or environmental conditions change, Wister asserted, social attitudes and personality types inevitably evolve in concert with them. Today, scholars refer to such ideas as social or environmental determinism. Wister, for example, observed that "Puritanism is the protest of one stage of civilization against another stage . . . [a situation at which Puritanism] . . . in its turn is bound to arrive" (1958, 37-38). Even though Wister was a political conservative, such social determinism is closely akin to the dialectical theories of Karl Marx. Even in his earliest writing, Wister asserted that the old heritage of the East was being replaced by the spirit of the frontier. He states in 1885, eight years before Turner presented his frontier thesis, that: "I feel more certainly than ever that no matter how completely the East may be the headwaters from which the West has flown and is flowing, it won't be a century before the West is simply the true America, with thought, type, and life of its own" (1958, 33).

Such theories, of course, bear a strong resemblance to the frontier thesis that gained currency among intellectuals after 1893; although Turner seems to have influenced Wister's later writing, it is significant that Wister independently articulated the essentials of the frontier thesis and did so long before Turner popularized the concept.

Wister was impressed with life on the plains and he visited it many times from 1885 to 1900. During these trips, Wister kept numerous notebooks and journals that provided much background material for his later writings. He was a careful observer who visited the plains when it was still a frontier; without this background, it is improbable that he could have achieved the stature in the field of Western American literature that he did. His observations are in journals which have been published and can be consulted by scholars (Wister 1958).

Around the same time that Wister was discovering the plains and visiting the frontier, Frederick Jackson Turner formalized his classic "frontier thesis" which argues that American history is best described as a series of conflicts which took place on the frontier as it moved ever westward. Because of the struggles and rigors of frontier life, Turner asserts, a distinctive personality type evolved in North America. By 1890, he continues, the frontier had been conquered and the first phase of American history ended. Nevertheless,

To the frontier the American intellect owes its striking characteristics. That coarseness and strength combined with acuteness and inquisitiveness; that practical inventive turn of mind, quick to find expedients; . . . that restless, nervous energy; that dominant individualism working for good and for evil, and with all that buoyancy and exuberance which comes with Freedom. (Turner 1920, 37)

Wister's connections with Turner's thesis are covert, but strong. Although he makes no direct reference to Turner in *The Virginian* (1902), Wister was an intellectual and he was aware of the influential theories of his times. Possessing a tendency to employ deterministic theories when explaining cultural evolution, Wister pushed Turner's theory to a logical conclusion by insisting that the individualist personality type born of the frontier gained personal prowess. In contrast to Cooper, Wister suggested that once this character had been developed, this personality type could leave the wilds and succeed in a modern, urban world. Wister made such assertions at the same time that "spokesmen for business enterprise, accepting the Turner Thesis . . . came to see in the cowboy, the last of the frontier types, a symbol of the American way (Boatright 1951, 163). Revealingly, Wister had a publishing agreement with a major spokesman for business enterprise:

Horace Lorimer, who took over the editorship of the *Saturday Evening Post* in 1898 and frankly made it the voice of American business, assembled a stable of Western writers, including Owen Wister, and through them kept before his readers the cowboy as a symbol of the rugged individualist that had made America great. (Boatright 1951, 161)

As Gary Scharnhorst has observed, the many parallels between the Virginian and George Washington indicate that Wister thought of his hero as an archetypical founding father of the United States (1984, 227-41).

Combining the Turner theory with his firsthand experiences on the plains, Wister produced the archetypical cowboy novel, *The Virginian*. For Wister, the frontier was a didactic proving ground that could be conquered only after the lessons of personal strength and individualism had been learned and put into practice. In Wister's novel, the hero is not displaced by the closing of the frontier; he leaves the plains, adapts to civilization, and becomes the central force within Eastern society. The frontier emerges as a forge where the frontier spirit is cast and as an incubator for an emerging American national character. Critics have increasingly recognized Wister's vision; thus, Sanford Marovitz observes that *The Virginian* is expressly a novel about America and ideal Americans rather that a regional fiction about plains life (1984, 214). Wister was fond of juxtaposing the pragmatic and independent Westerner with Eastern counterparts. Easterners, Wister believed, act in conventional ways without considering the specific situation in which they find themselves; Wister found fault with such people, both in his Western writings and in his more mainstream fiction.

East Meets West

A clue to Wister's vision is the fact that *The Virginian* is dedicated to Theodore Roosevelt, who had ridden his Roughrider fame to the White House (via McKinley's assassination). In the introduction, Wister speaks to Roosevelt: "Some of these pages you have seen, some you have praised, one stands new written because you blamed it; and all my dear critic [Roosevelt, himself], bear leave to remind you of their author's changeless admiration" (Wister 1902). In Wister's mind, Roosevelt represented the fruits of the frontier experience combined with the best of the civilized East; Wister more fully developed this thesis in *Theodore Roosevelt: The Story of a Friendship*, written many years later (1930).

Wister's distaste for effete Easterners is evident in his poetic denunciation of Woodrow Wilson, who is remembered as our most intellectual president. The caustic Wister states:

> You go immune, eased in your self-esteem
> The next world cannot scathe you nor can this.
> No fact can stab through your complacent dream.
> Nor present laughter, nor the future's hiss
> But if its father did this land control.
> Dead Washington would raise and blast your soul. (1916, 3)

This hatred of sterile, effete intellectualism can be found throughout Wister's work. *Philosophy Four*, published a year after *The Virginian,* is particularly revealing; it is a short novelette about Oscar, a tutor, and his pupils, Bertie and Billy. Oscar is a smug scholar who is incapable of thinking for himself and always bows to authority. An example of this tendency occurs when Billy and Bertie challenge Zeno's Paradox (that theorizes that objects cannot move) by reversing the logic to assert that moving objects cannot stop. Placing his entire faith in tradition,

The tutor must have derived great pleasure from his own smile for he prolonged and deepened and variously modified it, while his shiny little calculating eyes traveled from one to the other of his ruddy scholars. He coughed, consulted his notes, and went through all the paces of superiority. "I can find nothing about a body being unable to stop," he said gently, "If logic makes no appeal to you, gentlemen." (1903, 15)

Billy and Bertie, in contrast, do not blindly respect the past; they, for example, refer to the ancient Greek philosophers as the "Greek bucks" and Hobbes' school as "Hobbes and his gang." Instead of paying worshipful homage to the thinkers of the past, they are concerned with their own questions and their own interests. When the three students received their final examination scores: "Oscar received seventy five percent. . . . But Billy's mark was eighty-six and Bertie's ninety. 'There is some mistake,' said Oscar. . . . 'There is no mistake' said the professor" (1903, 92-93).

The initial success of individualism demonstrated by the philosophy examination foreshadows the fates of the three students: Bertie becomes treasurer of the New Amsterdam Trust Company, Billy becomes the superintendent of passenger traffic of the New York and Chicago Air Line,[2] while Oscar, unable to engage in original thought, became an intellectual. "He has acquired a lot of information. His smile is unchanged. He has published a careful work entitled *The Minor Poets of Cenquecento*, and he writes book reviews. . . ." (1903, 95).

Turning to *The Virginian*, we see a parallel exchange between the Virginian and the Schoolmarm. Molly Wood, with her Eastern upbringing, has accepted many of the conventional wisdoms of society and, like Oscar, she considered herself intellectually and morally superior to the roughshod individualist. In the final analysis, however, the Virginian's practical Western experience proves superior to the institutionalized knowledge of the East.

In Chapter 12, for example, Molly, obedient to her teachings, believes that "all men are created equal" (1902, 143), while the Virginian, uninhibited by cultural mores and conventional truisms, makes personal judgments, asserting "equality is a great big bluff . . . a man has to prove himself my equal before I'll believe him" (1902, 144). In the exchange that follows, the Virginian clearly wins the day and his victory is so great that Wister begins the next chapter with a short essay on the same observation, stating:

> . . . it was through the Declaration of Independence that we Americans acknowledged the eternal inequality of man. For by it we abolished a cut and dry aristocracy. We had seen little men artificially held up in high places and great men artificially held down in low places and our justice loving hearts abhorred this violence to human nature. Therefore, we decreed that every man should henceforth have equal liberty to find his own level. (1902, 147)

When the schoolmarm offers education to the Virginian, she does not symbolize knowledge which tames the frontier, as many critics suggest. Although she is initially symbolic of civilization, she is incapable of transforming the Virginian since Wister depicts him as superior to the East (which she initially represents).

The Virginian, therefore, is an intellectual force, not merely a primitive figure. As Moody Boatright has pointed out, "In spite of a good number of shootings, stabbings, and lynchings, physical violence is not abundant in Wister's works. His cowboys triumph by cleverness more often than by force. The Virginian outwits Trampas at every turn until the final showdown" (1951, 159). Another example of the Virginian's native intelligence is the fact that his game

> is poker rather than faro or craps or any other common Western game of chance. For poker is a strange game in which winning depends not only upon the hand one holds . . . but upon judgment. . . . Good cards alone do not win at poker . . . Wister again and again defines the unique character of the Western hero as precisely this ability to interpret the facts of life insightfully. (Folson 1966, 109)

It is incorrect, therefore, to depict the Virginian as a primitive, unsophisticated force who uses brawn without adequate reflection. Wister's hero represents a superior intellect honed on the frontier.

Molly's transformation from Easterner to Westerner occurs when she is forced to objectively evaluate the role of lynching, which Easterners consider to be an atrocity. Viewing the event in concrete situational terms, Molly eventually accepts that lynching, while distasteful, is appropriate for the circumstances; her transformation, however, is only possible after she abandons abstract moral standards. Wister clearly portrays the lynching as a "stopgap" measure: the only viable alternative where formal law does not yet exist. The lynching, incidentally, is a tragic event for the Virginian, who must allow his best friend to be executed; nonetheless, he rises to the occasion and completes the deed even though it profoundly hurts him.

Avoiding Racist Overtones

A close reading of Wister's depiction of lynching is important for another reason: Wister has long been accused of racial prejudice and even of justifying lynching for racist reasons. Philip Durham and Everett Jones have wrongly accused Wister of including no Negro cowboys within his works (Durham and Jones 1965). Even more damning is Moody Simms' statement that in *Lady Baltimore* Wister "hoped to convert his readers to the belief that craniology is an exact enough science which clearly distinguished superior from inferior races" (Simms 1970, 23-26). Simms' assertion is partly true: Wister was clearly a product of his times and he seems to have accepted certain racist aspects of social Darwinism. Nonetheless, Wister's intention in *Lady Baltimore* was not to justify prejudicial beliefs and actions but to demonstrate how many naive philanthropists and volunteer workers were doing poor and even counter-productive work among southern blacks. Wister's assertion is correct and has been well documented by later observers. In the field of folklore, for example, many of the missionaries who collected folklore only saw what they wanted to see and/or their black informants never shared their total culture with them. Thus, such collectors did not record whole genres such as toasts and blues. Wister is correct when he observes that the perspectives of these outsiders were profoundly limited.

In spite of Wister's social Darwinist views, he found racial exploitation and terrorist tactics repugnant. In *Lady Baltimore*, the hero, although, perhaps, convinced of black inferiority, refuses to accept the arch-racist's suggestion that the philanthropists "will get better results by giving votes to monkeys than teaching Henry Wadsworth Longfellow to Niggers" (1906). Hearing this, the hero tells the reader: "Retaliation rose in me. . . . I left the shop of the screaming [racist]" (1906, 171).

Although Wister's hero might be convinced by pseudo-science that blacks are inferior to whites, he nonetheless argues: "I am an enemy also of that blind and base hatred against him, which . . . [contributes] to the de-civilizing of white and black alike. Who brought him here? Did he invite himself? Then let us make the best of it and teach him" (1906, 175). In the final analysis, Wister found exploitation and terrorism every bit as intolerable as contemporary Americans do today. He states the South was "semi-barbarous" (1906, 434) because of racist lynchings. Nowhere does Wister condone inhuman treatment and he actively opposes it.

The most damning suggestion that Wister was a racist appears in Leslie Fiedler's *The Return of the Vanishing American*. Fiedler interprets the lynching scene in *The Virginian* as an apology for the murder of both blacks and American Indians. *The Virginian*, Fiedler argues, is about

the so-called Code of the West—the very same which set in motion these other white knights of the time, the Ku Klux Klan. . . . And just as Dixon's fictions were justifications for the oppressions of Negroes, so those of Wister and his imitators were . . . analogous justifications for the extermination of the Indian. (Fiedler 1968, 138)

Although Fiedler may be correct if he is suggesting that Wister's ideas were interpreted and reworked in such ways by other authors, Wister, himself, is immune from such critiques.

Looking at the text of *The Virginian*, for example, no supporting evidence for these assertions can be found. After the lynching, Judge Henry, himself once dedicated to the letter of the law, responds when asked if he thought "well of lynching" (1902, 433): "Of Burning Southern Negroes in public, no. On hanging Wyoming cattle thieves in private, yes. You perceive there's a difference, don't you . . . the south is semi-barbarous." Reading these passages, it seems obvious that Wister was well aware that his book might be read as a justification for Southern lynching and he took active steps to clearly demonstrate he opposed KKK tactics.

Wister goes on to depict a specific lynching which takes place on the plains as a quasi-legal or stop-gap device where formal law had not arrived. In Judge Henry's words:

In Wyoming the law has been letting our cattle-thieves go for two years. We are in a very bad way, and we are trying to make that way a little better until civilization can reach us. At present we lie beyond its pale. . . . Call this primitive if you will. But so far from being a defiance of the law it is an assertion of it—the fundamental assertion of self-governing men, upon whom our whole social fabric is built. (1902, 435-36)

The value of effective social control is underscored by a situation Wister mentions where cattle thieves eventually gain the upper hand; it proved to be a victory that "brought ruin on themselves as well, for in a broken country there is nothing left to steal" (1902, 434). An early critic of the lynching theme was Wister's own mother, who felt the book was of "doubtful morality" (Wister 1958, 17) because of the "justification of lynching." Wister answered his mother by observing that "lynching was perfectly successful in Montana and ended a reign of thieves there" (1958, 18). Wister knew that lynching was an imperfect system and he considers this issue in his short story "The Gift Horse" (1911), in which an innocent man is almost hanged. Thus, although a product of his times, Wister was also a humanitarian; unfortunately later critics (with their own agendas) have often ignored this fact. Wister's basic point is that during certain phases of the establishment of culture in a frontier region, extra-legal tactics may have to be relied upon in order to fill a gap where formal law does not yet exist. He does not equate these tactics with lawlessness or immorality; on the contrary, he portrays it as a means of establishing law and order even if the methods are imperfect and informal. When such methods are being used, individuals are making moral choices, not applying abstract codes of conduct.

Latent Individualism of the East

Although Wister believed that the East had become effete due to the forces of civilization, he also suggests that the spirit of the frontier covertly survives in the East and he believes it is possible for Easterners to reassert their true identity. Wister uses Molly Wood to portray this latent individualism reasserting itself when introduced to the frontier.

Indeed, to understand *The Virginian*, it is essential to view the heroine's embrace of her covert and repressed individualism. Although Molly's true spirit has lain dormant throughout her life, Wister depicts the frontier spirit as alive and well within her. It takes Molly a long time, for example, to come to grips with the concept of lynching as a stop gap measure in a lawless world, but ultimately she does and she and the Virginian plan to be married. Just prior to the ceremony, however, the Virginian discovers that he must meet Trampas in a showdown. Upon hearing the news, Molly again falls back upon her Eastern ethics, stating, "There's something better than shedding blood in cold blood. Only think of what it means . . . it's murder" (1902, 473). When she realizes that she cannot change his mind, she breaks the engagement. But after the showdown, " 'Oh thank God,' she said, and he found her in his arms. . . . Thus did her New England conscience battle to the end and in the end capitulates to love" (1902, 482).

Leslie Fiedler believes that Molly represents members of a morally superior society who "abdicate their roles as guardians of morality" (1960, 359-60). Fiedler goes on to suggest that Molly's acceptance of the Virginian after the showdown can be viewed as an "analogue for genocide" (1968, 139) and by extension Molly represents all seemingly moral individuals who look the other way in time of moral crisis. In an argument similar to Fiedler's, John Wilson observed "the school teacher, Molly Wood, is the figure of Emersonian compromise, the neither-good-neither-evil code-produced human beings whose salvation lies in the surrender of the intellect" (Williams 1961, 402).

These arguments, however, evaporate when we realize that Wister initially presents Molly as a reluctant and trapped member of Eastern society. Wister initially depicts her as pitiful; trapped and manipulated by the rhetoric of her culture, she lacks the ability to make decisions which reflect her true self and she cannot adequately respond to the situations into which she is thrust. As the novel progresses, however, Molly Wood doesn't surrender her intellect, she begins to use it. Initially a hapless victim of civilization, Molly transforms herself in the image of the frontier and combines the best of the wilderness with the benefits of civilization into what Wister portrays as an ideal composite. Her final capitulation to love might be emotional, but love usually is.

Wister, it should be added, did not believe that happy endings of this sort were inevitable or that they always occurred when West met East. In "Hank's Woman," Wister's first published story, the conflict between civilization and the frontier does not lead to a beneficial transformation, but to the death of both figures. In this story, Willomene, a female servant, is fired after losing a set of luggage keys. Finding herself stranded in the West, she marries Hank, a miner. Once they leave for the mining camp where Hank works, trouble breaks out. Willomene had never camped out before and her discomfort is evident. Hank, on the other hand, is irritated by his wife's personal habits, especially her religious devotions and her crucifix. At the end of the story we learn that after an apparent fight over the cross, Willomene kills Hank with an ax and goes on to fall to her death while attempting to dispose of the body (Wister 1892, 821-23). Thus, Wister did not portray the upbeat plot of *The Virginian* to be universal and inevitable.

In addition to demonstrating a positive compromise between the civilized East and the frontier West, Molly and the Virginian also represent different degrees of individualism. Molly's individualism remains unfulfilled as long as she is under the spell of Eastern civilization. The Virginian is well attuned to the frontier; nonetheless, until he gains a degree of sophistication, his options within the civilized world are limited.

Even though Molly initially represents culture coming to the plains, she herself is not a true representative of civilization. Molly is atypical because "it is not usual for young ladies of twenty to contemplate a journey of nearly 2,000 miles to a country where Indians and wild animals live unchained. . . . Nor is school teaching in Bear Creek a usual ambition for such young ladies" (1902, 90). Wister makes it obvious that Molly's move to the plains is a rejection of Eastern culture and not a desire to bring civilization to the West.

Molly, for example, was descended from an important colonial family with valuable social connections. "Had she so wished, she could have belonged to any number of those patriotic societies. . . . But she had been willing to join none of them" (1902, 90-91). Molly had been forced to become independent due to an economic disaster which had struck her family. Although she was forced to perform menial work, Molly refused to marry the wealthy Sam Bannett. People

declared that Sam Bannett was good enough for anybody who did fancy embroidery at five cents a letter. . . . Then certain members of her family began to tell her how rich Sam was going to be—was indeed already. It was at this time that she wrote Mrs. Balaam her doubts and her desires of migrating to Bear Creek. (1902, 94)

Although Molly Wood opposes the conventions of the Victorian middle class, she does not, as Fiedler has suggested, represent the "self-hate of the genteel Eastern sophisticate confronted with the primitive" (1960, 259). Wister goes to great lengths to demonstrate that Molly Wood is no genteel Victorian, but a descendant of Molly Stark, a Revolutionary War heroine. Wister uses Molly Stark, Molly Wood's ancestor and namesake, as a constant metaphor for describing the individualist qualities of his heroine. Molly Wood's prize possession is a miniature portrait of her grandmother. Before the young woman left Vermont, her great aunt had observed "My dear, you're getting more like the General's [General John Stark's] wife every day" (1902, 92). Wister then goes on to clearly tell us that, "if the ancestors that we carry shut up inside us take turns in dictating to us our actions and our states of mind, undoubtedly Grandmother Stark was empress of Molly's spirit . . . [when she left for the West]" (1902, 99).

Molly Wood is obviously a metaphorical duplication of the heroic frontier spirit born when the East was experiencing its own pioneer era. She exhibits vestigial remains which had once existed in the East but had moved westward with the expanding frontier. This echoes the Turner thesis, which depicts individualistic traits of the frontier being submerged beneath the veneer of society, but very much alive. Molly is the Eastern cousin of the Western individualist, not an example of the genteel Victorian middle class, as critics so often assume.

The spirit of Molly Stark is contained within Molly Wood, but for a time (when Molly decides to leave the West and return East), it appears that the Stark psyche will be repressed and thwarted. Then, by chance or by fate, Molly discovers the wounded and helpless Virginian as she rides alone on the plains. Even though she is in danger from hostile Indians, Molly, like her pioneer ancestors, risks her life in order to save the helpless Virginian, an action which ultimately reaffirms Molly's love of the

West and transforms her from a covert to an overt individualist. After this point in the novel, the frontier mentality gains the upper hand. Wister leaves no doubt that the frontier spirit of Molly Stark has finally prevailed; he names the transitional chapter "Grandmother Stark" (1902, 318).

Wister believed that the East had rejected the individualist spirit (that he represented with the Molly Wood/Molly Stark complex) and he felt that America was abandoning her true progeny when it did so. Wister demonstrates this theory in a parable contained within the cluster of chapters in which Molly is introduced to the reader. The parable is about a hen called "Em'ly" who has no chicks of her own. Wanting offspring to mother, she rolls seven potatoes together and is "determined to raise I don't know what sort of family . . . I've found her with onions and last Tuesday I caught her on two balls of soap. . . . She . . . seated upon a collection of green peaches" (1902, 71-76). In addition, Em'ly appropriates the offspring of other animals including two Bantam chicks, some turkey chicks, and even a litter of puppies. Finally hoping to give Em'ly a chick of her own the Virginian placed an egg under her, but when it hatched:

The little lonely yellow ball of down went cheeping along behind . . . following its mother as best it could . . . Emily . . . never looked at it. . . . Now she suddenly flew up in a tree. . . . Below the tree stood the bewildered little chicken, cheeping and making jumps to reach its mother. . . . We went to supper, and I came out to find the hen lying on the ground dead. (1902, 83)

This parable is obviously a metaphorical reflection of Wister's view of America. Like Em'ly, America at the turn of the twentieth century was willing to accept the offspring of any alien land. Millions of people were entering the country and like Em'ly, America was willing to accept them even while simultaneously ignoring its own heritage (the indigenous frontier individualist). Molly parallels Em'ly's chick, and like the chick, she found her needs unfulfilled in the East. Instead, both are ignored and thwarted. Wister ended his parable on a pessimistic note: Em'ly's death is somehow linked to the rejection of her true offspring. Wister allegorically suggests that America faces a similar disaster if it cannot come to grips with its own heritage. The ultimate success of the Virginian's and Molly's transformations, however, demonstrates how the heritage of the American frontier can be reintegrated into mainstream American society. Thus, as John Nesbitt has observed, *The Virginian* "asserts a debated marriage of values between east and west" (1983, 208). By 1902, however, the debate ceased and Wister's vision prevailed.

The Frontier Spirit

The Virginian, in contrast to Molly, represents the frontier individualist personified. Wister specifically suggests that his hero is not atypical or unique; instead he is depicted as an archetypical product of the American frontier. As Wister describes the cowboys of Judge Henry's ranch we learn that: "Those cow-punchers bore names of various denominations . . . and they came from farms and cities . . . but the romance of American adventure had drawn them all alike to . . . [the frontier and] . . . they bore a close resemblance to each other" (1902, 66).

Sam Bannett, a rival for Molly's love, is a pointed foil for the Virginian. Bannett is not a man of action and lacks the insight required to understand the dynamics of a social situation. On the train which takes Molly west, Sam asks if he can ride with her to Eagle Bridge; he obviously wants to make one last plea for Molly to remain in the East and marry him. At this moment, Molly seems not to have made a final, irrevocable decision. She, however, says "No" and Wister editorializes: "And Sam—what did he do? He obeyed her. I should like to be sorry for him, but obedience was not a lover's part here. He hesitated, the golden moment hung hovering, the conductor cried 'all aboard' the train went and there on the platform stood the obedient Sam, with his golden moment gone like a butterfly" (1902, 99). Sam, we must conclude, was both indecisive and unable to be appropriately forceful.

The Virginian, in contrast, takes decisive action when it is called for and he is insightful enough to realize that Molly can eventually love him. When Molly states, "I don't think I like you" (1902, 33), the Virginian realizes the true dynamics of the situation and responds, "You're going to love me before we get through" (1902, 133). And as the story progresses, events prove he is correct.

The Virginian is insightful and decisive in situations other than his love affair. The most famous example of this occurs when Trampas, the villain, calls the Virginian "a son of a [bitch]" (Wister 1902, 29). The Virginian recognizes this comment as an insult, but prefers to avoid a fight. He can't ignore the provocation, however, without losing face and responds by interpreting the phrase as merely an idiomatic expression and he advises Trampas to "Smile when you call me that" (1902, 29). By redefining the phrase in neutral terms, the Virginian avoids having to defend his honor and allows Trampas to withdraw the insult without losing face himself. Since Trampas chooses not to rephrase his polemical remarks in a more explicit manner, the matter is dropped and a fight is avoided.

Although the Virginian is a skilled social actor who is able to take appropriate action, he is the product of a dying world. In his introduction to *The Virginian*, Wister acknowledges that the American frontier is gone forever. As a result, the frontier personality, typified by the plainsman, must adapt or disappear. According to Wister, the individualist hero can adapt to civilization without abandoning his personality and character.

Throughout the novel, the hero evolves and grows under the influence of Judge Henry, his employer and future partner. Early in the novel, he is merely an ordinary cow-hand, but he gains sophistication and responsibility when given the opportunity to do so. These duties grow to include management and strategic planning; ultimately, he functions within Eastern society as an equal.

The Virginian's first experience with real responsibility involves transporting a two-train shipment of cattle to Chicago. His duties include quality control (watching after the cattle), management (he is in charge of the men), and strategy formation (he is instructed to persuade railroad officials to lower freight rates in order to stimulate trade). He is promoted to the position of "acting foreman." On the train ride back to the ranch, the Virginian meets the first real test of his executive ability when Trampas attempts to incite a mutiny with rumors of a newly discovered gold strike. The Virginian, however, is able to squelch the uprising by making Trampas look foolish by convincing him that there are frog farms where frogs, like cattle, are raised for slaughter. Having lost credibility in the eyes of the men because he is so gullible, Trampas is unable to lead the revolt and the Virginian returns home with all hands.

Because of his success in this enterprise, Judge Henry makes the Virginian permanent foreman. The Virginian soon displays that he has considerable insight regarding the character of hypocritical Easterners. An example occurs when Dr. McBride, a traveling preacher, comes to town for the yearly religious services. Although McBride claims to be dedicated to saving souls, the Virginian doubts his sincerity. To test McBride, he spends hours confessing imaginary sins in order to determine whether the minister would be willing to lose a night's sleep to relieve the conscience of a sinner. The minister, however, dislikes the prospect of being deprived of his rest for the sake of religion and he leaves the next morning. For all his pious talk, he isn't willing to lose sleep for the glory of God or the souls of men.

The message of the frog farm and the preacher anecdotes are foreshadowed throughout in the book by numerous practical jokes perpetrated by the Virginian. The latter two examples, however, demonstrate the Virginian's ability to act in a manner explicitly designed to control or direct a social situation. They suggest that the frontier personality can transform his existing skills into managerial tools and techniques and use them in dealing with the outside world.

The Virginian continues to educate himself. In time, "he could turn off a business communication about steers, or stock cars, or any other of the subjects involved in his profession, with a brevity and clearness that led the judge to confide three-quarters of his correspondence to his foreman" (1902, 275).

The Virginian's sophistication in the ways of civilization is demonstrated when he and Molly visit Molly's home town in Vermont. The people expect a semi-barbarian, but

Bennington probably was disappointed, to see get out off the train merely a tall man with a usual straw hat, and Scotch homespun suit of a rather better cut than most in Bennington—this was dull. And his conversation . . . seemed fit to come into the house. . . . Most of Bennington soon began to say that Molly's cowboy could be invited anywhere and hold his own. (1902, 499)

In addition to being able to pass in polite society, the Virginian is a success in business. Upon returning to Wyoming he becomes the partner of Judge Henry and survives a cattle war in which most of the other cattlemen are destroyed, and he emerges as an important person "with a strong grip on many various enterprises." The frontiersman leaves the environment which created him and succeeds in the civilized world while losing none of his independence or personal ethics. Thus, Wister believed the frontier spirit could survive the closing of the frontier and create a distinctive American civilization. He asks: "What has become of the horseman . . . ? Well, he will be here among us always, invisible, waiting his chance to live and play as he would like" (1902, ix).

In many ways, *The Virginian* is a typical turn-of-the-century success story. As Moody Boatright has observed,

In Wister's cowboys . . . we have both prowess and cleverness. But more importantly, the Virginian exemplifies the American vision of the myth of the faithful apprentice, the Horatio Alger story. Poor and obscurely born, he goes into the world—the West—to seek his fortune. (1951, 159)

The Virginian, however, is more complex than the Horatio Alger myth, since Wister also accounted for the origin of the individualist hero via the Turner thesis. Alger, like James Fenimore Cooper's Leatherstocking Tales, primarily dealt with a personality type *after* it had come into existence.

Wister, like Turner, believed the rugged individualist was a product of the West. He portrayed the individualist spirit as being forged in the wilds, but surviving the closing of the frontier to emerge as a pillar of American national character. The closing of the frontier necessitated a change but, he wrote, "such transition is inevitable. Let us give thanks that it is but a transition and not a finality" (1902, x). Wister believed the frontier hero continued to wield a strong influence. Henry James suggested to Wister that the Virginian should die at the end of the novel. Considering this suggestion, Neal Lambert observes, "Henry James thought Wister should have killed his Virginian. And in a sense he was right, too. For the figure of the cowboy is latent with possibilities for tragedy and so far as the Virginian does represent the cowboy confronted by the 'progress of empire,' he does contain tragic potential" (Lambert 1971-72, 106).

What Lambert fails to realize is that the frontier figure is tragic only if it loses in the confrontation with civilization. Lambert misses Wister's crucial point when he asserts that *The Virginian* is concerned with "residual wild places" (Lambert 1971-72, 106). On the contrary, Wister portrays the Westerner leaving residual wild places and emerging as an active force *within* Eastern society. It is easy to see why Henry James, an apologist of intellectual elitism, encouraged killing off the frontier spirit. *The Virginian*, however, was a product of the era of Frederick Jackson Turner and the frontier thesis. The novel was dedicated to Theodore Roosevelt, another hero who applied frontier tactics in socially acceptable ways. In 1902, neither Teddy Roosevelt nor the Virginian were viewed as tragic figures. Indeed, the Virginian evolved into an insightful businessman who buys land containing coal deposits because he realizes, "it won't be long before the new railroads need that" (Wister 1902, 502). He does not, as Forrest Robinson argues, "recoil from life" (Robinson 1986, 38). In complete contrast, Wister's hero enters the modern world with gusto and finds success there.

Discussion

By the end of the nineteenth century, the American West had largely been settled, but Americans continued to view their civilization as distinctive. In this atmosphere, intellectuals and social climbers from the New World sought parity with their European rivals. Given the ethos of the times, James Fenimore Cooper's vision of the frontiersman as a vulnerable vestigial remain was no longer appropriate, and this description conflicted with the tenets of the frontier thesis. Nonetheless, certain aspects of the plot formula created by Cooper continued to be attractive. First, Cooper created a vital heroic character who was depicted as a product of the American experience. Second, Cooper placed this hero in a conflict with the forces of the civilized European-like culture of the East. Both of these motifs appealed to the public; the ultimate message of displacement presented by Cooper, however, needed to be transcended.

Owen Wister embraced the heroic character of the frontier and pre-served the conflict with civilization; nonetheless, Wister went beyond Cooper's plotline in innovative ways by developing a mythic plotline that paralleled the prevailing frontier thesis that had been introduced by Frederick Jackson Turner. Wister's hero, hardly displaced by civiliza-tion, is able to return as a moral and all conquering force within society. Wister's frontier hero has learned the lessons of the frontier and, in the process, he represents a new breed which, while emerging from Old World roots, is able to surpass civilized Easterners as a result of an apprenticeship on the frontier.

The Virginian phrased this transition in epic form; as a result, the novel was a resounding success. In marketing terms, Wister adjusted the product of the frontier story that had become passé and was in decline. In doing so, he provided a new variant of the product which more clearly coincided with consumer desires and expectations. Wister restarted Cooper's frontier story on a new life cycle.

This basic version of the cowboy story was to remain current for many years, although, as is often the case, it came to serve the needs of those in the lower rungs of the adoption curve ladder. This process is the topic of later chapters. Certain innovations attempted to further trans-form this product; but until the worldview of the public changed, these further transformations could not be successfully established.

Notes

1. For examples of the degree to which Americans defined themselves in terms of the wilderness, consider the work of artist Thomas Cole and his Hudson River School of landscape painting, Henry David Thoreau's *Walden,* and the work of Ralph Waldo Emerson, especially his famous essay "Self Reliance."

2. Wister does use the term "air line" although the airplane had been invented in the same year he published *Philosophy Four.* I have no explanation for his use of words.

Works Cited

Boatright, Moody. 1951. "The American Myth Rides the Range: Owen Wister's Man on Horseback." *Southwestern Review* 36 (Summer): 157-63.

Durham, Philip, and Everett L. Jones. 1965. *The Negro Cowboys.* New York: Dodd, Mead.

Fiedler, Leslie. 1960. *Love and Death in the American Novel*. New York: Criterion.

——. 1968. *The Return of the Vanishing American*. New York: Stein and Day.

Folson, James K. 1966. *The American Western Novel*. New Haven: College UP.

Lambert, Neal. 1971-72. "Owen Wister's *The Virginian*: The Genesis of a Cultural Hero." *Western American Literature* 6.2: 99-108.

Marovitz, Sanford E. 1984. "Unseemingly Realities in Owen Wister's Western/American Myth." *American Literary Realism* 17.2: 209-15.

Nesbitt, John. 1983. "Owen Wister's Achievement in Literary Tradition." *Western American Literature* 18.3: 199- 208.

Robinson, Forrest. 1986. "The Virginian and Molly: How Sweet It Is." *Western American Literature* 21.1: 27-38.

Scharnhorst, Gary. 1984. "The Virginian as Founding Father." *Arizona Quarterly* 40.3: 227-40.

Simms, Moody. 1970. "*Lady Baltimore*: Owen Wister and the Southern Race Question." *Serif* June: 23-26.

Turner, Frederick Jackson. 1920. *The Frontier in American History*. New York: Henry Holt.

Twain, Mark. 1869. *Innocents Abroad*. Hartford, CT: American Publishing.

Warner, Charles Dudley, and Mark Twain. 1964. *The Gilded Age*. New York: Trident. Originally 1873.

Williams, John. 1961. "The Western Definition of a Myth." *Nation* 18 Nov.: 402.

Wister, Owen. 1892. "Hank's Woman." *Harper's Weekly* 27 Aug.: 821-23.

——. 1902. *The Virginian*. New York: Macmillan.

——. 1903. *Philosophy Four: A Story of Harvard University*. New York: Macmillan.

——. 1906. *Lady Baltimore*. New York: Macmillan.

——. 1911. "The Gift Horse." *Members of the Family*. New York: Macmillan.

——. 1916. "To Woodrow Wilson." *New York Times* 22 Feb.: 3.

——. 1930. *Roosevelt: The Story of a Friendship*. New York: Macmillan.

——. 1958. *Owen Wister Out West: His Journals and Letters*. Ed. Fanny Kemble Wister. Chicago: U of Chicago P.

7

ZANE GREY AND THE DEFEAT OF THE HERO

Zane Grey understood how to market fiction to mainstream people who believed the spirit of the frontier gave Americans and American society an inherent superiority. Grey routinized the basic plotline which had been crystallized by Owen Wister's fictional embracing of Frederick Jackson Turner's frontier thesis, and he transformed it into a formula which he replicated time and time again. The cowboy story has often been depicted as a completely predictable genre which features a virile and moralistic hero who confronts society. Grey standardized and codified what emerged as the classic formula of the cowboy story.

Grey was a successful popular author; his sales records are stunning. *U.P. Trail* was the number one best-selling novel of 1918 and *The Man of the Forest* topped the list in 1920. *The Lone Star Ranger, Wildfire, The Desert of Wheat, To the Last Man, The Wanderer of the Wasteland,* and *The Call of the Canyon* were among the top ten best sellers for their respective years (Hacket 1945). After his death in 1939, Grey's heirs continued to release one unpublished manuscript per year until 1962. His books remain in print today and are available via a Zane Grey book club.

Success did not come overnight, and it took a while for Grey to find his forte; early in his career, he experimented with contradictory literary formulas provided by James Fenimore Cooper and Owen Wister, his major precursors. Essentially, these efforts are a conscious duplication of the achievements of his predecessors. In the Ohio River trilogy (1903-1906), Grey emulated James Fenimore Cooper's Leatherstocking saga which depicted the displacement of the frontier spirit by an encroaching civilization. In *The Last of the Plainsman* (1908), in contrast, Grey pictured the frontier individualist as an all conquering hero in ways reflective of Owen Wister's *The Virginian*.

After these early efforts, Grey wrote a number of ambiguous novels—including *Riders of the Purple Sage* (1912), *The Rainbow Trail* (1915), and *The Desert of Wheat* (1919)—in which the rival themes of an all-conquering individualism and a suppressing society are uncomfortably intertwined. During this period of juxtaposition and experimentation, Grey developed a means of accommodating the rival philosophies of individualism and mass society that was to make his work distinctive.

Grey's masterpiece, *The Vanishing American* (1925), is the story of an extraordinary Indian who dies when he rejects modern society in favor of embracing his cultural heritage. As in Cooper's work, Grey's hero in *The Vanishing American* is an idealized person who cannot survive within the confines of society. The fate of this hero, incidentally, is more pessimistic than that of Cooper's Natty Bumppo because by the twentieth century the frontier had been closed and there was no "Great American Desert" to which the Bumppo-like individual could retreat. *The Vanishing American*, as we shall see, is the archetypical fatalistic frontier story and, although it was not acceptable in Grey's era, the formula has been successfully duplicated many times since 1960. Thus, Grey offered this plotline before it was acceptable to the public and it was rejected. In terms of marketing theory, it was marketed before its time and, as a result, it had a minimal impact.

Early Efforts

Grey's Ohio River trilogy, set in Ohio during the early frontier period, was purportedly based upon a diary written by Grey's ancestor Colonel Zane. Actually fictitious, the trilogy does contain many examples of family lore and legend. In addition to folklore and family history, Grey draws upon certain published accounts such as Charles McKnight's *Our Western Border*, a book he claimed to know by heart (Jackson 1973, 18). *The Last of the Mohicans* was one of Grey's favorite novels and he obviously relied upon Cooper while writing the Ohio River trilogy (Jackson 1973, 18).

Betty Zane, which starts the trilogy, is Grey's first novel. Although poorly written, it is of considerable interest because it demonstrates that Grey's heroines, like those of Owen Wister, are strong and individualistic . . . not faint of heart Victorian females.

Betty Zane is set in Fort Henry, a patriot outpost during the American Revolution; the plot centers around the love of Alfred Clarke, a patriot officer and Betty Zane, the daughter of the aforementioned Colonel Zane. Here, Grey reverses the love theme of Wister's *The Virginian* by presenting the heroine as a product of the frontier while Alfred, the hero, is an Eastern sophisticate transported to the West. Only after the Eastern male adjusts to his new Western environment and accepts the ways of the frontier and its women, does their love succeed.

Initially, Alfred objects to Betty's individualistic non-conformity, and he reprimands her behavior, such as leaving the protection of the fort. As commander of Fort Henry, he insists that Betty stay within the confines of the settlement, but doing so causes friction since she resents restrictions being put upon her freedom. Eventually, Alfred learns that Betty is capable of taking care of herself; during a siege of Fort Henry, the patriots run low on gunpowder and face defeat and death if the supply is not replenished; the men have but one hope, the chance that Betty might break through enemy lines and return with a fresh supply. Alfred, the civilized Easterner, cannot stand the thought of his woman risking her life; " 'No! No! Do not let her go!,' cried Clarke, throwing himself before them. He was trembling, his eyes were wild, and he had the appearance of a man suddenly gone mad" (Grey 1902, 270). Alfred, a product of genteel society, is horrified at the idea that a woman should subject herself to mortal danger while he, society's defender and protector, remains relatively safe within the confines of the fort.

Betty, however, dismisses fears for her own safety and makes a dash for the powder, remarking, "Now you can do nothing but pray God will spare my life long enough to reach the gate" (1902, 270). "The huge gate creaked and swung in. Betty ran out, looking straight before her" (1902, 270). She reaches Colonel Zane's cabin and says, "We are out of powder. Empty a keg of powder into a table cloth. Quick! I've not a second to lose" (271). Not burdened by an inappropriate sense of feminine modesty, she slips "off her outer skirt. She wanted nothing to hinder that run for the block house" (271). Colonel Zane, fully aware of the strength of frontier women, sends her on her way saying, "Brave girl, so help me God, you are going to do it. . . . I know you can. Run as you never ran in your life" (272).

The real challenge for Betty, however, is the trip back to the fort:

The cracking of rifles began. . . . The leaden messengers of Death whistled past Betty. . . . The yelling and screeching had become deafening. . . . The reports of the rifles blended in a roar. A hot, stinging pain shot through Betty's arm, but she heeded it not. The bullets were raining about. . . . A tug at the flying hair and a long black tress cut off by a bullet floated away on a breeze. Betty saw the big gate swing. . . . She felt herself grabbed by eager arms; she heard the gate slam. (272)

At this point, Alfred Clarke finally realizes the value and beauty of Betty's strength and independence. " 'God what a woman,' he said between his teeth as he thrust the rifle forward" (273). Thus, the Eastern-bred man comes to understand and appreciate the feminine version of the frontier hero, just as Molly Wood, the Eastern woman of Owen Wister's *The Virginian*, had learned to appreciate and understand the rugged Western male.

Although the love theme of *Betty Zane* is an analogous reversal of *The Virginian*, other aspects of the novel clearly parallel Cooper's Leatherstocking Tales. Grey's Indians, like Cooper's, were displaced or destroyed, and we learn that

the poor Indian is unmourned. He is almost forgotten; he is in the shadow; his songs have been sung; no more will he sing to his dusky bride; his deeds are done; no more will he boast of his all-conquering arm or of his speed like the North wind; no more will his heart bound at the whistle of the stag, for he sleeps in the shade of the oaks under the moss and the ferns. (289-90)

Wetzel, Grey's frontier hero, fades into oblivion with the establishment of culture and society in a manner reminiscent of Cooper's Natty Bumppo:

Wetzel alone did not take kindly to the march of civilization; but then he was a hunter, not a pioneer. He kept his word of peace with his old enemies, the Hurons, though he never abandoned his wandering and vengeful quests after the Delawares. As the years passed, Wetzel grew more silent and taciturn. From time to time he visited Fort Henry and on these visits he spent hours playing with Betty's children. But he was restless in the settlement and his sojourns grew briefer and more infrequent as time rolled on. True to his conviction that no wife existed on earth for him, he never married. His home was the trackless wilds. (288)

Betty and Alfred, the major characters of *Betty Zane,* eventually embrace society and Betty's fate is ultimately the fate of all former war heroes: although her deeds give her a degree of fame, she is expected to fit into the mainstream of society and live her life accordingly.

The Spirit of the Border, the second volume in the trilogy, tells Wetzel's story. To Grey, Wetzel is the true product of the wild frontier. He "was purely a product of the times. Civilization could not have brought forth a man like Wetzel. Great revolutions, great crises, great moments come, and produce men to deal with them" (1906, iv).

The reader learns that "When he was nearly eighteen years old a band of Indians—Delawares, I think—burned the old Wetzel homestead and murdered the father, mother, two sisters, and baby brother" (1906, 73). Wetzel, now a mature man, had "been devoted all these twenty years and more to the killing of Indians" (73). According to Grey: "Wetzel excels in strength and speed any man, red or white, on the frontier. . . . In brief, among all the border scouts and hunters Wetzel stands alone. No wonder the Indians fear him. . . . He is as swift as an eagle, strong as mountain ash, keen as a fox and absolutely tireless and implacable" (75).

Conflict arises when a missionary settlement, the Village of Peace, is endangered by renegade Indians led by Jim Girty, an outlaw white. Realizing that the settlement is in jeopardy, Wetzel goes to warn the missionaries and help save those living in the settlement. In spite of danger, the Reverend Wells, the leader of the community, is stubborn and refuses to leave; he responds: "You ask us to fail in our duty? No Never! To get back to the white settlements and acknowledge we were afraid to continue teaching the Gospel to the Indians!" (179). Wetzel, applying common sense to the situation, observes: "I advised you to go back to Fort Henry because if you don't go now the chances are against you goin'. Christianity or no Christianity, such men as you have no business in these woods" (179).

Under these circumstances, civilized outsiders find themselves marooned on the frontier and they face profound vulnerabilities:

Wetzel looked at the other men. No one would have doubted him. No one could have failed to see he knew that some terrible danger hovered over the Village of Peace. . . . Wetzel nodded and turned to depart when George grasped his arm, . . . "you are the man to kill Girty. Rid the frontier of this fiend. Kill him! Wetzel, kill him!" . . . Wetzel never spoke a word. He stretched out his long brawny arm and gripped the young missionary's shoulder. . . . Simply without words as the action was, it could not have been more potent. (180)

It is at this point that Wetzel abandons his quest for personal revenge in order to aid society and defend culture.

Wetzel's new role is further demonstrated when he encounters his arch-enemy, a famed Delaware chief: "There, within range of his rifle was his great Indian foe Wingenumd. . . . The Delaware's life was his to take and he swore he would have it. He trembled in the ecstasy of his triumphant passion . . . slowly he raised his black rifle" (180).

Wetzel soon discovered that Wingenumd was now protected under the umbrella of the white culture. Observing a funeral ceremony the old chief was performing for his daughter, Wetzel realized: "*Wingenumd was a Christian* . . . Suddenly Wetzel's terrible temptation, his heartracking struggle ceased. He lowered the long black rifle. . . ." (269; Grey's italics). Wetzel, as an agent of society, can no longer destroy one of its members, even for strong personal reasons. Although Wetzel is eventually displaced by society, Grey editorializes,

The Border needed Wetzel. The settlers would have needed many more years in which to make permanent homes had it not been for him. He was never a pioneer . . . to the settlers he was the right arm of defense, a fitting leader for those implacable and unerring frontiersmen who made the settlement of the west a possibility. (iv)

In *The Last Trail*, the theme of *The Spirit of the Border* is repeated. This time, however, the anti-social elements are white men, led by the infamous Simon Girty. Wetzel again serves society. "The story ended with the destruction of the horse thieves and with all the principal characters getting married except Wetzel, for whom marriage would have been completely out of harmony with his nature" (Jackson 1973, 27-28).

The Ohio River trilogy is similar to the Leatherstocking Tales in that in both, a frontier hero is displaced by culture and society. In one way, however, Grey differs from Cooper. Cooper constantly depicts society as amoral and even immoral. He depicts the frontier hero as morally superior to the culture which displaces him. In the early stage of his career, Grey did not yet deal with such negative aspects of culture and the positive alternative of individualism. He concentrated upon levels of social development and the inevitable displacement of the heroic frontier figure.

Buffalo Jones

After writing a trilogy in which civilization replaces the frontier and displaces the frontier hero, Grey visited the West and encountered the Western individualist firsthand. *Betty Zane* had not been a financial success, but the book made it possible for Grey to accompany Buffalo Jones, a famous adventurer, on a hunting expedition in 1907. According to Carlton Jackson,

Grey suggested that he go with Jones to Arizona and write an account of his experiences. Before giving his consent, Jones needed evidence that Grey could write so Grey gave Jones a copy of *Betty Zane*. As soon as Jones completed reading the book, he cordially invited Grey to accompany him to the west. This invitation opened a new world for Zane Grey. (1973, 28)

This world was one of strong men who depended upon themselves instead of on a cultural superstructure. The influence of this trip was similar to the impact of Owen Wister's western trips, and it led to a volume entitled *The Last of the Plainsmen*, a work which is similar in sentiment to Wister's *The Virginian*.

Jones, "the last of the plainsmen," was a prototype of the all-conquering hero. In 1908 he was 62, still in the prime of health and prowess, and for the most of his life he had been an outdoorsman. In his time he had

caught and broke the will of every well-known wild beast native to western North America . . . necessity had compelled him to earn his livelihood by supplying the meat of buffalo to the caravans crossing the plains. At last, seeing the extinction of the noble beasts was inevitable, he smashed his rifle over a wagon wheel and vowed to save the species. (1908, v)

Jones saved the buffalo from extinction by personally capturing calves and building up his own private breeding stock. The dangers inherent in catching wild buffalo alive are depicted in a chapter entitled "The Last Herd." Trouble brews among the men, who flatly refuse their orders: "Buffalo or no, we halt here. . . . Why, man, you're crazy! You didn't tell us you wanted buffalo alive. And here you've got us looking death in the eye" (1908, 54).

But Jones responds:

For two years, I've been hunting this herd. So have other hunters. Millions of buffalo have been killed and left to rot. Soon this herd will be gone, and then the only buffalo in the world will be those I have given ten years of the hardest work in capturing. This is the last herd, I say, and my last chance to capture a calf or two. Do you imagine I'd quit? You fellows go back if you want, but I keep on. (1908, 55)

In addition to the dangers of facing a hostile environment with uncooperative companions, there was a third hazard, " 'This is Comanche country. And if that herd is in here the Indians have it spotted! . . . That worries me some!,' said the plainsman, 'but we'll keep on' " (1908, 55). Sure enough the party soon catches sight of a group of Apache. "The leader [was] a short squat chief . . . Jones . . . knew the somber sinister broad face. It belonged to the Red Chief of the Apache. 'Geronimo,' muttered the plainsman through his teeth" (1908, 58). Discovery by the Indians would have meant sure death, but the party is well hidden and after the Indians are gone, they resume their search for the buffalo:

By the time the men discover their quarry, another problem arises: the weather is turning bad. The middle of the plain below held a ragged circular mass, as still as stone. It was the buffalo herd, with every shaggy head to the storm. So they would stand, never budging from their tracks till the blizzard of sleet was over. (1908, 61-62)

The weather continued to get worse: "Food had to be eaten uncooked. The long hours dragged by with the little group huddled under icy blankets. When darkness fell, the sleet changed to drizzling rain. This blew over at midnight and a cold wind penetrated to the very marrow of the sleepless men, made their condition worse" (62). Needless to say, Jones, unintimidated by the rigors of the chase or the danger of the hostile Indians, is not about to be done in by the weather:

Jones gloated over the little red bulls and heifers, as a miser gloats over gold and jewels. Never before had he caught more than two in one day, and often it had taken days to capture one. This was the last herd, this the last opportunity towards perpetuating a grand race of beasts. And with born instinct he saw ahead the day of his life. (1908, 64)

Because of his determination, Jones captures seven buffalo calves which soon become part of his private herd. Because of Buffalo Jones and hunts such as these, Grey tells us, the buffalo were ultimately preserved from extinction.

Buffalo Jones was able to beat fate, to forestall and prevent the inevitable extinction of the buffalo, and to demonstrate that the frontier spirit could prevail. It wasn't an Eastern conservationist who saved our wild heritage. No! It was the last of the plainsmen. The man who had the power to destroy also had the power to save and preserve. Grey wrote about Buffalo Jones numerous times throughout his career, and he always pictured him as an individualist hero of epic stature.

Like Owen Wister's fictional hero, the Virginian, Buffalo Jones was quite capable of taking care of himself in the civilized world. Jones had connections in publishing and introduced Grey to Ripley Hitchcock of Harper's (the publishing firm). Although Hitchcock disliked *The Last of the Plainsmen*, he did, two years later, accept *The Heritage of the Desert*, which proved to be Grey's first major literary breakthrough. Jones was also good at public relations and attended an autograph party celebrating the publication of *The Last of the Plainsmen*. Grey later recalled that Jones

was simply great that night and the crowd went wild. When my book was delivered each table got up with a roar . . . Jones . . . talked about the book, and [said] it was the most beautiful story ever written about a sporting event. When my turn came the roar that greeted me stunned me. (Jackson 1973, 31-32)

Like the Virginian, Buffalo Jones could handle himself well in urban culture and could easily make the transition between the frontier and the eastern intellectual scene.

Complexities and Inconsistencies

In his early volumes, Grey had written about two very different individualistic heroes. Wetzel, a vestigial remain of a fading era, could function only in the rugged frontier. Buffalo Jones, in contrast, was equally adept within society or on the frontier. For the next few years Grey intertwined inconsistent characterizations in a group of novels; in the process, he developed his writing skills, and earned a loyal audience.

The novels most representative of this phase of Grey's career are a two-volume series, *Riders of the Purple Sage* and *The Rainbow Trail*, and *The Desert of Wheat*, a novel concerned with the Industrial Workers of the World, World War I, and American agriculture.

Riders of the Purple Sage is Grey's most popular novel and one of his best. In some respects, it is Grey's most Cooperesque novel, even though the action is set in late-nineteenth-century Utah. The love theme, however, is essentially a duplication of that of Wister's *The Virginian* and the heroine, Jane Withersteen, largely parallels Molly Wood of that novel. Jane is a woman of personal strength and dignity who refuses to be repressed by her culture. She declines offers of marriage, despite the insistence by local religious leaders that she accept a husband. She refuses because her Mormon religion favors polygamy, a practice she finds appalling. Like Wister's Molly Wood, Jane incurs the wrath of society for not marrying properly. Following her personal ethics, Jane engages in taboo acts such as hiring the non-Mormon Berne Venters to help run her ranch. Venters had been oppressed by the Mormon establishment and had been financially ruined by Mormon plots. Like Wister's Molly Wood, Jane finds herself increasingly estranged from her heritage because she is a strong and independent woman who does not blindly follow the edicts of her culture. Jane does not feel disloyal to her Mormon heritage and ideals, but believes her own people abandon and wrongly punish her.

The hero of *Riders* is Lassiter, a skilled gunfighter who comes to Mormon territory on a mission of honor and vengeance: to discover the fate of his sister who was lured away by a Mormon. We are introduced to Lassiter when he prevents the Mormon leaders from whipping Berne Venters, Jane's hired hand. Lassiter soon becomes one of Jane's employees, and the relationship changes both of them for the better. Jane begins to discover an alternative to life within her culture and Lassiter, a loner, begins an intimate relationship with another person.

Grey also presents Lassiter in ways which parallel Wister's Virginian; the decision to kill the Bishop Dyer, for example, is presented in a manner strongly reminiscent of the Virginian's showdown with Wister's villain. (Grey, however, was more realistic than Wister in his portrayal of violence and he presents a long and bloody account of the slaying.) Jane, reflecting Molly, opposes the killing and pleads with Lassiter to spare Dyer:

> "I'll give myself to you, I'll ride away with you—marry you, if only you'll spare him!"
> His answer was a cold ringing terrible laugh.
> "Lassiter—I love you. Spare him." (1912, 238)

The strong and independent Lassiter, however, does kill Dyer and by doing so he destroys a symbol of Jane's oppression; as a result, he saves "her from herself" (1912, 240). Like the Virginian and Molly Wood, Jane and Lassiter become reconciled after the shooting.

In *Riders*, nonetheless, the protagonists are not conquering heroes and like Cooper's Natty Bumppo, they retreat to an isolated area where society cannot follow. Throughout the novel, we are given many examples of their inability to function within society. After Lassiter saves Venters from the unjust whipping, his horse is blinded by hostile Mormons. When Jane hires non-Mormon workers and refuses to marry, she is beset with the scorn of her neighbors. Jane's Mormon employees are forced to quit their jobs by the Mormon religious hierarchy, her cattle are stampeded, and the Mormon even make a deal with cattle rustlers to liquidate her herds. After the killing of Bishop Dyer (which Grey presents as a thwarting of illegitimate authority), the couple is compelled to retreat.

Like Natty Bumppo, Jane and Lassiter can only survive in isolation. Since there is no convenient "Great American Desert" for them to hide in, their only hope is a secret canyon, Surprise Valley; its one entrance can be blocked with a rock slide. There is a drawback to this strategy: once the entrance is blocked, those inside are marooned and cannot rejoin civilization and society.

Faced with this conflict, Lassiter weakens and remarks, "I've lost my nerve" (1912, 280). The strong woman must now take command, forcing a decision. "Lassiter! Roll the stone! . . . Roll the stone! Lassiter, I love you. . . . ROLL THE STONE. . . . From the depths there rose a long-drawn rumbling roar. The outlet to Deception Pass closed forever" (1912, 280). The strong feminine figure chooses isolation from the outside world and gives her man the strength to accept this alternative.

Riders of the Purple Sage is essentially an updating of Cooper's Leatherstocking saga; it is a generalization of the displacement theme and it demonstrates that both men and women are potential victims of an oppressive culture. In *Riders*, Grey underscores another Cooperesque theme: society is negative and immoral.

In *The Rainbow Trail*, a sequel, Grey tempers the conclusions of *Riders of the Purple Sage* and argues that democracy might eliminate the oppressions of local groups. The hero is a former minister named Shefford whose congregation had forsaken him. He states:

I had doubts of religion—of the Bible—of God, as my church believed in them. As I grew older, thought and study convinced me of the narrowness of religion as my congregation lived it. I preached what I believed. I alienated them. They put me out. Took my calling from me, disgraced me, ruined me. (1915, 55)

Like his former congregation, Shefford finds the local missionaries are oppressive; he becomes alarmed when they attempt to force their religion upon the Indians. Instead of helping the Indians in material ways, the missionaries merely provide religious dogma. The hapless Indians respond, "Me no savvy Jesus Christ! Me Hungry. . . . Me no eat Jesus Christ" (1915, 47). No one but Shefford empathizes with their plight. After Shefford objects to the missionary's approach, however, the clergyman "gave way to ungovernable rage and cursed Shefford as a religious fanatic might have cursed the most debased sinners" (1915, 149).

Luckily, the power of such oppressors is weakening as a strong central government rapidly encroaches upon their dictatorial powers. The institution of polygamy among the Mormons, for example, is undermined; thus,

All over Utah, polygamists have been arrested. . . . Over here in the wild canyon country there's a village of Mormon's sealed wives. . . . When the United States government began to persecute, or prosecute, the Mormon for polygamy, the Mormon over here in Strongbridge took their sealed wives and moved out of Utah, just across the line. They built houses and established a village there. (1915, 53)

The Mormons, who had once flaunted their polygamy, Grey argues, are forced to practice it in secret in secluded settlements called "sealed wife" villages. Although Grey's novel is fiction, he spent much time in Utah and used his knowledge to make the backgrounds realistic.

At one "sealed wife" village, Shefford meets Fay Larkin, Lassiter's niece, who accompanied Lassiter and Jane to Surprise Valley in *Riders of the Purple Sage*. During her life in the sealed wife village, Fay has been subjected to many of the same pressures which Jane had suffered

years before. In time, Shefford and Fay fall in love and, replicating the
flight of Jane and Lassiter, they flee the Mormon community and escape
to Surprise Valley.

Up to this point, *The Rainbow Trail* roughly parallels *Riders*. Social
conditions are different now as a strong central government is actively
engaged in destroying the powers of local oppression. Since Mormon
control is waning, Shefford, Fay, Jane, and Lassiter are able to abandon
their refuge and reunite with society. Lassiter and Jane move to Illinois
where Jane's former employee, Venters, has settled. Jane is reunited with
her two favorite horses who remember her and form a living link with
her past.

Considered as a composite, *Riders of the Purple Sage* and *The
Rainbow Trail* celebrate the ability of democracy to protect the rights
and freedoms of individuals by weakening the oppressive power of
local vested interest groups. Grey shows how a strong central government makes it possible for his protagonists to break the bonds of local
oppression and reunite with society. Grey's belief in a beneficial and
just central government, however, was rejected as time went on. Both
government and modern society become villains in his later novels.

The beginnings of this transformation can be seen in *The Desert of
Wheat*, a novel which depicts the Industrial Workers of the World, the
Wobblies, as a corrupt and pro-German labor union. In spite of this
theme, Grey hints that the individualist spirit was slowly being destroyed
and oppressed by the massive forces of the twentieth century. This is
explicitly stated when an IWW sympathizer laments,

years ago I was a prosperous oil-producer, I had a fine oil field. Along comes a
big fellow, tries to buy me out, and, failing that, he shot off dynamite charges
into the ground next to my oil field . . . choked my wells! Ruined me! . . . I
came west—went to farming. Along comes a corporation, steals my water for
irrigation and my land went back to desert. . . . So I quit working and trying to
be honest. It doesn't pay. The rich men are getting all the richer at the expense
of the poor. So now I'm a tramp. (Grey 1919, 168)

This inequity notwithstanding, the exploited tramp is urged to desert the
IWW and support his country in a time of need. Grey appears to have
been aware of gross injustices caused by mass society and big business,
but in 1919 he still believed modern society and government were essentially good.

The Desert of Wheat is also interesting because it closely resembles
the tone of Frank Norris' unfinished Wheat trilogy. In *The Octopus* and
The Pit, the two existing novels, Norris shows how the wheat caused

pain and misery all through the chains of production and distribution. Grey, in depicting the conflicts between the IWW and its opponents, does approximately the same thing. Norris, in his unfinished volume *The Wolf*, had planned to show how the wheat reaches its destination and serves mankind. Paralleling Norris' unfinished trilogy, Grey concludes:

America the new country became in 1918 the salvation of starving Belgium, the mainstay of England, the hope of France! Wheat—that was to say food—strength, fighting life for the armies opposed to the black hideous hordes of the Huns! . . . Fields and toil and grains of wheat, first and last, the salvation of mankind and the food of the world. (1919, 273)

The Desert of Wheat is a complex and busy book. In addition to the themes discussed above, there are other important subplots, such as a German-American who has to prove his loyalty to America, a romantic story, and the saga of a badly wounded veteran who is discharged from the service because it is assumed he would soon die. Like *The Rainbow Trail*, *The Desert of Wheat* celebrates America as a defender of individual freedoms, even though hints of Grey's increasing distrust of mass society and modern culture are evident.

After *The Desert of Wheat*, Grey increasingly associates culture and society with amorality or immorality. The oppressive nature of government and society are discussed in many of his later stories and novels. In *30,000 on the Hoof*, the hero and heroine are cheated out of a fortune by government agents. In addition, two of their sons are killed in World War I. Grey implies that the death of the strong and independent sons is caused by the fact that war is no longer a contest of man against man, but a game of technology, statistics, and machines. Upon seeing a newsreel of the war, the hero exclaims: "I sent my sons into that. . . . Good God! I reckoned they'd have a chance. Man to man with rifles, behind trees and rocks, where the sharp eye and crack shot would prove who was best! But that—God Almighty—what would you call that?" (Grey 1911).

In *Rogue River Feud*, the forces of big business are poised against the lone individual, a man who is disfigured because of a World War I injury. Ironically, Kevin Ball, this unfortunate hero, receives no government aid to compensate for his disability, while businessmen profit from the war and receive tax shelters and governmental subsidies. In addition, the businessmen rape and destroy the land and are rewarded by the government for doing so.

Unfortunately, such novels suffer from a basic flaw: they have happy endings which are contrived and at odds with the flow of the plot.

Just as James Fenimore Cooper ended many of his novels with unrealistic and compromised happy endings, Grey's heroes overcome impossible obstacles and emerge victorious.

Grey's Fatalistic Vision

In one novel, however, Grey allows the forces of society to defeat the heroic figure. In this story he pits two lone individuals against the immoral modern world. This novel is entitled *The Vanishing American,* and since it distills Grey's philosophy of society and the individual, it is his classic and most representative novel.

The hero of the novel is Nophaie, an Indian who was twice kidnaped when he was a young child. First sheep rustlers caught him so he could not alert the tribe that its sheep were being stolen. The rustlers, however, released the child as soon as they were safe. He was then found by white tourists who took him east, raised him and sent him to college, where he becomes an all American football player reminiscent of Jim Thorpe.

At 25 years of age, after 18 years among the whites, Nophaie goes back to the reservation and his people. His return coincides with the economic upheavals caused by World War I. On the reservation, he finds the war has caused temporary prosperity:

The war has brought false values. Wool is fifty cents a pound. Horses and sheep bring higher prices than Indians ever dreamed of. They think this will last always. They will not save. They live from day to day, and spend their money foolishly. And when the reaction comes they will be suddenly poor, with the traders prices higher than ever. (Grey 1925, 13)

In addition to the impersonal economic forces of a complex industrial society, the white teachers and missionaries constantly attempt to force their will and their culture upon the Navajo: "The injustice to them is the blackest of white man's baseness. The compulsory school system for the Indian boys and girls has many bad points. The bad missionary is the apostle of hate and corruption" (1925, 14). The head governmental official, a man named Blucher, proves to be pro-German and he encourages the Indians to circumvent governmental policies related to the war effort. Besides making the Indians a pawn in an international war, Blucher actively cheats the people he is paid to help:

For instance, the half-breed Noki Indian Sam Ween, is Blucher's interpreter. Blucher pays Sam twenty dollars a month when he pays him at all. I asked Sam. And I saw in government papers the amount appropriated by the government for Blucher's interpreter. (1925, 14)

Blucher actively spies on the people of the reservation and tampers with the mails. Blucher's confederates make sure that only the mail which is favorable to Blucher and Morgan, the missionary, reaches its destination.

Morgan, the missionary leader, is actually the dictator of the reservation: "He really is in control here. He boasts of having put the 'steam roller' over former superintendents of this reservation" (108). The chief activity of these white parasites is exploiting the Indians, whom they are paid to serve. Grey asks, "How can a man lie to the Indians, cheat them in money dealings, steal their water and land, and expect to convert them to Christianity?" (108).

If the condition of the Indians were not pitiful enough, they receive another "gift" from the white man, a deadly plague of influenza. "Three thousand Nopahs died of the plague, and from one end of the reservation to the other a stricken, bewildered, and crushed people bowed their heads. The exceedingly malignant form of the influenza and the superstitious convictions of the fatalistic Indians united to create a deadly medium" (282). Facing such obstacles, two strong people arise: Nophaie, the Indian, and Marian, the white woman he loves.

Like Grey's other heroines, Marian is a strong and independent woman. While in college, she had given Nophaie the strength to overcome his alcoholism: "I stopped drinking for you. And for an Indian to give up whiskey, once he knows its taste, is no small thing. . . . And I'm sure your influence kept me from the fate of more than one famous Indian athlete—Sockalexis, for instance, who ruined his career and health in one short year" (14). Again needing her assurance and support he requests, "Come, Marian, to Otjato—come to help me awhile" (15).

Marian, who also finds society to be debased, is happy to join Nophaie in an attempt to prevent the encroachment of white culture upon the Indians:

The farther she traveled the more untrue her situation seemed. Yet she was glad, deep within her stirred strange promptings. She strove to justify her actions in her own eyes. Surely one flight of freedom need not be denied her. . . . The prairie, the mountains, the sea, the desert all called to her with imperious voice. Some day she would surely have listened. (Grey 1925)

A major reason for Marian's flight to the desert is the hope of finding a mate who will treat her as an equal partner without denying her the benefits of domestic life: "I am my own master. I've always dreamed of love with honor—of marriage with children. Perhaps in vain! My aunt, my friends, would call me mad. They do not understand me. I am not throwing my life away" (1925, 18).

Unceasingly, Nophaie strives to find his true identity, to break through the veneer of white culture, and recover the long-suppressed Indian within him.

"I am an infidel," he said hoarsely. . . . "I did not know it when I came back to the reservation. . . . I tried to return to the religion of my people. I prayed—trying to believe in the Indian's God—I will not believe in the White man's God. . . . This Morgan kills the Indian's simple faith in his own God—makes him an infidel—Then tries to make him a Christian. It cannot be done." (1925/1953, 101)

Being strong-willed, Nophaie constantly seeks his true identity, but each time he fails. His old faith does not return.

Finally he too falls victim to the influenza and, although he becomes gravely ill, Nophaie does survive, and his cure rekindles a belief in his traditional God. In gratitude he sets forth on a pilgrimage to a sacred Indian shrine. As a result of over-exertion during the journey Nophaie suffers a relapse and dies. Nophaie rediscovers his personal identity and his God, but he dies as a direct consequence of his enlightenment; his death is linked to the fact that he paid homage to his own faith and his true self. Had he embraced the white religion, he might have visited the local church to acknowledge his cure and lived. Had he rejected the Indian God in the absence of any other, he might have stayed home and rested, and again he probably would not have suffered a relapse and died. Instead, he goes on a strenuous pilgrimage to celebrate himself and his traditions and he dies of a relapse precipitated by this pious overexertion. The disease, furthermore, is a malady introduced to the Indians by the whites.

The book ends with Marian, the strong-willed woman, left alone, a living loser in the struggle between society and the individualistic spirit. "It is symbolic," said Marian, "They are vanishing—vanishing. Oh! Nopahs! Only a question of swiftly flying time! Nophaie—the warrior— gone before them! . . . it is well" (1925, 308).

The theme of *The Vanishing American* is that those who choose to follow their own paths and adhere to their own standards will be destroyed by society. A corollary to this theme is that people will tend to survive if they play the game, capitulate, and obey established authority. Grey found the true individualist to be a heroic person and he depicted collective society in negative terms. Like Natty Bumppo, and the Virginian, Nophaie and Marian are of heroic stature because they stood up for what they believed and accepted their true selves. The fact that they failed had nothing to do with their personal worth, but with massive social forces beyond their control.

Discussion

For many years, Zane Grey vacillated between the conflicting themes of James Fenimore Cooper's pessimism, on the one hand, and Owen Wister's upbeat portrayal of the frontier thesis of American history, on the other. Throughout Grey's long apprenticeship, these themes were never completely reconciled. As a result, Grey often developed fatalistic themes, reminiscent of Cooper, only to conclude his stories with an inappropriate, unrealistic, and contrived ending in which the hero, nonetheless, prevails.

In *The Vanishing American*, however, it is possible to see the culmination of Grey's mature vision, which depicts a bleak and horrific oblivion for his strong individualist hero. The hero is not destroyed by equals in a fair fight. Instead defeat is inflicted by inferiors, analogous to the lowly virus which enters the region with the coming of civilization.

The Vanishing American is a fine novel, arguably Grey's best, and it was respected by the reading public. Nonetheless, it was viewed as an "offbeat Western"; Grey wrote in an era when the frontier thesis portrayed the west as the home and testing ground for invincible heroes and, as a result of these expectations, Grey's fatalistic plotlines could not emerge as a prototype for future transformations of the genre. The fact that the hero was an Indian, however, may have made the plot more acceptable to the reading public, since native people were often viewed as fading away as white society came to dominate the wilderness. Nevertheless, this scenario could not be generalized and embraced as a formula.

Written while the Wister/frontier thesis formula was still strongly established (in the maturity stage of the product life cycle), plotlines which overtly conflicted with this dominant product could not establish themselves. As a result, *The Vanishing American* had little impact and Grey, responding to public demands, reverted to writing upbeat novels which corresponded to the popular view of history.

Nonetheless, Zane Grey's *The Vanishing American* largely foreshadows and largely overshadows western stories of the 1960s and 1970s in which the noble hero, out of step with the world, must die. The message is clear. Moralistic individuals with unswayable visions are out of step with the world and cannot survive its onslaught. Even though Grey's novel revolves around a minority group, the American Indian, *The Vanishing American* is identical in structure and tone to important films such as *The Misfits*, *Ride the High Country*, *Lonely Are the Brave*, and *Butch Cassidy and the Sundance Kid* that embrace a fatalistic theme and portray strong individualists as heroic figures who are thwarted or destroyed by society.

The entire structure, ethos, and drama of these later fatalistic Westerns are contained within *The Vanishing American*, even though there is no evidence that Grey influenced them. Unacceptable in Grey's era because the death of the hero was in conflict with the audience's world view, by the 1960s such a pessimistic vision became the vogue and in this new environment the fatalistic Western could prevail as formula, not merely as an offbeat plotline.

Works Cited

Grey, Zane. 1902. *Betty Zane*. New York: Grosset and Dunlap.

——. 1906. *The Spirit of the Border*. New York: Grosset and Dunlap.

——. 1908. *The Last of the Plainsmen*. New York: Outing Publishing.

——. 1911. *30,000 on the Hoof*. New York: Harpers.

——. 1912. *Riders of the Purple Sage*. New York: Grosset and Dunlap.

——. 1915. *The Rainbow Trail*. New York: Grosset and Dunlap.

——. 1919. *The Desert of Wheat*. New York: Harpers.

——. 1925. *The Vanishing American*. New York: Grosset and Dunlap.

——. 1953. *The Vanishing American*. New York: Grosset and Dunlap. Reprint of 1925.

Hacket, Alice. 1945. *50 Years of Best Sellers 1895-1945*. New York: R. R. Bowker.

Jackson, Carlton. 1973. *Zane Grey*. New York: Twayne.

8

WALTER CLARK AND THE EMERGENCE OF THE ANTIHERO

Allegory or Western?

Published in 1940, *The Ox Bow Incident* put Walter Van Tilburg Clark on the literary map. A first novel, it won him immediate acclaim from both literary critics and the general public. Though it is overtly a cowboy story, critics have routinely argued that *The Ox Bow Incident* is some other type of literature and merely placed in a frontier setting. Some reviewers suggested the book, published during the regime of Adolf Hitler, was a thinly veiled statement on the Third Reich and the crackup of Western civilization. This theory casts a long shadow; Andrew Sarris, writing in the early 1970s, suggests *Ox Bow* is a topical film about "burning social issues of that time."[1] Robert Warshow views the film as a social drama which "makes the Western setting irrelevant, a mere backdrop of beautiful scenery" (1954, 198-99). Leslie Fiedler adheres to this general tradition of criticism by suggesting the story is actually about the South and the posse is analogous to the Ku Klux Klan. Fiedler argues that the lynching, directed by a former Confederate officer, replicates oppression and genocide directed at American blacks (1968, 142).

Such analysis notwithstanding, *The Ox Bow Incident* is firmly within the tradition of the cowboy story and the Western novel. The setting and action are typical, the requirements for heroic action are identical, and the moral message is parallel to the work of James Fenimore Cooper and Owen Wister, Clark's literary ancestors. The strength and valor required to oppose authority and collective action are the standards by which the protagonists of all three authors are judged. *The Ox Bow Incident* is atypical only because Clark suggests that in certain crucial situations, people must forsake moral, heroic action in order to survive. The novel demonstrates the same loss of optimism that prevailed in Zane Grey's *The Vanishing American*, in which the protagonist dies because he is too heroic for his own good. While Grey's protagonist is heroic because he remains true to his ideals, Clark's protagonists, in contrast, survive via a shrewd sacrifice of their personal integrity. As a result of this pragmatic compromise, they become antiheroes who survive. This chapter argues that products (examples of popular culture) are widely embraced when the public is ready for them. Thus, an innovative story that is in conflict with the basic beliefs of society will have little impact upon the public or upon the evolution of popular culture. In Clark's time, the "origin myth" of the frontier thesis (which depicts the cowboy as a moralistic and all-conquering superman who represented American ideals) was still strongly embraced by a large section of the population. These beliefs and preferences profoundly impacted the popular culture of the era.

Although *The Ox Bow Incident* was an offbeat story when published in 1940, in retrospect, it emerges as a prototype of the antiheroic tradition that was to emerge as an influential sub-genre in the 1960s.

A Question of Moral Leadership

The Ox Bow Incident concerns the lack of moral leadership which could have been provided by strong and uncompromising heroes. As a result of the void created by their absence, injustice prevails and three innocent men are hanged. The novel, however, is not an overt condemning of vigilante law, since lynching is portrayed as a legitimate method of social control. The formal laws of civilization and the religious edicts of the church, furthermore, are portrayed as ineffective in the untamed West.

Formal Eastern law is represented by the effete Judge Tyler, who is incapable of dealing with rustling and murder. The judge's personal appearance demonstrates his ineffectual nature. He is

wide and round, in a black frock coat, a white big collared shirt, and a black string tie, his large face pasty, with folds of fat over the collar, bulging brown eyes, and a mouth with a shape like a woman's mouth, but with a big pendulous lower lip, like men get who talk a lot without thinking much first. (Clark 1940, 79)

In addition to being pompous and having no real feel for the West, the judge is inexperienced: "The judge ain't had nothing bigger to deal with than a drunk and disorderly Indian since he got here" (1940, 122). In addition, there is no evidence that the judge is attempting to educate himself in the subtleties of the law. He does have "shelves of thick, pale brown books," but it appears they haven't been studied very much since "they were all pretty new looking" (1940, 79).

Besides Judge Tyler, however, society does have Sheriff Risley, a law officer who is wise to the ways of the West. Although some are disappointed with Risley's past performances, he is described as a "good man . . . and a good sheriff" (1940, 57). Unfortunately, Risley is out of town when needed: another demonstration of the ineffectiveness of the law; the frontier is too big for him to police alone.

In such a situation Judge Tyler refuses to provide meaningful leadership, stating: "It's not in my position. . . . It's not the place of either a judge or a lawyer. It lies in the sheriff's office. I have no police authority" (1940, 84). Although Tyler passes the buck, he objects when the sheriff's deputy tries to form a posse, observing, "You can't do it. . . . Risley's the only one empowered to deputize" (1940, 40). The law represented by Tyler cripples all attempts to deal with the problems at hand. When a posse is formed, furthermore, he becomes angry and swears to avenge himself.

Organized religion is equally incapable of meaningful action; the namby-pamby Reverend Osgood is as ineffectual as Judge Tyler. Instead of making a strong and vital stand, Osgood babbles, " 'They mustn't do this; they mustn't' . . . waving his hands and looking as if he were going to cry" (1940, 40). The cowboys have little patience with Osgood and his abstract notions of justice and respond, "Shut up, gran'ma. Nobody expects you to go" (1940, 40).

Desperate, Osgood launches into a sermon about the evils of lynch law:

"Men," he orated. . . . "Let us not act hastily, Let us not do that which we will regret. We must act, certainly, but we must act in a reasoned and legitimate manner, not as a lawless mob. It is not mere blood that we want; we are not Indians, savages to be content with a miserable sneaking revenge. We desire justice and justice has never been obtained in haste and strong feelings." (1940, 41)

Although Osgood's words are prophetic, he lacks the poise and personal strength to sway the men. After the speech it seems that he "intended to say more but he stopped and looked at us pathetically" (1940, 41). Eastern religion, like Eastern law, has not assimilated itself to the West and cannot play a decisive role.

A last representative of Eastern culture is Davies, the local storekeeper. Davies represents the coward; even though he is constantly a champion of restraint, he ultimately admits he is glad he didn't have a gun so he couldn't physically oppose the posse. He actually refuses the offer of a weapon so that he cannot challenge the posse.

Formal law, religion, and mainstream Eastern culture are unable to offer a viable alternative to lynch law. In a passage favoring the use of vigilante justice, the issues are made crystal clear:

"I don't know about the rest of you, but I've had enough rustling. Do we have rights as men and cattlemen or don't we? We know what Tyler is. If we wait for Tyler or any man like Tyler" he added glaring at Osgood, "if we wait, I tell you there won't be one head of anybody's cattle left in the meadows by the time we get justice." (1940, 43)

This rationale for lynch law is nearly identical to that of Judge Henry in Owen Wister's *The Virginian*. Judge Henry believes "the law has been letting our cattle-thieves go for two years. We are in a very bad way and we are trying to make that way a little better until civilization can reach us . . . far from being a defiance of the law it is an assertion of it" (Wister 1902). The justifications for vigilante law in *The Ox Bow Incident* and *The Virginian* are analogous; in both it is depicted as a legitimate stop gap method. Clark, therefore, sets up his story in ways which clearly reflect the classic cowboy story. The dilemma of establishing order in a lawless land is the theme of the novel. And lynching is portrayed as a method of social control which, although distasteful, is depicted as legitimate.

Immoral Forces Fill the Void

The paradox of *The Ox Bow Incident* is that, although lynching may be a valid method in the hands of reasonable people, the rank and file are ultimately manipulated by leaders who exploit the emotions of the moment for their own partisan purposes. Clark goes to great lengths to demonstrate that the leaders of the vigilantes are not fair and impartial. Instead of providing a fair trial, they inhibit justice in order to advance their own private motives.

The primary leader of the posse is Colonel Tetley, a former Confederate officer, a self-proclaimed leader who overreacts and treats a minor encounter involving some suspected cattle thieves as if it were the battle of Bull Run. Although the posse is attempting to capture only three men, Tetley maps out a battle plan with mathematical precision. Tetley's overblown use of elaborate military procedures punctuates the book at several places and each time they are inappropriate: evidence that Tetley lacks the temperament to respond appropriately to the situation at hand. In addition to treating a hastily assembled posse in a precise military manner, Tetley has a vested interest in the lynching: he hopes the incident will function as a rite of passage for his effeminate son and transform him into a man. Tetley's personality, methods, and personal agendas make true justice irrelevant to him; he is too engrossed with being obeyed and helping his son achieve manhood to be fair and objective.

A second leader, Farnley, is a good friend of Kincaid, who had allegedly been killed by the rustlers. Although Farnley isn't a bad man, he experiences an emotional frenzy after he hears that Kincaid is dead. His mission is one of blind vengeance brought on by grief. Before the capture of the supposed rustlers Farnley demands, "The son-of-a-bitch that got Kincaid is mine Tetley. Don't forget that" (1940, 183). During a raid of the suspects' camp, Farnley captures a Mexican who supposedly can speak no English. Finally after Farnley gestures with the rifle, the Mexican raised

his hands up. . . . "That's better" Farnley said, still grinning. "Though some ways I'd just as soon you hadn't, you son-of-a-bitch . . . " "No Sabby," The Mex said again.
   "That's all right brother" Farnley told him, "you will." (1940, 190)

Later, when it is suspected that the Mexican actually can speak English, a ghoulish Farnley volunteers to force him to speak. According to the narrator, "He was eager for it; he was so eager for it he disgusted me and made me feel sorry for the Mex" (1940, 198).

A third leader is Mapes, "a bully, and like most bullies he was a play the crowd man" (1940, 65). Even before a posse is formed, Art Croft, the novel's narrator, realizes Mapes is a poor leader. Once the alleged rustlers have been caught, Mapes inhibits any free and rational discussion that could have resulted in a just verdict. Every time Martin, the most articulate of the prisoners, attempts to plead his case, Mapes shouts, "Shut up" (1940, 211). Later, when Davies attempts to argue on behalf of the prisoners, Mapes takes him by the arm and pulling him away, aborts the defense. This seals the fate of the three men.

A last leader is Smith, a sadist who enjoys the prospect of killing and actually likes the idea of lynching the men. Upon first hearing that rustling has taken place, he jokes about lynching and performs parodies, of men dying at the end of a rope. After the innocence of the three victims is proven, Smith has not learned his lesson and wants to go out and lynch Colonel Tetley, the leader of the posse. He is a blood-thirsty sadist.

Such leaders should not dominate a life and death situation. As a result of their tenure, three innocent men die. This fact is clearly articulated by Art Croft when he observes: "It seems to me sometimes you have to change the laws and sometimes the men who represent them" (1940, 65). Although Clark argues that lynch law might play a valid role, he also emphasizes that it is easily perverted.

Coolheaded and emotionally balanced leaders who advocate lynch law do exist. Bartlett represents the intellectual rationale of vigilante justice; his justification for lynch law is virtually identical to that of Judge

Henry of *The Virginian*. It is Bartlett who, in a well-constructed and articulate speech, spurs the posse into action. He proclaims that Eastern law and religion cannot function on the frontier, points to precedents where lynch law had worked well in San Francisco and Texas, and concludes that the crime in question is not merely robbery, but cold-blooded murder. In Bartlett's words: "Let that go and I'm telling you, men, there won't be anything safe, not our cattle, not our homes, not our lives, not even our women. I say we've got to get them. . . ." (1940, 45). This speech, more than any other single action, causes the posse to be formed and provides a moral justification for their actions. Bartlett is the intellectual justification for lynch law.

Moore, in contrast, represents the pragmatic, grass roots, and practical basis of vigilante law. Moore is old for a cowhand and is "a sick man, though he wouldn't stand for having anybody ask how he felt" (1940, 14). He thoroughly understands the lawless cattle country and he is level headed. "His eyes were quiet and still, and he never blew off or got absent-minded no matter how bad he felt" (1940, 14). Moore symbolizes the honest, objective, and coolheaded person who could lend justice to vigilante law. Symbolizing intelligent people who are the backbone of any legitimate collective action, Moore is the man who appoints the head executioner of the posse (1940, 66).

When the illegitimate leadership, represented by Tetley, Farnley, Mapes, and Smith, call for a vote of execution, these two representatives of legitimate authority oppose the guilty verdict. They realize the trial has been a sham; they believe in the principle of lynch law, but they oppose hanging men under the present circumstances.

Inept Defenders of Justice

Only three other members of the posse champion the position taken by Bartlett and Moore. Unfortunately, all three are second-class citizens and incapable of swaying public opinion.

The first defender is Davies the storekeeper. Davies admits to the reader he is a coward and Clark presents him as a representative of effete Eastern culture. The second defender is Gerald Tetley, the effeminate son of Colonel Tetley. He is unfamiliar with the ways of the frontier, is bullied into submission by his father, and cannot defend legitimate authority. The last defender is Sparks, a Negro who is a second-class citizen for racial reasons; because of prejudice he can't emerge as a leader. The racial bias of the group is underscored when Art Croft apologetically tells the reader of his own bigotry.

Although Owen Wister's and Clark's portrayals of lynch law are similar, their conceptions of human nature are different. As a result,

Wister's lynching scene is honorable and just, while Clark's is dishonorable and perverted. In *The Virginian*, the entire posse is rational and humane, they are so fair that even Steve, one of the condemned prisoners, acknowledges he is being honorably treated. In Wister's portrayal, lynching emerges as an effective, fair, and humane method of social control in a lawless area.

Clark, in contrast, depicts the leaders of the posse as villains and the rank and file as passive followers who abandon reason in the excitement of the chase. It is hardly by chance that the posse is often described as a "pack" (1940, 132-34).

In Clark's story, furthermore, the most sane and equitable course of action would be for the posse to turn the prisoners over to the proper authorities. The second best solution would be for the posse to try the men, but only after more facts had been gathered. The prisoners are woefully outnumbered and their alibi can be easily checked. Under these circumstances, there is no reason to make a quick judgment and execute the men on the spot, but this is what happens. The result is not justice, but the whims of a chaotic "pack" spurred on by amoral leaders intent on advancing their personal agendas.

This theme is not inherently alien to the Wisteresque cowboy novel. Wister celebrated the moral choices made by an archetypical American hero who is identified with the frontier. The injustice of the mob could provide an arena where heroic action could be showcased, but so far, Clark has not veered from the dominant formula which is linked to Wister and the frontier thesis.

Potential Heroes

The failure does not lie with Davies, Gerald Tetley, or Sparks, even though Davies later blames himself. These would-be defenders lack the ability to effectively sway the posse. The fault lies with Art Croft and Gil Carter, men who are capable of acting, but fail to rise to the occasion.

Croft and Carter are young, used to danger, don't mind fighting, and are good with guns. Furthermore, since they are a good team, they can be effective against the posse, most of whom are but casual acquaintances. Clark implies that one strong man could prevent the lynching. Two young men comfortable with fighting and guns probably would have the ability to forestall it. Both men, furthermore, have doubts about the guilt of the men and feel that inquiries should be made. Gil Carter realizes the trial is improper and initially opposes Tetley, observing, "if you got any doubts, let's call this party off and take them to the Judge, like Davies wants" (1940, 208).

Tetley responds that since Carter is a stranger in the area it is "only very slightly any of your business" (1940, 208). Carter's retort implies a moral responsibility on the part of every person even if only "slightly" involved. "Hanging is any man's business that's around," he says (1940, 208).

Art also has doubts about the leaders of the posse and the way the prisoners are treated; he notices the posse is "mistreating" (1940, 210) the suspects and he is "disgusted" (1940, 198) by the way they are abused.

Both Art and Gil oppose the lynching and have the power to stop it. Nevertheless, both characters fail to act and they allow an unjust execution to proceed. The plot and the message of *The Ox Bow Incident* revolves around these two men and why they hesitate. To understand *The Ox Bow Incident*, the underlying motivations of Art Croft and Gil Carter must be understood. Literary critics, however, are in disagreement regarding these two men and, as a result, little consensus exists in interpretations of the novel.

Max Westbrook, a Jungian critic, believes Art and Gil act in archetypical fashion. To Westbrook, the posse represents the archetype of the collective and, in the final analysis, the two protagonists capitulate to the group and participate "in murder because they fear an inner reality" (1966-67, 116).

Westbrook de-emphasizes moralistic or political considerations and observes:

"Beyond all natural shyness, shame, and tact," writes Jung, "There is a secret fear of the unknown 'perils of the soul.' Of course one is reluctant to admit such a ridiculous fear." Jung's explanation of the danger of "secret fears" is strikingly relevant to *The Ox Bow Incident.* (1966-67, 116)

According to this paradigm, the novel becomes an example of the phantom of racial memory; Westbrook summarizes the message of the book as follows, "The tragedy of *The Ox Bow Incident* is that most of us, including the man of sensitivity and the man of reason, are alienated from the saving grace of archetypal reality" (1966-67, 110).

While Westbrook views Art and Gil as archetypal characters who slough off the veneer of civilization, Paul Stein feels they are locked in stereotyped roles common in the Western novel. According to Stein, Clark utilizes stock character types which have long existed within the genre. He accuses Clark of using "Types rather than individuals, clichés who suffer from a flattening of character and a dependence on label rather than content for flavor" (Stein 1970-71, 271).

Robert Cochran, in turn, repudiates Stein and believes *The Ox Bow Incident* concerns individuals and how they view their own nature. Cochran identifies two philosophies in the novel which are typified by Davies and Gerald Tetley. Tetley believes "man is more vicious and cunning than the wolf, more timid and fearful than the rabbit" (Cochran 1970-71, 257). Davies, in contrast, "is the spokesman in the novel for the civilized forces developed to hold in check the bestial nature of man" (Cochran 1970-71, 259).

Cochran believes Art and Gil (especially Art) are a "captive audience" (Cochran 1970-71, 260) and a sounding board for Davies and Tetley's views. Art's character, the argument continues, is blessed with a "Buddha-like contemplation" (Cochran 1970-71, 255) ideally suited for the role of listening and considering the two opinions. Cochran theorizes that both of these philosophers are eventually discredited and Art and Gil emerge as the survivors who live to tell the tale.

A more provocative analysis of *The Ox Bow Incident* is found in Robert Warshow's classic article on the Western film. He observes: "It is significant that *The Ox Bow Incident* has no hero; a hero would have to stop the lynching or be killed in trying to stop it" (Warshow 1954, 199). Warshow, as well as L. B. Saloman (1940, 344), an earlier reviewer of the novel, realizes that the plot lacks a hero. Warshow, however, makes the mistake of interpreting *Ox Bow* as primarily a statement on the evils of lynch law and that an heroic figure would have detracted from the real theme and "the 'problem' of lynching would no longer be central" (1954, 199).

None of these theories, however, deals with the dilemma which prompts Art and Gil's inaction. Unable to do this, such criticism fails to consider the central message of the book. The novel suggests that Art and Gil are in danger of losing their lives. They are in jeopardy of being lynched because they, too, are suspected of being cattle rustlers. When Art innocently asks Canby, the bartender, if there were any strangers in the area who could be rustling, Canby responds:

"There hasn't been, that knew cattle," said Canby, sitting back up on the counter, "Except you two."

"That's not funny," Gil told him and set his glass down very quietly. . . .

"Sure," Canby said, "I just thought I'd let you know how you stand." (Clark 1940, 15-16)

At the first talk of lynching, Art tells the reader that he is worried. "You can feel awful guilty about nothing when the men you're with don't trust you. I knew Gil was feeling the same way when he started to say something, and Canby looked back at him, and he didn't say it" (Clark 1940, 37). Art realizes that it is necessary to join the posse so he and Gil can vindicate themselves. He says, "We couldn't afford to stand in there behind Canby either. I pushed past him and went down onto the walk, Gil right behind me" (1940, 37). Once on the street, they become members of the posse.

Later, after the suspects are caught, Gil's defense of the prisoners is aborted when Tetley reminds him that he is a possible suspect. Gil is finally stifled when Tetley asks, "Have you a brief for the innocence of these men?" (1940, 208). Such proof could only be Gil's own confession that he is the murderer and rustler. After this challenge, Gil changes the subject and ironically argues that he isn't a coward.

Such characterizations and plot elements undermine Westbrook's archetypal argument. Art and Gil do not feel some unconscious archetypal threat as much as the overt and very understandable fear of being lynched themselves. If Westbrook wishes to pursue his Jungian argument, he must first grapple with the immediate danger in which Art and Gil find themselves. Without such an analysis, Westbrook's archetypical thesis falls like a house of cards.

Because of their very real fears, Art and Gil allow injustice to prevail and they emerge as antiheroes. Their guilt is demonstrated in Davies' final speech, a statement on the immorality of inaction. Although Davies blames himself, neither he, nor Sparks, nor Gerald Tetley have the ability to oppose collective authority. Davies' damning speech actually describes the guilt of those who have the power to oppose Colonel Tetley. The speech is a reflection on the inaction of Art and Gil.

Davies realizes that, even though the crowd makes a scapegoat out of the colonel, "Tetley couldn't help what he did. . . . Most men can't: They don't really think. They haven't any conception of basic justice: The really guilty people were those who saw the injustice of the trial but didn't stop it" (1940, 263-64).

Of all the characters in the book, only Art and Gil realize that the vigilante trial is unfair and have the power to stop the lynching. Art realizes his personal guilt and tells Davies: "If being able to think of all these things but not stop it . . . [is a symptom of guilt] . . . then I'm as guilty as you. More for that matter, I didn't even try to do anything" (1940, 267).

The Dark Side of Wister's Superman

The Ox Bow Incident parallels the lynching sequence of Owen Wister's *The Virginian*. Art, Gil, and the Virginian are intelligent and sensitive men. All become part of a lynching posse and allow men to be hanged without an official trial. In the two novels, as we have seen, the institution of lynching is presented as a legitimate method of social control on the lawless frontier. Here the similarity ends.

Although Warshow has noted such a similarity, he maintains *The Ox Bow Incident* is about "the illegality and injustice of the lynching itself" (Warshow 1954, 195). The lynchings in both *Ox Bow* and *The Virginian*, on the contrary, are circumstances into which Art, Gil, and the Virginian are placed. Thrust into these situations, they must choose to be either moral or immoral. Their morality or immorality is not caused by the lynching per se, but by the motivations which cause the three men to participate.

In *The Virginian*, the hero allows a lynching to take place even though it means the death of Steve, his best friend, and the estrangement of his lover. The painful choice is made because the lynching is an affirmation of democracy and is correlated with the emergence of law. The guilt of the rustlers is not an unresolved matter and the penalty of death is normal and expected. The Virginian allows justice to be carried out while being doubly hurt by it. He is not, as Warshow suggests, "stained by the killing" (Warshow 1954, 195). He does what he has to do and emerges as a greater hero by maintaining his resolve even while he is hurt by doing so.

In *The Ox Bow Incident*, the anti-heroic Art Croft and Gil Carter allow a lynching to take place because they have a vested interest in transferring suspicion from themselves to someone else. Fearing for their own safety, they fail to intercede even though they doubt the wisdom of the posse's verdict. As a result of their inaction, three innocent men are killed, Gerald Tetley and Colonel Tetley commit suicide, and Davies goes mad.

Ox Bow is representative of the Western genre because it concerns the individualist personality (typified by the cowboy) in conflict within a microcosm of society. The novel is antiheroic since the protagonists surrender to the will of the group merely to advance their own agendas. Art and Gil are willing to ignore moral considerations for personal reasons; they condone injustice because it is in their benefit to do so.

In spite of their emergence as antiheroes, Clark is sympathetic to his protagonists who choose a path which insures their survival even though that choice denies them heroic stature. Art and Gil will face death if they act according to their true feelings; *The Ox Bow Incident*, however, is not concerned with fatalistic heroics, but portrays the pragmatics of survival. Clark's protagonists live because they compromise themselves.

The requirements for heroism, however, are the same for Clark as they were for earlier Western authors. Thus, *The Ox Bow Incident* is a famous and highly regarded antiheroic western novel and it is an early prototype for the western in which the protagonists survive by compromising themselves and their ideals.

Parallel Themes

Perhaps Clark's opinions are best expressed in a short story entitled "Personal Interview" (Clark 1942). Published two years after *The Ox Bow Incident*, the story expands Clark's pessimistic vision while condensing the text to a scant three and a half pages. In *The Ox Bow Incident* Clark shows us Colonel Tetley through the eyes of Art Croft, who because of circumstances must adhere to the Colonel's self-serving schemes. In "Personal Interview" the narrator, Hal Carter, is similar to Tetley in character and temperament, but we see life from his perspective.

Carter is a high school football coach and, although he should teach young men the virtues of fair play, he has been accused by the high school principal, who Carter feels is a "fussy old hen," of "underminin' the kid's morals" (1942, 23). Hal has been successful as a coach and just signed a three-year contract with a major college.

As we soon discover, Hal has always been more concerned with coaching a college team than in instilling integrity into the boys he coaches. Getting a collegiate position wasn't easy because Hal made the mistake of playing pro football for a couple of years. Although he could have gotten into coaching immediately after graduation, he found himself forgotten and unknown. As a result, he had to start on the bottom (high school coaching) which at least allowed him to direct the whole show early in his career.

During the latest football season, Carter is assured of a perfect record if his team can defeat Orangefield. Unfortunately, the starting fullback, Randolph Barnes, has recently quit the team. Carter never liked Barnes and comments: "I never had much use for him. He's one of those honor students. Brains is all right, I always say, but give me a dumb guy with a heart and I'll give you a better football player" (1942, 24).

Carter is convinced that Barnes is cowardly after his knee is injured during one of the early games of the season. As it turns out Barnes wasn't faking since the knee actually did swell up, but Carter still thinks he is a coward. After the game Barnes confronts Carter, asking if he thinks football is "the Russian front" (1942, 24) and asking why he keeps players in the game when they're "all crippled up" (1942, 24). He also tells Carter that he is tired of his "slave-drivin'" (1942, 24). Hearing these challenges, Carter calls Barnes yellow and suggests he turn in his uniform. Barnes does and quits the team.

It is ironic that Carter condemns Barnes for something he himself had done in his own playing days. Carter states that after suffering a knee injury during his pro career for the Chicago Bears, "I wised up. That pro football's a tough racket, and don't you believe it ain't" (1942, 23).

Although Carter dislikes Barnes, he realizes that he needs him for the big game with Orangefield and he devises a scheme to blackmail Barnes into playing. At a pre-game pep rally attended by the whole student body, Carter says:

I'm sorry to have to say for the first time since I've been at Clareton, we got a quitter. . . . I think its too bad when one of the biggest guys on a team turns his suit in the first time the going gets tough and just when the biggest game in our history coming up. . . . There'll be a suit out for him Saturday if he wants to come and get it, but I'm not asking him. Only if he don't come . . . I guess I know what to think. . . . (1942, 25)

Carter knows his ploy is working because "the kids take it quiet, but saying Barnes' name you know and looking around at him" (1942, 25).

The strategy of the coach is parallel to that of Colonel Tetley. Just as Tetley implies that Gil is a rustler when he publicly asks, "Do you have a brief of innocence for these men?" (1940, 208), Hal publicly suggests that if Barnes doesn't rejoin the team he is a coward. In both cases the blackmail works; Gil rejoins the posse and Barnes rejoins the team. In both cases, however, the accused parties lose the very qualities they attempt to demonstrate by reuniting with the group. Art and Gil show they aren't murderers by participating in a lynching they know is wrong. Barnes, the one player courageous enough to openly confront an opportunistic coach, knuckles under because he is afraid his friends will consider him a coward.

His will to resist broken, Barnes rejoins the team for the big game and wins it through his own super-human efforts. Then he quits the team for good. By winning the game, however, Barnes gives Carter an undefeated season and a reputation which earns him a major college contract. Just as Art and Gil seal the doom of the three innocent men, Barnes seals the fate of Coach Hallum, the man Carter is destined to replace. Hallum is a "nice guy" who doesn't favor "professionalism" (1942, 26) in college sports. Carter plans to do away with Hallum's idealistic approach and recruit like everybody else. After all "you gotta meet your competition" (1942, 26).

Because "Personal Interview" is told in the first person, Clark is able to bring home one last chilling observation: Carter never realizes that he is corrupted and that he is an opportunist and immoral schemer. Carter even congratulates himself and imagines himself to be a superior person because he is skilled in manipulation (which he considers "psychology"). Even though *Ox Bow* is pessimistic, it contains a ray of optimism. Colonel Tetley is finally made to suffer for his evil deeds. Gerald, his only son, commits suicide after it is proven the victims are innocent, and a heartbroken Colonel Tetley joins his son in suicide. Gil also seems to have learned his lesson and decides not to pick a fight with the man who had stolen his girlfriend. The coach, however, shows no signs of remorse and is actually rewarded by society, not punished, for his immoral behavior.

The Ox Bow Incident, as amplified by "Personal Interview," presents a chilling antiheroical message. To survive and succeed, we are told, people must abandon personal morality and capitulate to the whims of the group. To do otherwise is to flirt with disaster.

Discussion

As was true in the case of Zane Grey's fatalistic Western, *The Vanishing American*, Walter Clark's *The Ox Bow Incident* did not exert any significant impact upon the evolution of the cowboy story. Clark wrote in an era when the prevailing view of American history depicted the frontier as a proving ground and as a catalyst which spawned a distinctive American culture possessing both prowess and morality. Since a significant segment of the reading public embraced this worldview, plotlines which overtly conflicted with this central origin myth could not establish themselves.

According to Clark's vision, the forces of society were all powerful. As a result, individuals must adjust themselves to these forces or be destroyed. This process of accommodation, unfortunately, can lead to amoral and self-serving decisions. Nonetheless, Clark seems to suggest that this kind of opportunistic submission is inevitable.

While these views conflicted with the popular worldview of Clark's era, such sentiments clearly parallel perspectives that emerged after World War II and which became particularly dominant in American thought around 1960. In *The Organization Man*, for example, William Whyte argues that although individualism is an American ideal, in order to survive, people must increasingly compromise themselves by embracing the will of the group. Such behavior, Whyte continues, creates a "double bind" for people: they can either remain true to themselves and fail or compromise themselves and succeed. This creates a "no win" situation for modern-day Americans.

In the 1960s such beliefs began to overpower the frontier thesis; when this happened, the saga of the antihero (the man who must abdicate the heroic role for pragmatic reasons) emerged as a popular and viable scenario. In Clark's era, however, such beliefs were not the vogue. As a result, *The Ox Bow Incident* was merely a random occurrence—a message before its time.

Note

1. Andrew Sarris, *The Primal Screen* (New York: Simon and Schuster, 1973), 34. The film version of *The Ox Box Incident* is different in certain respects to the novel. The most important differences are the fact that in the film, Art and Gil vote against the lynching while in the novel, they go along with the posse. In addition, Gerald Tetley does not commit suicide in the film, while he does in the novel. Finally, in the film Colonel Tetley commits suicide because he loses face, while in the novel, his suicide is caused by grief over the death of his son. The message and tone, however, are the same.

Works Cited

Clark, Walter van Tilburg. 1940. *The Ox Bow Incident.* New York: Readers Club.

——. 1942. "Personal Interview." *New Yorker* Dec. 12: 23-26.

Cochran, Robert. 1970-71. "Nature and the Nature of Man in *The Ox Bow Incident.*" *Western American Literature* 5.4: 253-64.

Fiedler, Leslie. 1968. *The Return of the Vanishing American.* New York: Stein and Day.

Saloman, L. B. 1940. Review of *Ox Bow Incident. Nation* Oct. 12: 344.

Sarris, Andrew. 1973. *The Primal Screen.* New York: Simon and Schuster.

Stein, Paul. 1970-71. "Cowboys and Unicorns: The Novels of Walter Van Tilburg Clark." *Western American Literature* 5.4: 266-76.

Warshow, Robert. 1954. "The Westerner." *Partisan Review* 21.2 (March/April): 190-203.

Westbrook, Max. 1966. "The Archetypical Ethic of *The Ox Bow Incident.*" *Western American Literature* Summer: 105-18.

Wister, Owen. 1902. *The Virginian.* New York: Macmillan.

9

THE FATALISTIC WESTERN:
ALIENATION AND CULTURAL EVOLUTION

In 1925 Zane Grey portrayed the lone individualist marooned in an increasingly immoral society and, abandoning his usual veneer of optimism, Grey allowed his hero to be destroyed in *The Vanishing American*. His readers, however, rejected a steady diet of this message and, catering to public pressure, he abandoned his pessimistic realism. Elsewhere, however, such thoughts persisted; consider a poignant letter which appeared in *Adventure Magazine* in 1926:

I am writing you to obtain the following information which I have tried in vain to acquire for some time.

Would like to know about cattle companies which are operating in Mexico, and which are running cattle under conditions and methods the same as those employed in the U.S. range sections in former years.

Would like to locate in a good range section, work for a large company on the range, learn the language, people, and country, and in future years work into an outfit of my own.

Pardner and I have worked on ranges from Pecos to Montana so are no pilgrims looking for Mecca, but old conditions restored to thirty years ago. We understand Mexico is the place. (1926, 180)

The response to this request was not encouraging: "I would suggest that if you have a good job to stay with it, for you could not better yourself by going to Mexico if cattle running is what you expect to do. . . . Times have changed in Mexico in the past few years . . ." (1926, 180). Like Grey's *The Vanishing American*, this letter and its response indicate that the frontier had closed and that people were better off adjusting (preferably with a socially acceptable "good job"). The wisest strategy was to forget the past and accept the present. Many people, however, were unable or unwilling to do so. Although these feelings of displacement were widely felt and were expressed both in pulp magazines and in occasional best-selling novels (such as Walter Clark's *Ox Bow Incident*), it was 30 to 40 years before the fatalistic Western story, in which the noble hero dies, was to become a viable plotline which the public could accept as an established part of the genre.

Social conditions and beliefs prevented such prototypes from transforming the cowboy story; Americans still believed that they could determine their own destiny and they were unwilling to openly confront the fact that they had little control over their lives. Zane Grey, himself, acknowledges this in an obscure article which appeared in the December, 1932, issue of *Modern Screen Magazine*:

In view of the fact that twelve million of my books have been sold, and that they have been translated into 16 foreign languages, I think I may say I ought to know a little about what the general public likes to read, to see, and to feel. . . . They want to see virtue triumph and vice downed. In a word they long to see life that is not hopeless—to see chivalry in men and chastity in women, to see the struggle for good against evil, to prove the truth of friendship, kinship, honor, and God. (Grey 1932)

Grey anticipated public taste and responded to it; aside from an atypical foray into a pessimistic plotline in *The Vanishing American*, he adhered to a profitable and upbeat formula.

High Noon: *An Overture*

Through the 1940s, the cowboy story continued to be an arena where the noble, individualist hero could remain moral and victorious. By the 1950s, however, conditions were changing and people increasingly felt they were pawns in a game that was much bigger and more powerful than they were. Perhaps Carl Foreman's screenplay for *High Noon*, released in 1952, is a prologue to this emerging fatalism.

The action of the drama is precipitated by the pardon of Frank Miller, a convicted murderer who swore to kill Kane, the law officer who had brought him to justice. Although Miller is a deranged man and an incorrigible criminal, the politicians "up North" commute his sentence and now, after only five years, he is free. Miller has scheduled the showdown to take place on a Sunday morning; that happens to be Will Kane's wedding day and the day he has promised his Quaker bride to give up his guns. Immediately after the wedding, a telegram arrives stating that Miller has been freed. To make concerns even more immediate, it is reported that Ben Miller, Jim Pierce, and Jack Kolby, three of Miller's old gang, have arrived in town and are waiting at the depot for Miller, who is expected to arrive on the noon train.

The marshal's life begins to fall apart when Amy, his wife, insists that he not fight. Amy, a woman whose father and brother were killed in the Civil War, observes that her family had been on the right side but they died anyway and now she is strictly anti-violence. Amy, who cannot stand the thought of waiting an hour to see if she is to be "a wife or a widow," abandons her husband, and buys a train ticket to St. Louis.

Although deserted by his Quaker wife, Kane feels confident that he will be able to get help and affirms, "This is my town. I've got friends here. I'll swear in a bunch of special deputies and with a posse behind me maybe there won't even be any trouble."

We then learn why people refuse to help Kane in a life-and-death situation. A prologue of things to come is provided by Judge Clarkson, the man who presided over Miller's trial. The judge is cynical, but survival oriented, and is too busy packing his courtroom furnishings to help Kane. When Will asks why the judge is so distrustful of the townspeople, he responds:

No time for a lesson in civics, my boy. In the fifth century B.C., the citizens of Athens, having suffered grievously under a tyrant, managed to depose and banish him. However, when he returned some years later with an army of mercenaries, these same citizens not only opened the gates for him, but stood by while he executed members of the legal government. A similar thing happened about eight years ago in a town called Indian Falls. I escaped through the intercession of a lady of somewhat dubious reputation and the cost of a very handsome ring, which had once belonged to my mother. Unfortunately, I have no more rings.

Society, the judge underscores, is fickle and ultimately so is the justice which he and his courtroom trappings represent. He has been a judge before and probably will be again, but not by depending upon society to protect him and uphold justice. The judge then encourages Kane to follow his example and get out while the getting is good. As Kane is soon to discover, the judge's assessment of the townspeople is correct— when the chips are down, they will not raise a finger to help him.

Fear paralyzes some into refusing to help. One man observes that he pays taxes to hire lawmen, but now that the going is rough, he is asked to risk his neck. Some are openly ashamed of their cowardice, but even Herb, an unsolicited volunteer, eventually backs down when he realizes the cards will be stacked against him. Fear, however, is a minor factor; personal greed and opportunism are far more significant.

Harvey, Kane's deputy, for example, decides to use the Miller incident as leverage to get the job as marshal and he refuses to help unless

Kane puts in a good word with the town council. When Kane won't be blackmailed, Harvey quits.

In addition, Kane has enemies who would like to see him dead. The town has been "respectable" for only a few years and the rowdy population of earlier days resents him. These sentiments are best expressed by a hotel clerk who openly admits he dislikes Kane for "lots of reasons. One thing, this place was always busy when Frank Miller was around. I'm not the only one. There's plenty people around here that thinks he's got a come-upons comin'."

Although it is understandable that the town rowdies would resent Kane, the marshal hopes the law-abiding citizens will rally to his aid. After all, he has made the town a decent place to live and a community in which women and children are safe. When Kane goes to the local church for help, several men immediately volunteer. After a moment of reflection, however, a debate begins on the pros and cons of aiding Kane, who technically is no longer marshal. When the parson, the symbol of established morality, is asked to comment, he cannot take a meaningful stand and states: "I don't know . . . The right and wrong seem pretty clear here, but if you're asking me to tell my people to go out and kill and maybe get themselves killed, I'm sorry. I don't know what to say. I'm sorry."

The next speaker is a prominent citizen and a successful business-man. He begins by praising Kane and acknowledges "what this town owes Will Kane we can never pay with money and don't ever forget it." As he continues, however, it becomes increasingly clear that his real concern is for his own financial security. He reminds the congregation that:

People up north are thinking about this town . . . thinking mighty hard. Thinking about sending money down here to put up stores and factories. It would mean a lot to this town, an awful lot. But if they're going to read about shooting and killing in the streets, what are they going to think? I'll tell you. They're going to think this is just another wide-open town and everything we've worked for will be wiped out.

When the congregation realizes the economic ramifications of protecting Kane, they reject him and he is urged to leave town so his death will not adversely reflect the town's lack of civilization . . . an ironic paradox.

Only two people offer to help Kane and each does so for his own personal gain. Both lack manhood and hope to gain stature by aiding the marshal. One of them is a boy of 14 who lies about his age and claims to be a good shot. Facing Miller would be his first assertion of adulthood.

The other would-be ally is old one-eyed Jimmy, a man whose alcoholism has drowned his last vestige of manhood. Jimmy hopes that standing up against Miller will allow him to regain the self-respect alcohol has taken. In Jimmy's words: "I want a gun. I want to be with you when the train comes in. . . . It's chance. See? It's what I need. Please, Kane, let me get in on this." Kane refuses both offers.

Kane's last plea for help is to Mark, a retired marshal and Kane's best friend. But Mark, like the judge, is embittered by society and describes the job of marshal as "a great life. You risk your skin catching killers and juries turn 'em loose so they can come back and shoot at you again. If you're honest, you're poor your whole life. And in the end you end up dying all alone on some dirty street. For what? For nothin. For a tin star."

Just as the judge's speech is the prologue of Will Kane's dilemma, Mark's speech is the epilogue. Both characters are mature men with long tenures of civil service and both understand humanity. They know the townspeople are selfish and Kane is wasting precious time by depending upon them.

High Noon concludes when Amy abandons her abstract moral structure in favor of defending her husband. She returns to town in the midst of the gunfight and kills Miller's last ally. Thus, Kane is saved by his wife and in spite of their religious differences they are reunited. Sickened by the selfish indifference of their supposed friends, the couple leaves town after Kane throws his marshal's badge in the dirt, symbolizing his disgust for the town he once loved. Immediately after the film's release, critics interpreted it both as a universal story of morality and as a parable of American international relations.

Howard Burton suggests in "*High Noon*: Everyman Rides Again" (1953-54, 80) that the film is a reworking of the religious drama of the Middle Ages. Drawing parallels between the stereotyped Western and morality plays (both of which present abstract characters who represent good and evil), Burton suggests that the hero, Will Kane, is a symbol of good who overcomes evil and death. These superficial similarities, however, can be made only when one looks at the film in isolation and not with reference to the evolution of the genre.

Harry Schein, more provocative than Burton, makes the mistake of viewing *High Noon* in isolation. Schein, a Swede, asserts the story is a parable about the plight of the United States in the late 1940s and early 1950s:

I see *High Noon* as having an urgent political message . . . like the United Nations before the Soviet Union, China, and North Korea; moral courage is apparent only in the very American sheriff. He is newly married; he wants to have peace and quiet. But duty and the sense of justice come first, in spite of the fact that he must suddenly stand completely alone. . . . *High Noon*, artistically, is the most convincing and likewise the most honest explanation of American Foreign Policy. (Schein 1955, 316)

It is perhaps natural that Schein, a European, would view *High Noon* in international terms. Certainly the 1950s was an era when America perceived its role to be the world's military watchdog. In a more localized sense, however, the 1950s was also a time when people were being increasingly alienated by mass society, a factor which is largely responsible for the evolution of the public's literary tastes and a concomitant evolution of the Western.

To further muddy the waters, there are two additional sets of contradictory interpretations of *High Noon;* one views it as an archetypical Western, the other interprets the film as a "social drama" which merely happens to have a Western setting.

Robert Warshow acknowledges that *High Noon* contains most of the trappings of the Western genre and that the motif of the story belongs "to the established form (there is even the fallen woman who understands the marshal's position . . .)" (1954, 199). Because of this, Warshow realizes the film is a good "companion piece to *The Virginian*" (Warshow 1954, 199) and is an example of how the genre has evolved. When the chips are down, however, Warshow defines the film as outside the Western genre. He states, "We are in the field of the 'social drama'— of a very low order, incidentally, altogether unconvincing and displaying a vulgar anti-populism . . ." (1954, 199). Here, as in other places, Warshow shows us the flaw in his approach to the Western. Instead of empirically searching for what the Western is, he deductively states what motifs and plots belong in the genre. Any Western film which goes beyond his postulated criteria is defined to be something else, usually a "social drama." Warshow's method smacks of a heavy-handed use of idealism and ultimately fails for that reason even though he does provide significant insights.

While Warshow argues that *High Noon* is a social drama, J. A. Barsness (1967, 32-37) suggests that it is the most archetypical Western of them all. Viewing the film as mythic and unrealistic, he juxtaposes it with *The Misfits*, a film he considers to be an excellent example of the realistic Western.

Although numerous critics have analyzed *High Noon*, they have not dealt with it in terms of the slow and steady evolution of the genre. Instead, *High Noon* tends to be viewed in isolation in order to advance various theories, many of which are only vaguely concerned with the Western per se.

Actually, *High Noon* retains many of the conventions popularized by Owen Wister which typify the classic cowboy story. Society, for example, is depicted as amoral and inept.[1] The only people to act morally and meaningfully are the frontier hero and his wife. These characterizations closely connect *High Noon* to other earlier prototypes associated with Cooper and Wister.

High Noon contains many aspects of the displacement theme popularized by James Fenimore Cooper in the 1820s. When Cooper's Natty Bumppo and Foreman's Will Kane abandon the law, they are cast out of society. Bumppo disregards a local ordinance for just reasons while Kane, once a law officer, gives up his job as marshal. Because Kane no longer has a position within society, the community is no longer willing to protect him. Amy and Will Kane's rejection of society is similar to Natty Bumppo's decision to live and die away from civilization. Both Bumppo and the Kanes have the option of returning to their society but refuse.

It is worthwhile to note that "The Tin Star" (Cunningham 1975), the short story upon which *High Noon* is based, has an opposite message; it suggests that the lawman should remain within society and that he is morally bound to do so. "Star" begins when old Marshal Doane is saddened to hear that his understudy, Deputy Toby, has decided to abandon his career as a law enforcement officer. Toby notes that there is no money in the profession and that everybody else gets rich while he remains poor. In *High Noon*, Toby's sentiments are not stated by an inexperienced novice, but by Mark, a seasoned ex-lawman; in the film, Mark's cynicism is the product of sophistication, not selfishness. As "Tin Star" continues, Doane and Toby are drawn into a gunfight in which Doane sacrifices his life to save his friend. This heroic action reaffirms the deputy's respect for the law, and with Doane dead, Toby accepts his badge; Doane's heroic example brings the straying Toby back into the fold. *High Noon*, in contrast, ends with Kane scornfully throwing the star in the dirt and riding off.

"Tin Star" is a story of "passing the torch" of law to a "prodigal son." The message is "the law is dead—long live the law." The plot closely parallels numerous World War II war films, such as *The Immortal Sergeant,* in which a reluctant hero rises to the occasion in spite of his previous indifference to become a leader. "The Tin Star," published only two years after the end of the World War II, seems closely tied to this tradition. Scriptwriter Carl Foreman, however, completely eliminates such sentiments in *High Noon*. Society is depicted as depraved and the old marshal is depicted as correct to reject society. *High Noon* is a film of rejection, not acceptance; of disassociation, not embrace.

High Noon is clearly a transitional piece. It suggests that the individual is thwarted or undermined by a selfish society, but this change is not depicted as universal or inevitable. Instead, *High Noon* portrays a society that has forgotten its former virtues. The Kanes become estranged from their friends because society abandons the common virtues which should prevail in any culture. It is worthwhile to mention that this was the last screenplay written by Carl Foreman before he was blacklisted during the McCarthy era; his next film was *Bridge On the River Kwai*, for which he received no credits. From this perspective, the script is obviously autobiographical in theme. Foreman's plight is analogous to Kane's: Foreman's friends did not intercede on his behalf and he had to fight alone and eventually "leave town."

Building upon such themes, the fatalistic western film emerged artistically in the early 1960s. In such films, the heroes are incapable of effectively dealing with modern society even though they are superior to it. Three such classics in this tradition are *Ride the High Country*, *The Misfits*, and *Lonely Are the Brave*. Numerous other films of their general structure and theme have also been produced; while some (such as *Butch Cassidy and the Sundance Kid*) emerged as blockbusters, nonetheless, they seem largely redundant to the developments and innovations so apparent in these early innovations.

The Peckinpah Vision

Of the three, only *Ride the High Country* deals with the actual closing of the frontier. The heroes are two aging ex-marshals, vestigial remains of another era. Gil Westrum has accepted changing times and has a job performing parodies of himself in a traveling side show. Posing as the "Oregon Kid" for curiosity seekers is hardly a noble profession, but he at least can get free drinks at the local saloon.

Steve Judd, in contrast, wants to remain true to "the code of the West" and, except for age and hard times, he is the same man he had been 20 or 25 years ago. The rapidly modernizing West, however, has little use for him; to earn a meager living, he guards an occasional gold shipment.

These old friends, whose paths had long since separated, are drawn together once more when they are hired to guard a shipment of gold. Throughout the trip, Westrum hints that they should steal the gold and retire. After all, both men have defended the law for most of their lives and they have nothing to show for it. Now they are aging and their futures are insecure. Although Westrum's arguments are compelling,

Judd retains his personal integrity and rejects the opportunity. When Westrum observes that nobody, not even the bankers, will suffer from the robbery, Judd retorts that he would suffer, because he would have to compromise himself and tarnish his reputation. When Westrum asks Judd what he wants, Judd replies, "I want to enter my own house justi-fied." It is important to note that this line, scripted by Peckinpah during a rewrite, was the paraphrase of a Bible verse Peckinpah learned from his father and never forgot (Callenback 1963-64, 7).

On the way to the mining camp, the party stops at the home of Joshua Krudsen, a religious fanatic. When they leave, Krudsen's daugh-ter Elsa joins them to escape her domineering father and to marry one of the Hammond brothers. The Hammonds, however, are despicable and Elsa soon realizes her mistake, but she too late. She is already married and "the property" of her husband. Elsa's plight demonstrates that abstract law is amoral since it eliminates justice, ethics, and decisions based upon the situation. It is obvious that Elsa has made a mistake because she has been overly protected all her life. The Hammonds are depraved animals, and she will be horribly mistreated as long as she is forced to stay with them. The amorality of modern society is further underscored by the character of Judge Tolliver, the man who performs the marriage ceremony. The judge, obviously a drunk, is incapable of any positive action. Elsa is an interesting reversal of the role of the whore in a television play entitled *Jeff*, which was scripted by Peckinpah before he broke into feature films. *Jeff* concerns a woman who is immoral, corrupt, and beyond redemption. As in *Ride the High Country*, the hero fights to free the woman from exploitative men. After Jeff wins the woman's freedom, however, he learns she will not accept his offer of a new life. In *Ride*, Elsa clearly does want that choice and is grateful for it.

In this situation, Westrum and Judd take Elsa with them. The Ham-monds, enraged, and with the law on their side, give quick pursuit. Although outnumbered and opposing established law, Judd and Westrum stand and fight for what is just; the Hammonds are killed, but the moral-istic Judd is mortally wounded.

Westrum, the survivor, now has the option of stealing the gold as he had earlier planned. In the fight to save Elsa, however, his ideals are restored and he decides to be true to his code of ethics. Just before Judd dies, Westrum assures him that the gold will be delivered. Although Nigel Andrews has suggested Peckinpah constantly illustrated "that a moral code produced by one age or society is not necessarily valid in another" (1973, 70), the film actually stresses that the hero's morality is inherently superior even as modern society rejects and overshadows it.

Although Westrum makes a choice which will leave him poor and forgotten, he achieves heroic stature by doing so.

In *Ride the High Country*, Peckinpah emphasizes that culture, by its very nature, tends towards depravity, and the moral individual raised on the frontier is inherently superior to an amoral society. Peckinpah states, "My work has been concerned one way or another with . . . individuals looking for something besides security" (Callenback 1963-64, 8). In the showdown with the Hammonds, Peckinpah metaphorically presents a last struggle between modern society and the frontier and, although the frontiersmen win, it is unlikely they will fight again. The old fade in truly heroic fashion as a new ignoble order emerges, by default, to fill the void.

Although *Ride the High Country* possesses more optimism than some of the later fatalistic Westerns, it is still fatalistic in tone. In such stories, the frontiersmen, aging and obsolete, are being displaced by society. They are inherently superior to the breed which is destined to replace them and, after a final heroic battle, precipitated by matters of conscience, they die or fade into oblivion.

Peckinpah's better known *The Wild Bunch* resembles *Ride the High Country* in many ways. The primary motivation of the heroes, however, is ambiguous. On the one hand, the protagonists die to avenge the brutal murder of a friend; on the other hand, they seem to consciously choose to commit suicide because the frontier is gone and there is no place left for them. To the extent that they are actively seeking death, the film concerns a desperate form of capitulation to forces beyond one's control: suicide.

Closely paralleling *Ride the High Country*, *The Misfits* and *Lonely Are the Brave* depict the plight of the frontier personality within the modern world. In these films, the frontier has long been closed and the heroes are displaced remnants of that bygone era.

Arthur Miller and The Misfits

The Misfits is an important film for a number of reasons. It contains the last performances of Clark Gable, Marilyn Monroe, and Montgomery Cliff. It is also important because it was scripted by Arthur Miller, who was married to Monroe when the script was written and the film was made. (Miller and Monroe were divorced immediately after the film was completed.) *Misfits*, furthermore, is "noteworthy as a serious attempt for a serious playwright to conceive a work directly for the screen" (Alpert 1961, 26). In addition, the film has an autobiographical aspect. The plot concerns divorce and the adventures of those who come to Nevada merely to end their marriage. Years before, Miller had done this in his own life and he drew upon these experiences when scripting the film. Miller was also trying to understand his wife, who played the female lead, and the script can be seen as a reflection of their marital difficulties (Weatherby 1961, 26).

When viewing the *Misfits* as a Western, it is worthwhile to remember that Arthur Miller (like Owen Wister and Zane Grey) was a product of civilization who went to the frontier, lived among Western people, and later wrote about them. While getting his divorce, Miller had "lived at Pyramid Lake, went to Reno only for his laundry and a little shopping, and spent much of his spare time with the friends he made among the cowboys" (Weatherby 1961, 26). These experiences are the raw material out of which *Misfits* was created. Miller was truly able to capture the spirit of the West as he saw it; when an old cowboy associate of the Pyramid Lake period visited Miller during the filming of *Misfits*, he inspected the sets, talked to Miller about the script, and "said, deeply moved, 'you've made it all mean something'" (Weatherby 1961, 26).

Miller had passed the severest test; actual cowboys realized his story had meaning. This exchange reminds me of an anecdote in the introduction of Owen Wister's *The Virginian*. Wister read the manuscript of a story to a cowboy friend: "Was that the Crow Reservation?, he inquired at the finish. I told him that it was no real reservation and no real event. . . . And I could no more help telling him that this was the highest compliment ever paid me than I have been able to help telling you about it here" (1902, x). Just as Owen Wister took pride in hearing this friend's response, Miller is entitled to be self-satisfied by hearing his own friend's comments. Whatever else critics suggest, the old cowboy's words demonstrate that *The Mitfits* is essentially a Western.

The Misfits concerns a cowboy who is forced to realize that the modern world is inherently destructive to him, his kind, and everything he represents. Gay Longland (Gable), charming and intelligent, spends most of his time in Reno, Nevada, entertaining women who have come to Nevada to get a divorce. In the modern world, Gay is still able to use the skills of the frontier to earn a living: he occasionally goes onto the desert to catch mustang horses which he sells for pocket money. But even here modern technology has interceded; an airplane and a pickup truck aid in the chase. Nevertheless, Gay, Perce Howland, a has-been rodeo rider, and Guida, the pilot, earn a living.

On one such hunt, Gay and his sidekicks allow a divorcee, Roslyn Taber, to accompany them on their search for wild horses. Roslyn, played by Marilyn Monroe, proves to be an outsider with an objective eye; she realizes a cold, hard fact which the three men have ignored, forgotten, or repressed. The noble beasts they capture, the last of a species typifying the frontier, are destined to be made into cat food. After a long moralistic debate, the horses are freed.

The underlying theme of *The Misfits* is that Gay and his friends are analogous to the mustangs they have been sending to their deaths. The noble beasts become pet food while noble men are reduced into a temporary pastime for women who come to Reno to get a quick divorce. The products of the frontier, the men and the horses, are wasted and destroyed through catering to the whims of the modern world.

The Misfits ends on a slightly positive note. The horses are freed and, although they may eventually be recaptured, they have been give a stay of execution. Gay decides not to perform symbolic suicide by participating in the destruction of a breed of horse which, like himself, is a remnant of a bygone era. In the last scene, Gay and Roslyn drive into the desert and a strong bond seems to be forming between them. If it continues, perhaps Gay will not return to the bars of Reno to become the toy of women between husbands. The film never shows what eventually happens to Gay and Roslyn, but it does suggest a possible salvation. In order to survive, they must reject the modern world and reassert their true selves. This alternative seems to be an option even in the modern world.

Kirk Douglas' Vision

If *The Misfits* contains a ray of qualified optimism, *Lonely Are the Brave* is completely pessimistic and overtly links an amoral modern society with the death of the frontier hero. The action starts when Jack Burns, an aging cowboy, and his horse are disoriented by fast-moving automobiles. This prologue is similar to the beginning of *Ride the High Country*, where Steve Judd is nearly knocked down by a horseless carriage. It is interesting to note that these two films were released at almost exactly the same time.

Using the ethics of a bygone era, Burns decides to help his friend, Paul Bondi, escape from prison. Bondi, a noble man, had been found guilty of helping illegal aliens. Inventing a means of getting arrested himself, Burns finds that Bondi rejects a chance for illicit freedom since his prison term is fairly short; realizing that society is stronger than the individual, he chooses not to blatantly oppose established authority for a second time.

His mission completed, Burns escapes from jail and becomes a hunted man, tracked down by a posse under the direction of Sheriff Johnson. Johnson does his duty even though he respects Burns and obviously hopes Burns will escape. Although Johnson has the aid of U.S. Army helicopters, Burns is able to elude his pursuers; he is inherently superior to the men of civilization.

Throughout the film, on the other hand, we are shown numerous glimpses of a tractor trailer hauling a load of toilet bowls—the ultimate symbol of modern culture. The truck is slowly traveling from east to west. Burns (the symbol of the frontier) and the truck (the symbol of modern culture) are inevitably drawn to the same stretch of highway. When Burns attempts to cross the highway, the last obstacle to his freedom, he is hit by the truck and killed; although a superior individual, he cannot survive in a struggle against the modern world.

Lonely is a film which Douglas passionately wanted to make. He recalls: "I found *Lonely Are the Brave* as a paperback called *The Brave Cowboy*. The picture on the cover had nothing to do with the story inside. I loved the book and engaged Dalton Trumbo to write a screenplay" (1976). *The Brave Cowboy* (Abbey 1956) was written by Edward Abbey, who says of himself: "The army made an anarchist out of me and what with one thing or another, I've been living off the government ever since" (Abbey 1956a). Abbey's hero is the antithesis of his creator. Burns was born and bred a frontier anarchist and he has never taken anything from the government except hard knocks. There appears to have been an uncanny meeting of the minds between Abbey, Trumbo, and Douglas, since "the very first draft of Trumbo's screenplay was the one we shot. This is very unusual. Usually one goes over and over many drafts" (Douglas 1976).

Although Douglas was enthusiastic about the film:

Lonely Are the Brave was a picture that the studio disapproved of. I was allowed to do it by keeping it on a low budget. I disagreed with their releasing pattern. . . . I pleaded with them to put it in one little theatre in New York and just wait and see what happens. Instead, they released it to a large number of theatres like an old fashioned Western which, of course, it wasn't. (Douglas 1976)

Lonely Are the Brave is an interesting companion piece to *High Noon*, since *Noon* was the last script to be completed by Foreman before he was blacklisted, and *Lonely* was written by Dalton Trumbo after returning from prison and the stigma of the blacklist. While the hero is rejected by society in *Noon*, he is destroyed in *Lonely* primarily because he won't allow himself to be caged in by society. Another interesting comparison is between *Lonely* and Sam Peckinpah's *The Ballad of Cable Hogue*. The symbolism and plot of *Ballad* in many ways duplicate that in *Lonely*. In both films, motor vehicles, the symbol of a new age, kill the hero, a symbol of a bygone era.

Discussion

The fatalistic messages of *Lonely Are the Brave* and *Ballad* are explicit. Modern people are inferior to the products of the frontier, but modern culture is invincible. Anyone who opposes it will be destroyed.

Carl Foreman, who provided a transitional prologue to the fatalistic Western in *High Noon*, remained interested in the ultimate eclipse of the heroic figure. In 1961 he scripted *The Guns of Navarone*, a film concerning a heroic commando mission supervised by Mallary, a man with "an Anglo-Saxon sense of decency." This decency has caused him much trouble; as a humanitarian gesture, he once gave a safe conduct pass to a troupe of German soldiers who claimed to be on a mission of mercy, but once behind enemy lines, they went on a rampage of killing and destruction. The family of Mallary's arch enemy, Andrea, was killed by this German patrol.

Besides Mallary, the moralist, and Andrea, the vengeful realist, *Guns* also concerns Miller, the product of amoral technology. Miller mouths expediency, but when the chips are down, he has no stomach for killing men face to face. He even refuses an officer's rank because he does not want to be responsible for making decisions. He is the man who makes the bombs and like bomber pilots, he doesn't mind killing if he doesn't have to see it. In his words, he prefers to "leave the killing to someone like you, an officer."

Mallary's response to Miller indicates that morality includes decisions, no matter what the consequences may be: "Someone has to take responsibility if the job's going to get done." The mission is successful because Mallary gives a wounded ally false information knowing he will be captured and that the Germans will torture the information out of him. Although Miller finds this ploy reprehensible, it is the only way to accomplish the assignment.

The film ends with Mallary and Andrea, the old antagonists, shaking hands. The vengeful realist has become more moral, while Mallary's "Anglo-Saxon decency" had been tempered and made more pragmatic. After *Guns*, Foreman considered a sequel. He "thought of advancing the surviving characters two or three years later in the war and making them feel hopelessly outdated by the tremendous technological advances war always creates and by the development of very young men for specialized commando work" (Foreman 1969, 14-16). Although this would not have been a Western, Foreman's idea parallels the developments in the Western in which there is no place for the old style hero. *MacKenna's Gold* (1969) is a later Western scripted by Foreman which is not considered here because it is not fatalistic in tone. Instead the hero is spared by divine intervention because he is honorable.

After the early 1960s when these three classic fatalistic Westerns were made, the saga of the displaced cowboy confronted by modern culture became formula driven. In *Butch Cassidy and the Sundance Kid* (Gertner 1974, 277), two famed outlaws are chased from the United States by a group of well-organized guards hired by a millionaire and then killed in South America where they are vastly outnumbered by a rag-tag army. In *The Wild Bunch*, a gang of outlaws, displaced by the modern world, flee to Mexico and are killed while revenging the brutal death of a friend. These films, and many others like them, embrace the plotline provided by the three early classics but do little to expand or develop the genre. Like the imitators of James Fenimore Cooper, or Owen Wister, they essentially rephrase an established plot formula; the message, the sentiment, and the impact are identical. The protagonists all face dilemmas which parallel the plot of Zane Grey's *The Vanishing American*—they confront an encroaching society and are destroyed. Although identical in tone and structure to Grey's classic, these films are not influenced by it. In the 1920s society could not embrace *The Vanishing American*'s fatalistic message and the story was forgotten. By the 1960s, the fatalistic plotline reflected the prevailing worldview and in such an environment it was independently reinvented and it thrived.

Note

1. Western fiction and film, of course, commonly characterizes society in this way. Prime examples are James Fenimore Cooper's *The Pioneers* and Owen Wister's *Lin McLean*.

Works Cited

Abbey, Edward. 1956. *The Brave Cowboy: An Old Tale in a New Time.* New York: Dodd, Mead and Company.

——. 1956a. Dust Jacket of *The Brave Cowboy: An Old Tale in a New Time.* New York: Dodd, Mead and Company.

Adventure Magazine. 1926. Letters to the editor section Oct. 8.

Alpert, Hollis. 1961. "Arthur Miller, Scriptwriter." *Saturday Review* Feb. 4: 26.

Andrews, Nigel. 1973. "Sam Peckinpah." *Sight and Sound* 42.2 (Spring): 69-75.

Barsness, J. A. 1967. "A Question of Standard." *Film Quarterly* 21.1: 32-37.

Burton, Howard. 1953-54. "*High Noon*: Everyman Rides Again." *Quarterly of Film, Radio, and TV* 8: 80-86.

Callenback, Ernest. 1963-64. "A Conversation with Sam Peckinpah." *Film Quarterly* (Winter): 3-10.

Cunnningham, John W. "The Tin Star." *The Western Story: Fact, Fiction, and Myth.* 1975. Ed. D. Durham and E. Jones. New York: Harcourt Brace, and Jovanovich.

Foreman, Carl. 1969. "A Sense of Adventure." *Films and Filming* Nov. 14-16: 14+.

Grey, Zane. 1932. "A Plea for Westerns." *Modern Screen Magazine* Dec.: 20+.

Schein, Harry. 1955. "The Olympian Cowboy." *American Scholar* 24 (Summer): 309-20.

Warshow, Robert. 1954. "The Westerner." *Partisan Review* 21.2 (March/April): 190-203.

Weatherby, W. J. 1961. Rev. of *The Misfits. Saturday Review of Literature* 44 (4 Feb.): 26-27.

10

THE MODERN ANTIHEROIC COWBOY:
SURVIVOR IN AN AMORAL DESERT

Just as Zane Grey provided an early prototype for the fatalistic Western in which the noble hero dies, Walter Van Tilburg Clark's *The Ox Bow Incident* contains all the trappings of the contemporary antiheroic Western in which survival is won at the price of sacrificing personal integrity. Clark's novel, which presents the antihero as both the victim of social pressures and the perpetrator of injustice, remains every bit as relevant today as when first published in the 1940s.

Although *The Ox Bow Incident* is a powerful and compelling novel, it was written before its time. Like Zane Grey's innovative *The Vanishing American*, *The Ox Bow Incident* was highly acclaimed but it had little if any impact upon the evolution of the Western genre, even though it independently foreshadowed the antiheroic Western films of the 1960s and 1970s.

John Ford and a Prologue to the Antihero

While Walter Clark anticipated the antiheroic Westerner in fiction during the 1940s, director John Ford did so, in film, during the 1950s, the decade before the antiheroic Western came to full flower. In specific, Ford's *The Searchers* revolves around antiheroic themes; it concerns a hate which borders on insanity and a lust for revenge which can best be described as fanatical obsession.

The film, furthermore, is an anomaly in Ford's career and it is awkwardly sandwiched between his other Westerns. About five years prior to *The Searchers*, Ford had been involved with John Wayne's "Cavalry Trilogy" which focused upon the epic of the frontier. *The Searchers* (released in 1956), in contrast, depicts the frontier in terms of hatred, murder, and bigotry. By 1961, Ford had gone full circle and *The Man Who Shot Liberty Valance* portrays the Western hero in a most sympathetic light. After experimenting with an antiheroic theme, Ford reverted to "printing the [heroic] legend," not the truth (as the newspaper editor had urged in the closing scenes of *Liberty Valance*).

The plot of *The Searchers* can be easily summarized; Ethan Edwards' brother and his family are attacked by Indians and all but Lucy and Debbie, two of Ethan's nieces, are killed. The tragedy takes place while Ethan is away stalking rustlers. Stealing the cattle, however, had merely been a ploy devised by the cunning Chief Scar who used it as a diversion in order to lure the able bodied men away from the ranch so it would be vulnerable to attack.

The search party includes Ethan Edwards and Brad Jurgensen. Jurgensen meets a pointless death when he, crazed with grief, mounts a suicide attack against the Comanche singlehandedly. Ethan, in contrast, represents an even more insidious form of rage. Although obsessed, Ethan never loses his rationality. His hatred does not dissipate with time; it takes Ethan five years to find his quarry, but his hate never wavers.

Ethan's hatred grows so intense that he forgets his true purpose: rescuing his niece. When he does find her, his love vanishes since he finds she has lived with the Indians and, in his mind, she is tainted by the experience. Andrew Sarris acknowledges, but de-emphasizes, these anti-heroic themes by wrongly asserting that the film primarily concerns American wanderlust, and he falsely asserts that, by the end of the film, Ethan "is miraculously delivered of all the racist revenge—seeking furies that have seared his soul" (1971, 58).

Ethan is not Ford's typical hero, but he is not a clear-cut villain either. Instead, he commits atrocities for reasons that are disturbingly understandable; such portrayals were, no doubt, especially upsetting in the wake of the World War II Holocaust. *The Searchers,* for example, shows Ethan acting in ways that parallel the horrors of that era. In some of Ford's other films the audience is comforted with an obvious dichotomy between good and evil (as in *The Man Who Shot Liberty Valance*). *The Searchers*, in contrast, contains a disturbing ambiguity. Recognized today as an important film, it was 15 years before critics gave it serious attention. Why did recognition come so late? At first glance, the film seems to be the pointless story of a lone misanthrope, not a serious and seminal rephrasing of the myth of the West.

Indeed, the promotional campaign of the film emphasizes wild obsession. Ethan's insanity is exploited in a promotional campaign which repeated key phrases. Three days before the New York opening, for example, a newspaper ad warned, "Don't ask him what he saw. Don't ever ask him what he saw." For the next three days we learn, "He had to find her. . . . He had to find her. . . ." We also learn that the film is about someone who would do "whatever it took, whatever it took him." Finally, the reader is told that the obsession is not a short-lived phenomenon since the epic "sweeps from the great Southwest to the Canadian border." To further emphasize the insanity involved, an illustration shows two lone riders dwarfed by Monument Valley, guns in hand, looking . . . looking . . . looking (*New York Times* 1956). In this way, the film was presented more as an idiosyncratic response to tragedy than as a rewriting of the origin myth of American culture.

Released the same year as the last *Lone Ranger* film of the era which was described as "endless cattle rustles, slashing fist fights and Western clichés" (Crowther 1956, 12), *The Searchers* was born during the death of the juvenile B Western. Turning his back on stereotyped, childish visions, Ford created a misunderstood masterpiece, which was ignored because it came before its time. Adult Westerns which "made it" in the 1950s either rephrase the cowboy myth as in *Shane* or were interpreted to be allegorical films such as *High Noon* and *Rio Bravo* which are conscious political statements. A 1950s Western dedicated to exploring the antiheroic impacts of the westward movement could not influence the evolution of the genre, although it could foreshadow it. In that era, *The Searchers* was not the stuff from which new formulas could be forged.

Delmer Daves' *Broken Arrow* is an adult Western of the post World War II era which is clearly antithetical to *The Searchers*. Daves' film is positive and optimistic; the Indians are not stick men and their culture is shown as having worth and dignity. Even marriage between an Indian and a white (a controversial topic in the 1950s) is depicted as a humanizing experience. It hardly needs to be mentioned that liberals loved *Broken Arrow*.

Ford's film, in contrast, gave liberals little comfort. Ethan's hatred is so profound that it bares his soul and destroys the love he once had for his own flesh and blood. To make matters even more disturbing, Ethan is not a mere stick man or a conventional villain; perhaps we can see a little of ourselves in him and his obsessions.

In 1956, not only was *The Searchers* unappreciated for what it was, *Broken Arrow* went on to become a weekly TV series. It is significant that Ford's reality was rejected while Daves' more politically correct fairy tale was rephrased for the masses and beamed over network TV into homes throughout the nation. *The Searchers* was released during the genesis of another major social upheaval of post World War II America—the generation gap. Although this phenomena did not reach epidemic proportions until the mid-1960s, the seeds were certainly sown in the late 1940s and were taking root in the 1950s. The conventional wisdom of the mid 1950s asserted that the generation gap was merely a "phase" all children go through. Hollywood obediently ground out films based on this premise. Even John Wayne followed this general trend; his *She Wore a Yellow Ribbon* and *Rio Grande* both deal with troublesome youths who ultimately follow in their father's (Wayne's) footsteps.

In *The Searchers*, however, Ford presents a profound conflict between Ethan (an uncle but really a thinly disguised paternal figure), and Debbie (a surrogate daughter). In the film, Debbie joins an Indian band, a social group which Ethan hates. Even though Debbie had little choice in the matter, she becomes a member of a despised long-haired communal group which lives close to nature. Upon learning of her conversion, Ethan becomes enraged and he wants to kill her. Significantly, *The Searchers* was released just one year before Jack Kerouac published *On the Road*, the counterculture manifesto which foreshadowed the hippie movement which ranged from San Francisco to Greenwich Village and profoundly impacted American history and culture.

In short, *The Searchers* was released in the midst of a number of monumental social upheavals: Americans were beginning to question the glorious mythology of the frontier, civil rights campaigns were gaining momentum, and people increasingly believed the past was wrought with injustice. The post World War II generation gap, furthermore, was in its infancy but was already a source of anxiety among many adults. *The Searchers* portrayed, in an unvarnished way, exactly what people didn't want to confront. *The Searchers* was not a trend setter because it conflicted too strongly with the mindset of the American people.

The Amoral Man with No Name

But times were changing, and before another decade had passed an unknown, Italian director Sergio Leone, was to capitalize upon the antiheroic protagonist who came to be identified with Clint Eastwood. Neither Leone nor Eastwood predicted *A Fistful of Dollars* would be a blockbuster success in both Europe and the U.S. The film, however, filled a void and became a classic. Vietnam was gaining momentum and was often envisioned as a cowboy war in which the Vietcong were "Indians." Even John Wayne of *The Searchers* starred in *The Green Berets*: a tribute to U.S. troops in Southeast Asia. Films like *Little Big Man*, furthermore, suggested that raw hatred, arrogance, and racism were key ingredients of the westward movement.

Both young and old became estranged. As a result, films such as *Culpepper Cattle Company* depicted socialization as the process of being brainwashed into accepting the callous side of life. Because of crucial social changes in the 1960s, relatively unknown personalities rose to fame by replicating what John Ford had done in *The Searchers* during the 1950s. Perceptive artist that he was, Ford anticipated the trends of the 1960s and 1970s, but *The Searchers* did not profit from his insight. It was simply the right film at the wrong time.

The rise of the antiheroic tradition in the modern Western is best typified by the early career of Clint Eastwood, an actor whose roles run the gambit from traditional cowboy hero to archetypical antihero to rogue cop. Eastwood came to public attention as the co-star of *Rawhide*, a long-running TV series about a cattle drive transporting a herd from Texas to Oklahoma. In *Rawhide*, Eastwood portrayed Rowdy Yates, a conventional hero whom Eastwood described as a "sheepish, nice guy" in a 1961 interview. *Rawhide* aired for over seven years (1/9/59–2/8/66) and established Eastwood as a recognizable Western actor. Possessing these credentials, he was able to land the role of "the man with no name" in the now classic *A Fistful of Dollars*. Up until this point, Eastwood had a wholesome image.

In developing his portrayal of No Name, however, Eastwood transformed the westerner. Although a script for *Fistful* existed when he was hired, Eastwood was largely left to his own devices because there was a language barrier between him and his director, Sergio Leone. In Eastwood's words:

I developed it from what was in the screenplay. A lot of it was taken from the frustration of doing *Rawhide* year in and year out, where I played sort of a conventional hero, nice guy type. I made the character more—antiheroic—just be more of a guy who was a gunman out for his own well-being, placed himself first, and didn't get involved in other people's problems unless it was to his benefit. (Kaminsky 1974, 29)

Although Eastwood's antiheroic role was innovative, he capitalized upon an aspect of the Western genre that has often been utilized: mysteriousness. This was a conscious choice. Eastwood observes: "I dropped dialogue. . . . I felt the basic strength of the character. . . . I felt you don't dissipate the strength by talking too much or too much exposition. . . . I felt that the less people knew about him, the better" (Kaminsky 1974, 31).

To interpret the transformation of the No Name personality, it is necessary to discuss four films: *A Fistful of Dollars* (1964), *For a Few Dollars More* (1965), *The Good, the Bad, and the Ugly* (1966), and *High Plains Drifter* (1973). The first three were made in the mid 1960s and established the modern antiheroic tradition in the Western genre. *High Plains Drifter*, made in the 1970s, gives a greater social context to the antiheroic personality by showing how and why he develops his cynical, antiheroic attitudes.

A Fistful of Dollars, incidentally, was a remake of *Yojimbo*, a samurai film directed by Akira Kurosawa, the internationally acclaimed Japanese director. Such influences are especially noteworthy when it is recalled that *The Magnificent Seven* (1960), a popular Western about a band of socially displaced gunmen, is a remake of *Seven Samurai*, another Kurosawa film.

Leone clearly believes that although *Yojimbo* was a Japanese production, its inspiration came from America. He observes: "I had seen the Kurosawa film, *Yojimbo*, where a theme from the American detective cinema had been transposed into a samurai story. With this perspective, I then proceeded to return the story to its native land by placing it in the context of a Western" (Kaminsky 1974, 39).

The plot of *A Fistful of Dollars* revolves around a mysterious stranger who enters the town of San Miguel to find two rival clans, the Rojos and the Baxters, fighting for control of a smuggling business. No Name, a clever opportunist, is quick to observe, "There's money to be made in a place like this." He then kills four members of the Baxter contingent and, as a result, is hired by the Rojos who have just ambushed a gold shipment and massacred its military escort. In order to get the gold, No Name pretends he has found two survivors from the ambush and negotiates with both the Rojos, who want to kill the only witnesses to their crime, and the Baxters, who hope to use the survivors as leverage against their rivals. With the help of this ploy and an improvised bullet-proof vest, No Name emerges as the victor and in possession of the gold.

Although Eastwood had gone far to create an antiheroic protagonist, he was somewhat inhibited by the script, which in certain ways makes the character inconsistent. In a most blatant example, No Name altruistically helps Marsol, Ramon Rojos' mistress, and her husband to escape and he suffers a brutal beating as a result.

In *For a Few Dollars More*, No Name becomes a bounty hunter who allies himself with Colonel Douglas Mortimer, in pursuing El Indio, a drug-crazed outlaw. The two are perfect foils; No Name is motivated purely by a mercenary's desire for money while the Colonel is directed by what he considers a moralistic mission: avenging the murder of his sister. Thus, No Name's faint glimmerings of humanity are totally eliminated.

In *The Good, the Bad, and the Ugly*, the basic No Name figure follows the same amoral and opportunistic strategies. The setting is the Civil War and No Name makes money by turning his partner, a wanted criminal, into the authorities, collecting the reward, and finally saving his friend from jail. Eventually No Name tires of the gimmick, abandons his friend, and leaves him behind bars.

What follows is a game of cat and mouse in which the forsaken partner, out for revenge, stalks No Name. Intertwined with the revenge sub-plot is the search for a fortune buried in a cemetery. As in *A Fistful of Dollars*, No Name is essentially an amoral figure with a strong instinct for survival. He does, however, occasionally deviate from this norm, such as when he spares his former partner and shares the fortune with him.

In these films, No Name evolves from the proto-antihero, to the total antihero, and finally in *The Good, the Bad, and the Ugly* he begins to transcend his antiheroical tendencies. In doing so, Eastwood evolves a distinctive portrayal of the frontier antihero. He is an amoral pragmatist who survives. In Eastwood's words, he "initiated the action—he shot first" (*New York Times* 1967). No Name is selfish and ruthless, and usually not inhibited by morals or compassion. He will do almost anything as long as it is to his benefit. The old-fashioned Western hero tended to be too honorable, too good, and too brave to be believable; No Name is the alter ego of such contrived characters. Just as Eastwood reacted against his role as Rowdy Yates, the viewing public was equally willing to embrace an alternative to the clean-cut cowboy image. These parallel disenchantments were not only critical to Eastwood's career, they led to the dawn of a new trend in the Western movie; the establishment of the antiheroic Western as a recognizable sub-genre.

Many western antiheroes who resemble No Name are incomplete and imperfect. No Name is unrealistic because in real life people aren't usually that callous, opportunistic, antisocial, deranged, and disturbed unless they are suffering from serious mental disorders. As a result, No Name emerges as an idiosyncratic misanthrope, not a symbol of a phase of history or distinctive personality type. In addition to being an anomaly, No Name's background is purposefully hidden. He is from nowhere. His life reflects neither the modern world nor the past; the character lacks a rooting in society and a social relevance. It is true that the motif of the mysterious stranger is common in the Western, but usually such protagonists represent the anonymous frontier spirit which is fading into the sunset (moving further West). In such circumstances, the mysterious stranger is conceived of as part of the historical past and not as an antisocial outsider.

Eastwood Expands the Antihero

Eastwood appears to have realized such limitations and in 1973 (nine years after the production of *A Fistful of Dollars*), he produced, directed, and starred in *High Plains Drifter*, in which the stranger is nested within a social context. The film is significant because it was a more or less conscious remake of *High Noon*; both films concern towns which profess to be civilized but are willing to abandon morality and humanity during a crisis.

High Plains Drifter begins when a stranger comes to town and is drawn into a gunfight. After the battle in which his three opponents are killed, we learn that the dead men had been hired to protect the town from ex-convicts who, upon their release from prison, have sworn to return for revenge. The town had sent the convicts to prison years before, but they are now free and out for blood. Their protectors dead, the townspeople ask the stranger for help. Although unknown to the townspeople, the stranger is actually a ghost: the spirit of the sheriff who had been abandoned by the town and killed by the same revenge-seeking convicts he is now being asked to oppose.

The stranger accepts the town's offer, but only on his terms. He will teach the citizens to defend themselves, but he will not actually do their fighting. In the ghost's words: "You don't want to get shot. You don't want your women touched. You don't want anything to happen except you're afraid to do anything about it or you don't know how." He then provides the townspeople with a crash course in self-defense.

The ghost does some things which are blatantly symbolic. He renames the town "Hell" and appoints the town dwarf mayor. Making a stigmatized and deformed person the official representative of society allegorically underscores the fact that, morally and ethically, the citizens are disfigured. Finally the whole town is painted blood red.

When the showdown occurs, the people are unable to fend off their foes; they waited too long to learn self reliance and the town is burned. At the last moment the ghost reappears and destroys the three men who had murdered him when he had been sheriff.

Both *High Plains Drifter* and *High Noon* dwell on the amoral nature of society. The plot of *High Noon* concerns a man who initially believes in society and is slowly and relentlessly shown that his friends cannot be trusted. In *High Plains Drifter*, the protagonist had been deserted and killed years before and he has no false illusions. And, when the people do not learn to embrace justice, "Hell burns."

In the three early Leone films, No Name functioned outside of society and with few exceptions his close associates have no moral pretensions. In *High Plains Drifter*, as in *High Noon*, however, the town represents a society which pretends to be civilized and moral. By placing the stranger within such a hypocritical environment, Eastwood ceases to portray an idiosyncratic antihero and the film emphasizes the amoral nature of society. In Eastwood's words, the townspeople weren't "totally evil, they were just complacent and they just sat back and let their Marshal get whipped to death" (Kaminsky 68). Eastwood believes such amoral apathy is an evil in our society and the film can best be viewed as a commentary on this potential.

At the time *High Plains Drifter* was made, furthermore, Eastwood realized that many of his viewers possessed what may be called a revenge fantasy. In 1973 he observed: "It's not the blood-letting or whatever that people come to see in the movies. It's vengeance. Getting even is a very important thing for the public. They go to work everyday for some guy who's rude and they can't stand, and they just have to take it. Then they go see me on the screen and I kick the shit out of him" (Eastwood 1973). Sensing this emotion in his audience, Eastwood made and starred in *The Outlaw Josey Wales*, a film about a vengeful man who must overcome a lust for revenge before he can become a worthwhile member of society. *Josey Wales*, therefore, emerges as a mature Western that explores the antiheroic theme and provides an important commentary regarding modern America.

The story begins in Missouri, Jesse James' homeland, and Josey bears some superficial similarity to the legendary outlaw. Jesse and Josey—even their names sound alike—are victims of Union atrocities during the Civil War. Unlike Jesse, however, Josey eventually overcomes his hate and alienation and finds an idealized microcosm of society which he can trust.

In the film's prologue, Josey's family is needlessly killed by Redlegs, a Union guerilla. Shortly thereafter, Josey's comrades-in-arms are murdered by Redlegs under a flag of truce. Even Josey's former commanding officer, Bloody Bill Anderson, compromises himself by personally gaining when he arranged the surrender (Anderson, however, hadn't been told his men would be killed, and, therefore he is not responsible for the atrocity). Eventually Redlegs and Anderson are assigned to capture Josey, the last Confederate holdout. By this, time, however, Josey is the leader of a small segment of society and he teaches his flock how to defend themselves. Unlike *High Plains Drifter*, the high point of *Josey Wales* occurs when this group defends Josey in his time of need.

The significance of this theme to Eastwood is emphasized by the fact that it does not appear in Forest Carter's novel *Gone to Texas*, the novel upon which *Josey* is based. In *Gone to Texas*, Josey is a protector whose moral deeds are not repaid. It is hardly an accident that in the film Josey is saved by guns that are thrust through cross-shaped holes in the window shutters of the house they are defending. This symbolism underscores the fact that crosses (traditional symbols of morality) have power only when people use them in a forceful and moralistic way.

The theme of the film is best expressed in Josey's speech to Comanche chief Ten Bears when he makes peace with the Indians. In Josey's words: "Governments don't live together. People live together. Governments don't always give a fair word or a fair fight. . . . I'm not promising you anything extra. I'm just giving you life and you're giving me life. And I'm saying men can live together without butchering one another."

Although Josey has been saved by his friends, he is still unable to join their society because of his hatred, typified by his brutal slaying of Redlegs late in the film. After the killing, Josey enters the local saloon and encounters Bloody Bill, his last foe. Anderson is accompanying two Texas Rangers who are in the process of declaring Josey legally dead. Anderson recognizes Wales but says nothing; as a result, Josey is able to gain a new identity.

After the rangers depart, Anderson does not acknowledge that he recognizes Josey, but says, "I think I'll go down to Mexico to try to find him. He's got the first move, I owe him that. I think I'll try to tell him the war is over." Josey chooses to end his feud and acknowledges that all have suffered. He responds "I reckon so . . . [the war is over] . . . I guess we all died a little in that damn war." The vengeance dies and Josey and Anderson go their separate ways in peace and Eastwood transcends the totally antiheroic protagonist.

A Broader Context

Since the popularity of Eastwood's classic antiheroic No Name Westerns, several other antiheroic westerns have been made which develop the personality of the antihero and place it within a social context. Three important second-generation anti-heroic Westerns are *Bad Company*, *Pat Garrett and Billy the Kid*, and *Doc*. Each develops antiheroes who are best interpreted in social terms.

In *Bad Company*, set during the Civil War, a noble youth, Drew Dixon, goes West to avoid military service. Although he, like the stranger in *The Good, the Bad, and the Ugly*, deserts his country in a time of need, Drew's draft dodging is depicted as a reasonable (not an immoral) action. Once in St. Louis, however, Drew becomes involved with Fagin, an immoral thief and a petty con artist. Through his relationship with Fagin and a covey of youthful criminals, Drew learns the ways of a world without moral standards. On the sterile prairie, far away from culture, the world becomes increasingly dehumanized. The boys encounter a man who sells them the sexual services of his wife. One of their party is brutally killed when he attempts to steal a pie. Nobody trusts anybody and everybody is exploited by everyone else. The boys eventually turn against one another.

In *Pat Garrett and Billy the Kid* such themes are more fully developed as Pat Garrett chooses not to resist the flow of history and he drifts into the twentieth century by debasing and compromising himself through the killing of his friend Billy. Director Sam Peckinpah's conscious utilization of Garrett as a symbol of the modern antihero is demonstrated by comparing Peckinpah's own knowledge of Garrett's life with the portrayal of the film, which presents Garrett as an antihero who commits evil acts in order to survive. Peckinpah believed that Garrett ultimately redeemed himself and, like Billy, he died as a result. In Peckinpah's words: "The same people who had hired Garrett to kill Billy, years later had him assassinated because as a police officer he was getting too close to their operation. They had already killed a judge and his son in New Mexico and Garrett had indicted people for their murder. So he was assassinated" (Aghed 1973, 65). These facts contradict Garrett's symbolic role in the film, in which he survives because of his amoral capitulation.

It is significant that Peckinpah's vision of the American West is rooted in the fading of the frontier. Born and raised in Madera County, California, which was then a vestigial remain of the frontier, Peckinpah lived a rugged boyhood. He observes: "My earliest memory is of being strapped into a saddle when I was two for a ride into the high country . . . the whole family, the Peckinpahs and the Churches, had been wandering in that country since moving out from the Midwest in the middle of the 19th century" (Peckinpah 1972).

Peckinpah was taught to be independent; his father, for example: "claimed that all the animals on his land were his to do what he liked with. I was twenty years old before I knew there was a such a thing as a hunting season or a game warden and I was thirty before I began paying any attention to it." Not realizing the frontier was rapidly closing, Peckinpah "rode and fished and hunted all over that country. We thought we'd always be a part of it" (1972).

After World War II and the post-war population boom, things quickly changed. Peckinpah laments:

It's mostly gone now. Fresno's like a little L.A. today and the country around it is chopped up with new roads and resort facilities and overrun with all those shit-ass tourists and campers. My brother Danny and I were in on the last of it. A lot of the old-timers dated back to when the place had been the domain of hunters and trappers, Indians, gold miners—all the drifters and hustlers. . . . I did like that period in American life. And I liked the period I grew up in, the Thirties. It was a different America. We hadn't run out of ground. (1972)

Because he was raised on a dying frontier, the displacement of the cowboy by a lesser breed emerges as a recurrent aspect in Peckinpah's work. This theme is apparent in *Pat Garrett and Billy the Kid* even though the film's final editing proceeded against the director's wishes.

Doc, in contrast, was written by Pete Hamill, a native of Brooklyn. While Peckinpah's work is typified by a personal relationship with the old West, *Doc* resonates off the mythic impact which the Western genre has for the Eastern urbanite. Hamill notes that:

The Western had become the primary American myth by the time I was growing up in the movie house dark. . . . I suppose we all needed some myth of chivalry in those days. The Depression remained with millions of Americans; where I grew up it did not really end until the early 1950s. Men, especially in the cities, had learned that other men did not always move on their best instincts, they could be mean-spirited, cruel, evil. The Western showed us, in some basic way, that there could still be men who operated with a code of basic honor; or more properly, that there were once men who did. (Hamill 1971)

Thus, while Peckinpah's vision stems from a frontier heritage and emphasizes the fading of a world he knew, Hamill's West was a mythic Utopia where men had once been free and honorable. As a young adult, Hamill became disillusioned. He observes:

I was a New Yorker who loved my city and the people who lived in it, and I suppose I would have been a very different writer, a kind of minor-league Damon Runyon, if it hadn't been for Vietnam. . . . We were continuing to fight because of some peculiar notions of national macho pride, self-righteousness, and the missionary spirit. (Hamill 1971)

Although Hamill doesn't spell it out, it can be inferred that he found himself caught between the real and the ideal. His first novel, *A Killing for Christ*, for example, is a spy thriller about Catholicism which juxtaposes the real with the ideal church. In *Doc* Hamill debunks the idealistic myth of the West by showing long lauded heroes in a most unflattering light. The fate of the antihero is similar to that of Peckinpah's Pat Garrett; both Doc and Pat are sensitive men who ultimately must compromise themselves in order to survive.

Doc has significant flaws because the film attempts too much. Hamill simultaneously undermines so many aspects of the Western myth that the impact of the script becomes diffused and, thereby, weakened. Perhaps this is because the actual writing was, according to Hamill, an almost spontaneous creative effort. Hamill states that after wrestling with the project for months, "The film started mysteriously coming out of the typewriter . . . It was as if the film I had in my head was unspooling before me, as if I were a spectator instead of the writer. . . . Nine days after I started . . . I finished the script" (Hamill 1971). Nonetheless, an hour and a half film is too short a time to debunk the Earp-Holliday legend; develop the theme of latent homosexuality; suggest the Earp boys were infantile; and develop the overworked metaphor of a closing frontier. By scattering these numerous subplots throughout the script, Hamill dilutes the real achievement of the script: the creation of an antihero who suffers because he is essentially human.

The film begins when Doc Holliday, a long dead Doc Holliday, is surprised by our presence in a lonely and barren purgatory. All he has is a table, a stool, and a deck of cards. These are the tools of gambling, his profession, but since he exists alone, he cannot ply his trade. In an attempt to entertain his unexpected guest, Doc begins to talk about the old days, the period of the gunfight at the OK Corral. The film, therefore, uses the flashback approach.

We first see an impersonal and amoral Doc who wins the sexual services of Kate Elder in a card game. Kate had been the "property" of Ike Clanton; Doc wins her by betting his horse against the woman. Kate's wishes (and the horse's) are obviously unimportant to both men. After spending the night with Kate, Doc wants to leave her at a lonely unnamed cantina run by a fat, despised "greaser." Kate, however, nags, pleads, and cries until Doc allows her to accompany him as far as Tombstone. Later a more humane side of Doc's character manifests itself. During a dance:

The band starts to play a waltz. Doc takes Kate in his hands and wordlessly begins to dance. This is a Doc we haven't seen before, standing tall and elegant, moving in graceful precise steps, his movements evidence of a past that is irretrievably behind him. (Hamill 1971)

For a while it looks like Doc's humanity will return. Alone in his hotel one night he is reminded of Kate when he hears a waltz playing in the bar below. Suddenly, a feeling of love overwhelms him and in truly heroic fashion he breaks into the whorehouse where Kate works, kidnaps her, and begins to live with her. Doc, obviously in love, sincerely attempts to set up a home with Kate. He rents a disheveled adobe hut which is humble but can be improved. He buys Kate the trappings of domestic life, including kitchen utensils and a supply of food. Kate is also willing to change her ways and settle down. When Doc is out of town she transforms the hovel into a home. Doc returns to find "there are silk purple sheets on the bed, and a full pillow, and the brass is gleaming and polished. There are curtains on all the windows. . . . There is a thick woven rug on the floor and a tablecloth with a candlestick on the table." Even more important, Kate has abandoned her whorish ways and is dressed in a "modest gown, no cleavage" (Hamill 1971). At this point it appears that both Doc and Kate have been transformed: "We see Doc coming out of himself, as if the dead branches of trees had been given a second chance. And we see Kate freed of cynicism, so obviously in love with her flat-assed tubercular Doc that she seems a very young and open girl. The whorehouse seems behind her forever" (Hamill 1971).

This idyllic scene, however, is shattered by Doc's relationship with the Earp brothers. Wyatt hopes to make a fortune by being elected sheriff and having Doc run the gambling concession of the Alhambra Saloon. Upon hearing about Wyatt's opportunistic scheme, Doc matter-of-factly observes, "You sound like a bad people, Wyatt." (The construction of this statement mocks Wyatt's description of the Clantons as "bad people.") Although they are longtime friends and business associates, Doc has little respect for the Earps and considers them to be the "Snopeses of Tombstone" (Hamill 1971).

Doc, furthermore, resists becoming a participant in the infamous gunfight at the OK Corral. One of his potential opponents is Kid McLowery, Doc's friend and admirer. The Kid, who is like a younger brother to Doc, swore never to kill him. In addition, Doc knows that if he joins the Earps in the carnage, he will lose Kate. Doc, however, is like a moth drawn to the flame and when Wyatt asks, "You ain't gonna walk away from me now, are you John?" Doc "fatalistically, with a touch of exhaustion" responds, "I guess I'm not" (Hamill 1971).

When the gunfight ends, the Kid has a chance to kill Doc, but as he had promised he lowers his gun and refuses to shoot. As soon as the gun is lowered, Doc raises his revolver and shoots the Kid dead. The reason for this unnecessary killing is that the Kid "reminded me of too many things." As Doc says earlier in the film, "I'm sick of killing. I'm sick of seeing young kids gun down old men to prove something about their manhood. I'm sick of seeing people shot down for bullshit reasons." To Doc, killing the Kid is an act of humanity, not brutality. Because he dies in his youth, the Kid will never become an antihero such as Doc. In *Doc*, the Kid, killed in his youth (he is still embarrassed by the overtures of a prostitute and drinks beer, not whiskey), is never allowed to become a debased, antiheroical figure. Holliday leaves Tombstone after the gunfight. The story is finished, and the scene shifts back to Doc's lonely purgatory. The film ends when Doc pitifully begins to waltz alone, pretending he is dancing with his beloved Kate. Hamill's antihero is fully developed. Not only are his actions shown to be the result of his situation, but he is depicted as a real and human personality. His evil deeds affect both his foes and himself.

Conclusion

The evolution of the antiheroic Western is completely opposite that of the fatalistic Western where the heroic figure refuses to compromise and must die. Sergio Leone's initial antiheroic Westerns are imperfect because Clint Eastwood plays stick men, not vital and realistic characters. Although the antiheroic traits which Eastwood overemphasizes had often been ignored in the Western, real people are not usually as callous as the antiheroes he so often presents. Surely, some deranged or antisocial individuals do exist who resemble the "Man With No Name," but they are not representative of the old West. Before the antiheroic Western could reach maturity, the protagonists had to be portrayed as real people with human feelings and emotions. Such antiheroes may be evil, but they are still human beings with histories and feelings who become villains for reasons which we can understand.

As the antiheroic Western has become established, several explanations for the genesis of evil were offered. In *Bad Company*, a noble youth evolves into an antihero because he is forced to live on a wild frontier devoid of any law except survival of the fittest. In *Pat Garrett and Billy the Kid*, the ending of the frontier and the arrival of "corporate society" results in Pat Garrett capitulating. In *Doc*, a man is trapped by his own past and by social entanglements he cannot avoid.

The antiheroic Western has not evolved into a routine, predictable formula. One reason for this may be that various rival plot structures of the antiheroic subgenre are based upon different philosophical concepts which cannot easily be reconciled. Nonetheless, antiheroic Westerns routinely parallel Walter Van Tilburg Clark's *Ox Bow Incident,* published in 1940, even though they were not directly influenced by it. As the antiheroic cowboy protagonist ceases to be a stick man and becomes a realistic person, he begins to have more in common with Walter Clark's Gil Carter and Art Croft: the potential heroes of *The Ox Bow Incident* who reluctantly compromise themselves in order to survive.

By adjusting these themes in ways which could be embraced by the public, the emerging pattern eventually developed into the antiheroic Western: a subgenre which is recognizable and achieved a large popular following. Changing circumstances and responses to them by both creative talents and the consuming public transformed the Western in ways which were relevant for the times. As a result, the Western was started on a new product life cycle.

Works Cited

"Actor Clint Eastwood's Star: Risen." *Washington Post* 24 April 1973: Section 8: 11.

Aghed, Jan. "Pat Garrett and Billy the Kid." *Sight and Sound* Spring 1973: 64-68.

Crowther, Bosley. "Review of *The Lone Ranger*." *New York Times* 11 Feb. 1956: Section 12: 1.

Eastwood, Clint. *Hollywood Reporter* 13 July 1961.

Hamill, Pete. 1971. *Doc: The Original Screenplay*. New York: Coronett.

Kaminsky, Stuart. 1974. *Clint Eastwood*. New York: Signet.

New York Times. Advertisements for *The Searchers* 27-30 May 1956.

Peckinpah, Sam. "*Playboy* Interview with Sam Peckinpah." *Playboy Magazine* 19 (Aug. 1972): 65-76.

Review of *Fistful of Dollars*. *New York Times* 2 Feb. 1967: 29.

Sarris, Andrew. "On *The Searchers*." *Film Comment* Spring 1971: 58.

11

THE COWBOY STORY, 1820-1970:
A COMPOSITE ANALYSIS

In this monograph I have tried to demonstrate that the discipline of consumer research has much to contribute to popular culture scholarship and vice versa. Popular culture scholars have long been interested in the "marketplace" where consumption occurs; they, however, have tended to use intuitive and independently invented concepts of marketing and consumer response. When they do so, unfortunately, they fail to benefit from advances in marketing and consumer research, disciplines which are centered around the study of this kind of phenomena.

Consumer research and marketing, in turn, have increasingly become involved in borrowing concepts and research methods from the humanities in order to expand their methodological toolkit. As argued above, however, these scholars have tended to focus upon critical methods which derive from existential philosophy. As a result, over-arching culture-wide models have not been adequately applied to the field. By employing the myth and symbol method, this monograph presents an example of how structural/cultural models can simultaneously be applied to both consumer research and to popular culture scholarship.

In chapters 4 through 10, a number of authors/phases of Western American literature were analyzed. In each of these chapters, important aspects of the history of the cowboy story were interpreted and discussed through combining the methods of marketing/consumer response and literary criticism/popular culture scholarship. The result is a useful cross-disciplinary analysis that would not have been possible if these disciplines had operated independently of each other. Nonetheless, by limiting the discussion of each chapter to a particular author/phase of Western American literature, the full potential of evolutionary discussions, so crucial to both popular culture scholarship and consumer research, could not be fully accomplished.

In order to demonstrate the potential for evolutionary/historic analysis, this chapter will discuss the entire evolution of Western American literature in one self-contained discussion. The analysis, while based on earlier discussions, is completely freestanding. As a result of the freestanding nature of this chapter, parts of the theoretical underpinnings presented earlier will be repeated; dong so facilitates a self-contained presentation of the model which is used here. Starting with a discussion of the myth and symbol method and relevant theories from consumer research, a fully integrated treatment of the genre is presented in ways which respond to the needs of both popular culture scholarship and consumer research.

The Myth and Symbol Method

Literary criticism, American studies, and popular culture scholars often examine people's responses to cultural products in order to better understand the nature of North American civilization. This scholarly tradition is a focused and well established research stream which analyzes American culture and behavior patterns identified with it. The myth and symbol method provides an important intellectual framework for literary criticism, American studies, and popular culture scholarship which assumes that an overarching entity (which is usually envisioned as "American national character") exists and that it predisposes many, if not most, Americans to respond in roughly parallel ways to examples of popular culture. A favorite technique of the myth and symbol method is to suggest that American literature and popular culture embody a distinctively American content consisting, in large part, of myths and symbols. A high percentage of Americans are viewed as responding in almost identical ways to this material. Those seeking an overview of the method are encouraged to consult Smith (1957), Slotkin (1986), and Sklar (1975). In the minds of many critics (including the present writer), literary critic Leslie Fiedler is a master of this method.

A classic example of the myth and symbol school is Henry Nash Smith's *Virgin Land* (1950). As the title suggests, *Virgin Land* is primarily concerned with the image of the frontier and with its impact upon American self-identity. Smith forcefully argues that the image of the nineteenth-century West provided a number of myths and symbols that profoundly impacted American culture and the worldview which Americans embrace. By examining these symbols (in artifacts such as literature and popular culture), Smith argues that the essence of American society can be better understood. (Smith concentrates, more or less, upon "high brow" culture while numerous other scholars, such as Leslie Fiedler, evaluate popular culture.) Thus, literature is a secondary variable that is impacted and influenced by a primary variable consisting of American national character. By examining popular culture (the secondary variable), the primary variable, which is reflected therein, can be usefully analyzed.

As time has gone on, there has been a tendency for literary critics and American studies scholars to concentrate upon specific subgroups. This has led to the establishment of various schools of American studies such as neo-Marxism (Lears 1985; Jameson 1981; Williams 1977), "interpretative social science" that includes semiotics and structuralism (Rabinow & Sullivan 1979; Hawkes 1977; Bernstein 1978), and post-structuralism (Hartman et al. 1979; Johnson 1980; Arac et al. 1983). Many of these later approaches largely ignore the significance of national character in order to concentrate upon the uniqueness of specific sub-groups (that may be defined by gender, economic, racial, or ethnic identities, etc.). According to this later research stream, a focusing upon American national character is seen as directing attention away from specific groups and ignoring crucial issues concerning them. As a result of these contemporary research initiatives, the myth and symbol school has lost prestige in recent years and, currently, it is not a particularly fashionable method. It still stands, however, as a sophisticated and legitimate research technique.

While the myth and symbol school has fallen from favor in some circles, it continues to be a productive paradigm for scholars such as Richard Slotkin (1973, 1985, 1992), whose work, ironically, is a frontal attack upon Smith and the theme of Smith's *Virgin Land*. Slotkin, however, seeks to counter Smith's upbeat portrayal of the frontier myth by concentrating upon negative aspects of American life (such as the destruction of the wilderness, the genocide of native peoples, and the exploitation of the masses) which, Slotkin suggests, is also a legacy of the West. Although Slotkin profoundly disagrees with Smith on substantive matters, he continues to embrace the basic strategies of the myth and symbol method; the quality of Slotkin's work and the respect it has earned demonstrates the continued value of the myth and symbol method.

The myth and symbol method may be summarized as:

1. It possesses a willingness to analyze various genres of literature, film, and popular culture (or deal with several genres simultaneously) as required by a research project.

2. It analyzes the content of literature, film, and popular culture in order to explore and interpret culture via an analysis of motifs, character developments, etc. and how they evolve or remain stable in different times and places.

3. A relatively long time frame is used in order to spot trends, inconsistencies, and to project the future.

A key component of the myth and symbol method is that it carefully analyzes the content of literary art and popular culture and interprets them from cultural and sociological perspectives. Although the myth and symbol method has been infrequently utilized in recent years, it remains a powerful tool that has many contributions to make to both popular culture and consumer research.

The Life Cycle of Products and Their Diffusion

As suggested above, the myth and symbol method can be used to demonstrate how the fluctuating popularity of literary products can provide clues regarding the culture and the evolving consumption patterns of its members. These abilities are somewhat paralleled by concepts in marketing and consumer research, such as the product life cycle and the diffusion of innovations model. By linking the myth and symbol method with these marketing/consumer research techniques, a useful integration of the two fields can be established.

The concept of the product life cycle (initially developed by Everett Rogers in 1962) is a related model that draws an analogy between the career of a product and the history of a living organism (which is born, matures, and eventually dies). Although a wealth of variations in the product life cycle have been discussed (Michael 1971; Sproles 1981), a general and recognizable pattern (or some might say metaphor) has emerged. First, there is an introduction phase that corresponds with birth (when the new product is young and helpless). During this period, sales levels are low and the product tends to be adopted primarily by a small group of elite individuals. As time goes on, however, the product moves through the growth and maturity stages. When this occurs, the more mainstream members of the society begin to adopt the product. Responding to new target markets, the product must be adapted to them and adjusted to fit their pocketbooks.

Eventually, the product falls into a decline which might result in residual sales to a small segment of "diehard" customers; on other occasions, the product "dies" and it ceases to exist in the marketplace. Any significant innovation of the product or its marketing, however, may result in the product being "reborn" which starts it on a new product life cycle. Although its value has been debated (Dhalla & Yuspeh 1976), the product life cycle has emerged as one of the most useful formulations in marketing and consumer research. While contemporary observers often suggest that it must be applied with insight and caution, the product life cycle is routinely employed by both practitioners and scholars.

Well-established, the diffusion of innovations and the product life cycle models are poised to help analyze how specific genres of popular literature evolve through time and predict who will consume literary products at specific times. Since literature, film, and popular culture are products, various theories from marketing and consumer behavior may be employed when analyzing them. Doing so can be accomplished in tandem with the use of humanistic theories.

Combining marketing theories and the myth and symbol method, this discussion suggests that genres of literature, film, and popular culture (like other products) go through "life cycles." These life cycles, furthermore, can be restarted via a significant innovation which gives the product (genre of popular culture) a new lease on life. Certain identifiable classes of people, furthermore, are prone to adopt products at specific times during its life cycle.

In addition, literature, film, and popular culture often have symbolic meanings that can demonstrate the underlying and evolving belief system held by significant segments of the culture. By viewing specific creative artists and their products within this social context, literary critics/popular culture scholars can merge relevant theories from marketing and consumer research in mutually beneficial ways.

The Cowboy Story: An Overview

As indicated above, the myth and symbol method examines literature, film, and popular culture in order to document and analyze aspects of culture and society. Various mainstream critics have included popular Western or cowboy stories[1] within the sample of works they analyze. By doing so, critics gain a greater flexibility than if they had concentrated solely upon so-called "serious literature." Some popular culture scholars have specialized in analyzing the cowboy story. Continuing this tradition, the present paper examines the cowboy story as a genre of popular culture that has been distinctive from the time of James Fenimore Cooper.

The work of Richard Slotkin, used as a touchstone, will prepare the reader for the synthesis of consumer research and popular culture scholarship that follows. Slotkin has written an impressive multi-volume review of Western American literature and culture (which he calls "mythology"). To a large extent, Slotkin's writing is a reaction against that of Henry Nash Smith's upbeat and positive portrayal of the American West as a garden of Eden. Slotkin, in contrast, questions this depiction and concentrates upon the negative heritage of the westward movement.

Slotkin is an excellent writer and the general strategies which he embraces are representative of the myth and symbol method. At the beginning of *Regeneration through Violence*, for example, Slotkin observes: "The mythology of a nation is an intelligible mask . . . of national character" (1973, 3). Having made this statement, Slotkin examines this "mythology" of the West and the frontier in order to understand American culture. Thus, Slotkin finds mythology to be a secondary variable that is impacted by national character, the primary variable. By examining and exploring this secondary variable, therefore, key aspects of the primary variable (the subject of interest to the scholar) can be better understood.

By looking at this technique, so well demonstrated by Slotkin's work, it becomes possible to quickly grasp the methodology to be used here:

1. This discussion seeks a greater knowledge of how the American national character and/or the belief structure typically held by Americans have evolved through time.

2. It is assumed that the propensity to consume examples of popular culture that embrace specific myths and symbols is, to some degree, influenced by the prevailing belief structure and national character held by the members of a culture.

3. Since it is possible to investigate the popular culture of earlier generations and how the public of those eras responded to it, consumer researchers can chart how changes in national character and/or belief structures have impacted changes in the consumption of certain types of popular art.

The discussion of the modus operandi of the technique (above) lays the methodological foundation which is embraced in this culminating chapter.

James Fenimore Cooper: The Introduction Stage

James Fenimore Cooper, the first major American novelist, created an immortal heroic figure who possesses an uncompromising morality but is profoundly vulnerable to the amoral forces of society. Cooper's frontier fiction concentrated upon the plight of strong-willed and moral individuals who live in an immoral world. Cooper believed that the noble and self-reliant hero would ultimately be displaced by a society that he depicted as amoral at best. Such sentiments can be seen as a partial reworking in America of Jean-Jacques Rousseau's concept of the noble savage as merged with Cooper's vision of morality and coupled with perspectives that were influential in Cooper's time.

Cooper's most profound achievement was to create a distinctive frontier protagonist who was ultimately recast as the cowboy hero

(Walle 1973; 1976). Cooper, like later writers, nested the fate of the hero into what can be viewed as the flow of history. So doing, the Leatherstocking Tales (Cooper's five-volume frontier saga featuring Natty Bumppo, the frontiersman hero) and especially *The Pioneers* and *The Prairie* (two volumes in the series) emerge as a symbolic/mythic epic that caught the imagination of Cooper's contemporaries. The consuming public accepted the flow of Cooper's plotlines and his work emerged as the popular literature of his era.

In *The Pioneers*, Natty Bumppo, the noble hero, has long helped the people of Templeton (presented as a symbolic microcosm of the emerging sedentary culture) to establish themselves in the wilds of upstate New York. Bumppo represents the frontier personality who has the misfortune of being displaced by the coming of civilization. Throughout *The Pioneers*, Natty evaluates people, statuses, rights, and privileges using his own standards; as a result of his personal style, he must eventually go West where society has not entrenched itself and where he can act according to his beliefs. The climax of *The Pioneers* is a case in point: Judge Temple is the leader of the society that is entrenching itself in upstate New York. He is the owner of the land, the maker of the laws, and the self-styled judge of other people. Natty, using frontier logic, kills a deer in violation of Judge Temple's arbitrary laws and, in the eyes of the established legal system, he becomes an outlaw. As a last straw, Natty disrupts the decorum of established law and is banished to the wilds where his character is not at odds with the prevailing regime. He and his dog are last seen retreating into the untamed forest where society has not yet reached. This plotline connects the idea of the noble savage with views of society which were held by the social elite of early nineteenth-century America.

Many noted critics view Cooper as a true visionary. In this regard, Francis Parkman, the acclaimed historian of the American West and author of the ever-popular *The Oregon Trail* (1846), observes:

Of all American writers, Cooper is the most original, the most throughly national; His genius . . . [sprang] from the soil where God planted it, and rose to a vigorous growth . . . [although Cooper had faults as a writer]. A rough diamond, and he is one of the roughest, is worth more than a jewel of paste, though its facets may not shine so clearly. (1852)

Cooper's fiction resonates with the spirit of the times and it symbolically depicts the prevailing world view held by the elites of early nineteenth-century America. The consuming public embraced Cooper's work because it symbolically portrayed (even as it helped to define) a prevailing belief structure.

In *The Prairie* (sequel to *The Pioneers*, where Natty Bumppo had earlier been banished to the wilds), he finds a permanent home in "the Great American Desert" where organized society cannot usurp him. In accordance with the worldview of the times, Cooper depicted the prairie as a desert where sedentary, "civilized" life cannot establish itself. Cooper, accepting the conventional wisdom of his times, falsely depicted the Midwest as an uninhabitable desert which, in reality, was not the case (Flanagan 1941). Finding a haven in the barren prairie, Cooper's strong-willed and highly moral Bumppo is able to live out his days without being dispossessed by the encroachment of an effete and amoral society.

Cooper's literary innovation, represented by the combined plotlines of *The Pioneers* and *The Prairie*, therefore, has four basic components:

1. The hero is a moral person whose very morality makes him the antithesis of established culture. He is somewhat (but not totally) related to the concept of the noble savage.

2. Due to conflict between the individualist hero and a culture based on conformity and compromise, society rejects the noble hero.

3. The hero retreats to where society cannot usurp him.

4. This plotline flows in accordance with the prevailing worldview held by the elites of Cooper's era.

Cooper's work satisfied his market. Both *The Pioneers* and *The Prairie* were best-selling novels of their day and established Cooper's reputation as a major literary talent and taste maker. Many years later, primarily because of public demand coupled with Cooper's financial needs, he wrote additional Natty Bumppo novels that deal with the hero's younger days. As with the prequels of many authors, however, these latter works are not of the same quality as the originals and they do not advance Cooper's vision.

As is often the case when new, innovative products are first being marketed, Cooper's original customers (his readers) were educated, affluent, and of relatively high social class; they emerge as "innovators" according to the diffusion of innovations model. And, as is also typical of the adoption curve, as time went on the product was embraced by other groups ranging from "early adopters" to the "late majority." A product variant aimed at the late majority is the so-called "dime novels" of the late nineteenth century.[2] These cheap uninspired versions of Cooper's original plotline were marketed to poor, uneducated people of low social class. A good discussion of this phenomena can be found in Daryl Jones' *The Dime Western Novel* (1978), which analyzes the popularity of specific plot formulas.

Thus, although the typical customers for this product (the cowboy story) changed over the years, its basic structure did not change. Quality, however, sank lower and lower. And, in line with the diffusion of innovations model, those who consumed this product ceased to be the elite, as the product became embraced by those on the lower rungs of society. As is usually the case under such circumstances, the product (1) became tailored to the demands of the late majority as (2) quality fell.

Cooper, therefore, created a major innovation by portraying the frontier hero as a noble, but overspecialized, product of the wilds destined for eventual oblivion and banishment as society asserted itself. Cooper's original customers can be viewed as the innovator class and Cooper went to great lengths to cater to this group. Other groups embraced the product as it was abandoned by the elite. For seventy years after its introduction, Cooper's plot formula remained current although, in accordance with the theories of consumer behavior, the people buying the product evolved from social elites to the lower classes. By the turn of the twentieth century, the product survived primarily in low quality magazines and cheap novels aimed at the masses.

The Cowboy as Superman: A Restart of the Product Life Cycle

As indicated above, by the late nineteenth century, the product (the cowboy story as represented by Cooper's original plot formula) was in the later stages of the product life cycle. And, in accordance with the diffusion of innovations model, the product was primarily embraced by individuals who were members of what consumer researchers call "the late majority": lower-class individuals, the last to adopt a product. Thus, Cooper's innovation exhibited all the earmarks of a product in serious decline. By and large, the literary elites had gone on to other things, such as the psychological novel (as developed by elite writers such as Henry James). Although Cooper's variant of the frontier or cowboy story survived in cheap fare marketed to the lower classes, the future for the product looked bleak. A plotline that suggested that the frontier personality cannot make the transition to the modern world became passé. In addition, the symbolic displacement of the distinctive American hero undercut the attempt of the North American elite to assert that North American civilization existed on a par with (if not actually superior to) older European society. Since Cooper believed that civilization and the frontier were incompatible, his plot formula seemed to depict European-derived civilization as superior to that of the new world. As a result,

Cooper's plotlines came to contradict the vision of the late nineteenth-century American elite (who increasingly viewed the frontier heritage as the catalyst which gave Americans a distinctive superiority). The 1890s was the era which codified the "frontier thesis" of American history that argued that Americans had evolved a unique and superior civilization due to the impact of the frontier experience. According to historian Frederick Jackson Turner (1893), the existence of a rugged frontier and 400 years of Americans being in contact with it had created a new breed of person and a new type of culture. The ancestry of most Americans came from the old world where, Turner suggested, individual strength had become submerged beneath the dictates and priorities of a complex culture and an overbearing society. Nonetheless, Turner continued, the challenge of a raw frontier helped such civilized weaklings to regain a degree of self reliance and personal strength that had atrophied in a more sedentary Europe.

The frontier, Turner continued, had closed about 1890 and although occasional pockets of wilderness survived, they are surrounded by civilization and will inevitably be annexed by it. Nonetheless, Turner insisted, the heritage of the frontier experience would continue to impact American culture and society for many years to come since it had given rise to a strong and virile personality type and created a national character which led to greatness.

Originally formulated in 1893, the frontier thesis was quickly embraced by the American elite. For many years, Americans had been made to feel like second-class intellectuals by Europeans who suggested that American achievements were but pale reflections of more sophisticated European prototypes. The frontier thesis, in contrast, reversed the tables by asserting that on the wild frontier Americans had honed their skills to an edge far sharper than that of their European counterparts and in the process they had created a distinctiveness all their own. Clearly this new vision needed to be portrayed in a symbolic way. Published in 1902, Owen Wister's *The Virginian* phrased this emerging worldview in fictional form in what many critics believe is the seminal or archetypical cowboy story.

Significantly, Wister borrowed some aspects of the Cooper formula while discarding and adjusting others. The personalities of Cooper's Natty Bumppo and Wister's Virginian, for example, are identical; both are strong men who are willing to use their own personal morality as a guide, even if doing so results in transcending the norms of mainstream society. While Cooper's and Wister's heroes are largely interchangeable, their fates are profoundly different. Cooper's Natty Bumppo is cast out of society and forced to survive in a hinterland where society has not been established. Wister's Virginian, in contrast, learns the practical and moral lessons of individualism while living on a wild frontier. After this apprenticeship, he is able to rejoin society and emerge as superior to it.

The Virginian was quickly embraced by the social elites because it updated Cooper's formula using perspectives provided by the frontier thesis. As often happens in marketing, an innovation in an existing product restarts its product life cycle; as a result, the product is again successful and influential. While keeping the personality of the frontier hero constant, Owen Wister transformed his protagonist from a weak person banished to the hinterland to an all-powerful superman who, having learned the lessons of the frontier, returns to civilization vital and triumphant. At the end of *The Virginian*, for example, Wister observes: "[The Virginian] was an important man with a strong grip on many various enterprises" (1902, 506). While Cooper's Natty Bumppo had to hide out in the desert, the Virginian returned East and became a pillar of society. Not only is the Virginian a strong moral influence, he is able to forcefully achieve pragmatic goals in his dealings with society.

Becoming established around the turn of the twentieth century, this updating of the cowboy story originally appealed to social elites who were looking for an apology for capitalism and for a means of portraying American civilization on a par with (if not altogether superior to) older European cultures. Since European intellectuals often asserted their superiority and depicted the New World as provincial, American elites needed a means of blunting Old World claims of supremacy. The frontier thesis provided an intellectual rationale for doing so and *The Virginian* emerged as a symbolic articulation of these beliefs.

Wister, himself, was a "blueblood" and socially connected; he had many elite tastemakers as personal or family friends. Revealingly, *The Virginian* was dedicated to Wister's personal friend, Theodore Roosevelt (who was president of the United States when the novel was published and whose flamboyant life demonstrated how a strong dose of the frontier could lead to both personal success and profound achievement). Equally significant is the fact that Roosevelt personally took a hand in fine-tuning this emerging American "myth." Speaking directly to Roosevelt in his dedication, Wister observes: "Some of these pages you have seen, some you have praised, *one stands new-written because you blamed it*" (1902, iv, italics added).

Owen Wister's cowboy hero, via his social Darwinistic portrayal of the frontier thesis, provided the American elite with the intellectual justification its members needed to portray themselves as superior to their rivals from the Old World. It also intellectually justified the economic system that was beginning to dominate in early twentieth-century America. The elite were concerned with both issues and they found a symbolic working out of these tensions in the cowboy story. According to Moody Boatwright, Wister had a publishing contract with publishers who were dedicated to advancing the worldview of the elite:

Horace Lorimer, who took over the editorship of the *Saturday Evening Post* in 1898 and, frankly, made it the voice of American business, assembled a stable of Western writers, including Wister, and through them kept before his readers *the cowboy as a symbol of the rugged individuals that had made America great.* (1951, 151, italics added)

As time went on, popular writers and various forms of mass communication (movies, radio, and TV programs) brought Wister's innovation to a wider audience. As in the case of the later variants of Cooper's plotline, furthermore, Wister's heroic figure came to be embraced by people who were further down the rungs of the diffusion of innovations ladder. In addition, the Wisteresque hero became involved in a long series of morality plays directed primarily at children. Thus, although a few examples of "the thinking man's Western may have survived," Wister's innovation increasingly become known as a genre for people of low social class and for children. This situation remained until the 1960s when the formula again changed.

Aborted Innovations

As is widely acknowledged within consumer research, creating a significant innovation does not insure success in the marketplace. Besides providing a new option, innovations must be made available at a time when the public is willing to embrace them; otherwise consumers will not accept the product even if it is "superior." If the timing is wrong, innovations cannot be successfully marketed.

In the history of the twentieth-century cowboy novel, there are at least two classic examples of high quality innovations that failed because the public rejected them. They are represented by Zane Grey's *The Vanishing American* (1927) and Walter Van Tilburg Clark's *The Ox Bow Incident* (1940). Both novels significantly transcended Wister's social Darwinistic/frontier thesis plotline by updating its message to new realities. Both are excellent examples of fiction created by acknowledged writers. Neither, however, was able to make an impact on the evolution of the cowboy story in any meaningful way. From a consumer research point of view, both were unsuccessful innovations because they were presented to a public which was not ready to accept them.

Zane Grey, of course, was a wildly successful author of cowboy novels that were targeted towards the general public. For many years,

Grey provided his readership with tales in which the hero, after overcoming great obstacles, emerges victorious. On one occasion, however, Grey experimented with an innovative plotline in which the noble hero fails and dies. This notable innovation, *The Vanishing American* (1927), was viewed as offbeat and Grey reverted back to upbeat plotlines in order to please his paying customers.

In *The Vanishing American*, the hero, a Navajo, finds himself pitted against government agents who administer the reservation. Many immoral actions of the debased Eastern bureaucrats are chronicled as are the hero's attempts to correct them. At book's end, the strong, noble individualist totally embraces his indigenous (read frontier) culture and in a traditional rite of passage, performs a ceremony involving exposing himself to the elements. As a result of this ritualistic ordeal that indicates his maturity and a positive embrace of his heritage, he catches influenza—a disease brought by the whites—and dies. Symbolically, the novel asserts that those who are noble and true to themselves will be destroyed by an inferior, but dominant culture, metaphorically depicted by the lowly virus which has been brought by the white man. In recent years, the plight of the American Indian has been increasingly recognized and discussed in both fiction and nonfiction. The reader is encouraged to consult Berkhofer (1978) and Drinnon (1997) for relevant background. Although these themes regarding Native Americans have only recently been forcefully articulated in fiction and nonfiction, they were anticipated by Grey, who strategically abandoned them when they proved to be unpopular with the reading public of his era.

The message of *The Vanishing American* is that even a strong, noble, and superior individualist is no match for the impersonal forces of society. Just like Cooper's Natty Bumppo, the cards are stacked against Grey's hero and he can't win; both are fatalistic heroes who although glowing with individualism and "self-actualization" (to use Abraham Maslow's term), are ultimately defeated. Death comes as a direct result of a positive asserting of one's true self. Viewed objectively in terms of writing quality and plot development, *The Vanishing American* is a high point in Grey's career (Walle 1976). Such plotlines, however, were not demanded by the reading public of Grey's era and he adjusted accordingly; he never replicated this pessimistic plotline and he reverted to upbeat stories which were popular with his audience and provided consumers with what they wanted to buy and experience.

While Grey's aborted innovation depicted the noble hero who remains true to himself and dies as a result, Walter Van Tilburg Clark created amoral potential heroes who are forced to capitulate in order to live. Clark's *The Ox Bow Incident* (1940) was one of the most celebrated Westerns of the twentieth century. Made into a highly successful movie, the antiheroic message reached a wide audience. Today, it is highly regarded by literary and film critics.

In the *Ox Bow Incident*, three innocent men suspected of murder and cattle rustling are hanged at a lynching. In large part, the story is an analysis of the interworkings of mob rule. The plot, however, is much more complex than that; more central to our chain of thought is the fact that there are two decent men in the posse who doubt that the suspects are guilty. They alone can save the doomed prisoners from the irrational mob. Why don't they? Precisely because they are strangers in the area and, therefore, they are the only other possible suspects. By not interfering with the posse, these capitulaters allow the mob's vengeance to be dissipated in a way which does not threaten them. "The *Ox Bow Incident* is about the eclipse of morality by personal interest . . . [the main characters] allow a lynching to take place because they have a vested interest in transferring suspicion from themselves to someone else. . . . As a result of their inaction, three innocent men are hanged" (Walle 1995, 60-61). Thus, while the hero of *The Vanishing American* confronts evil and dies, the antiheroes of *The Ox Bow Incident* abandon the code of virtue and act in ways which insure their own partisan interests.

Although *The Ox Bow Incident* was a best-selling novel and although it is still highly regarded by literary and film critics, it did not undercut the dominance of the Wisteresque cowboy story that depicted the hero as a moralistic superman whose prowess was wrought on the frontier. Instead critics viewed the novel as "serious fiction," which merely used the conventions of the western as a literary device. Some critics even described the novel as a symbolic tale about Nazi Germany set in the old West. In a similar way, Leslie Fiedler suggests the plotline is actually about race relations in the American South and the posse is analogous to the KKK. Fiedler argues that the lynching, authorized by a former Confederate officer, replicates oppression and genocide directed at black Americans (1968, 142).

Clark rode the waves of *The Ox Bow Incident*'s success to an impressive literary career, but he made a professional transition from writing cowboy stories to catering to literary elites by writing "serious fiction" and other, more "high brow," literary forms. As in the case of Grey's *Vanishing American*, Clark's *Ox Bow Incident* came and went without influencing the genre of the cowboy story or the tastes of the general public.

Consumer researchers are aware of many examples of seemingly superior innovations that ultimately proved to be unsuccessful among consumers because the public was not ready for them. In such cases, a product might be ranked as "superior" based on many criteria, but still be unsuccessful in the marketplace. In many cases, a product, although "superior," according to yardsticks of evaluation held by the producers, may not win sales and loyalty. Clever marketers often develop specific techniques for overcoming resistance; thus, Microsoft's Windows 95 is a superior product, but its developers realized that the market might resist it since parts of the product were "new" and "strange." Microsoft's solution was to allow the user to merely push a button in order to make the new innovative product "look like" the old, familiar Windows 3.1. *The Vanishing American* and *The Ox Bow Incident*, in contrast, reflect the potential failure of products which cannot be adjusted to mesh with the expectations of consumers and their demands. Both were excellent works of fiction and each, in its own way, advanced the formula of the cowboy novel by adjusting it to an evolving world. Both, however, were rejected by the public because the timing was off; the content did not mesh with the tastes and expectations of the audience. As a result, neither innovation was able to transform the cowboy story and restart it on a new product life cycle.

In the 1930s and 1940s, the frontier thesis that argued that the frontier had honed American national character to a new level of greatness, was still a strong and widely cherished belief. *The Vanishing American* and *The Ox Bow Incident* undercut these popular vision by suggesting that the strong moral force wrought on the rugged frontier faces two un-enviable alternatives: (1) remaining true to itself and dying (2) and/or capitulating to the immoral forces of society in order to survive. Because these innovative products contradicted the popular worldview of the times, both were rejected by the public even though literary critics have praised them.

A Final Restart of the Cowboy Story "Product Line"

Consumer researchers agree that innovations (even if superior and skillfully wrought) will not impact a product or influence potential consumers if they are offered at the wrong time or in an inappropriate context. As has been argued, in the 1920s through the 1950s the fatalistic and antiheroic western plotlines were innovations that were out of sync with popular belief. As a result, these products were rejected by the consuming public and they failed to exert a lasting impact upon the product line of the cowboy story.

Ultimately, there was nothing "wrong" with these innovations; the timing was merely off. As American culture evolved, however, these plot formulas came to symbolically portray a worldview which became increasingly popular with a sizable segment of society. When this occurred, the fatalistic and antiheroic product variants were able to restart the product life cycle of the cowboy story.

In post World War II America, an evolving view began to undercut the frontier thesis that asserted that the rugged individualist was an all-conquering hero. A number of notable monographs analyzing American culture, including William Whyte's *The Organization Man* (1956), David Riesman's *The Lonely Crowd* (1950), and Philip Slater's *The Pursuit of Loneliness* (1970), pointed to the fact that many Americans were hurtfully cut off from others and unable to successfully function in isolation. *The Organization Man,* written in the 1950s, reflects the changing temper of the times; its basic premise is that although Americans hold rugged individualism as an ideal, in the modern world of bureaucracies, it becomes increasingly difficult to successfully live by such a code. According to Whyte, post World War II Americans found themselves in the untenable position of having to either (1) abandon their individualistic ideals in order to survive/succeed in the modern world or (2) live an individualistic life and become a dysfunctional failure as a result. Note how these two orientations parallel the plotlines of Grey and Clark.

If *The Organization Man* is used as a barometer with which to chart a major adjustment in the American worldview, a turning away from the Turner thesis by a significant segment of the market can be seen. This emerging worldview acknowledges that individualism does not inevitably lead to success and that it can prove to be counterproductive within society. In some ways, Whyte's orientations are a re-embrace of James Fenimore Cooper's belief that the strong-willed individualist could not function effectively in a collective, social world.

In the 1960s, as this worldview became popular among Americans, the fatalistic and antiheroic innovations of the cowboy story, unacceptable from the 1920s to the 1950s, emerged as viable products. The fatalistic Western used the cowboy to symbolize a vestigial remain that might be noble and heroic but is ill-equipped to function in the modern world. Perhaps the classic and most popular example of the genre is Paul Newman and Robert Redford's *Butch Cassidy and the Sundance Kid.* (The seminal films of this type are Samuel Peckinpah's *Ride the High Country* [1961] and Kirk Douglas and Dalton Trumbo's *Lonely Are the Brave* [1962].) In this highly regarded blockbuster film, the lives of two rough and tumble, devil may care Western individualists face an encroaching civilization. Increasingly unable to compete in the modern world which is emerging, the heroes (like Natty Bumppo) retire to vestigial hinterland retreats. Mass civilization, however, relentlessly pursues them and they are finally unceremoniously gunned down by an army of lackluster automatons. Although individually, Butch and Sundance are portrayed as superior to the "organization men" who destroy them, their death is depicted as the inevitable result of their refusal to adjust to changing times.

While the fatalistic Western chronicles the displacement and/or death of the noble, individualistic product of the frontier, the antiheroic

Western demonstrates how people can survive if they abandon heroic virtue. Clint Eastwood's early Westerns are classic examples of this genre; in these films, Eastwood portrays a Westerner who has abandoned the last vestiges of nobleness associated with the "white hatted" cowboy hero. Although (and possibly because) they have rejected a noble life, Eastwood's characters survive. Eastwood's characters capitulate and/or compromise themselves; and, as a result, they don't have to die like Butch and Sundance.

Although these fatalistic and antiheroic Westerns closely parallel the earlier prototypes of Grey and Clark, they were not influenced by them. Instead, they sprang from the minds of writers, directors, and actors who were influenced by changing times not by literary history. By the 1960s, America had changed to such an extent that scenarios dealing with a flawed hero were popular with the public and made sense of it. When applied to the cowboy story, these plotlines emerged as viable innovations that restarted the product life cycle of the cowboy story.

Both of these subgenres, furthermore, were embraced by what can best be viewed as "innovators" or "early adopters" before reaching a mainstream audience. In this case, innovation is largely associated with youth. The Western plot formula associated with Owen Wister and Frederick Jackson Turner was increasingly unappreciated by young people. The adult population, however, tended to prefer the older plot formulas. Such preferences reflect the findings of consumer researchers Holbrook and Schindler (1989; 1994), who find that "tastes for popular culture" are formed at "sensitive periods" of individuals, typically during their early twenties. According to Holbrook and Schnidler, such orientations are useful in predicting consumer demand for products. The segment of the population which reached adulthood prior to the 1950s were introduced to the Wisteresque version of the cowboy story at a "sensitive period" in their lives and, as a result, they developed a preference to it.

Those who came of age in the post World War II era, in contrast, were more likely to be influenced by worldviews which militated against the symbolic view of American history presented by Turner and Wister. By the 1950s the white-hatted cowboy hero, who was noble and invincible, had emerged as a stickman marketed primarily at children and not to be taken at face value by adults. It became all too easy for the baby boom generation to view the Wister-type cowboy story as juvenile and to discard it.

The present author can personally remember various conversations during the 1960s in which some people objected to antiheroic and fatalistic westerns because of a belief that the cowboy should (1) maintain his virtue and (2) should succeed. The logic of such observations hinged around a perceived need to preserve the noble image of the cowboy so it could be mimed by children. Even in "adult Westerns," however, the Wister formula fought against pessimistic revisions; John Wayne and Howard Hawks, for example, explicitly made *Rio Bravo*, a conventional Western where virtue prevails, in order to rebut *High Noon*, a proto-fatalistic Western in which the hero, abandoned by the town he loves, develops a contempt for civilization because he was abandoned in his time of need. As is often the case when new products are being developed, some people do not realize when a restart of the life cycle is taking place. Wayne and Hawks seemingly viewed *High Noon* as a random event and not as a prelude to the evolution of the genre.

Others foresaw the transformation for what it was: a restart of the cowboy story on a new product life cycle. In the case of *Lonely Are the Brave*, for example, Kirk Douglas clearly realized his fatalistic film, scripted by Dalton Trumbo, marked a departure from earlier westerns. In this low budget, but influential film, the hero (a symbol of the rugged individualism associated with the old West) comes in conflict with society and faces minor legal proceedings brought on by his disrespect for authority. When he escapes from jail, however, this insignificant trouble escalates and he becomes a wanted man being hunted down by a well-organized and well-financed posse. Nonetheless, the individualist hero is able to thwart all attempts by "organization men" to defeat him. When he attempts to cross a highway, his last hurdle to freedom, however, he is struck and killed by a truck full of toilet bowls. The truck and its cargo (flush toilets are symbolically used to depict civilization) demonstrate that although the hero is superior to the specific "organization men" who he faces, the onslaught of modern civilization is unstoppable and individualistic people who stand in its way will be destroyed.

Douglas, aware that the film was a significant transformation, wanted to initially cater to innovators. He states: "I disagreed with their [the studio's] releasing pattern. . . . I pleaded with them to put it in one little theater in New York and just wait and see what happened. Instead, they released it to a large number of theaters like an old fashioned western which, of course, it wasn't" (Douglas 1976). In an ill-conceived marketing blunder by the film distributors, *Lonely Are the Brave* was not released to innovators as Douglas had hoped but dumped on a mainstream audience that was not ready for it. As a result, the film was not financially successful when it was released. Today, however, it is recognized as a masterpiece of the fatalistic sub-genre.

Within a few years of the release of *Lonely Are the Brave*, new plotlines had proceeded through the diffusion of innovation cycles and the fatalistic *Butch Cassidy and the Sundance Kid* emerged as a blockbuster at the box office. Thus, between 1820 and 1970 the cowboy story went through various permutations which reflect both the product life cycle and the diffusion of innovations model. This transformation is best understood by using a social interpretation which links the myth and symbol method with models of consumer research.

Discussion

The basic analytic device employed here is derived from the myth and symbol method of American studies and popular culture scholarship combined with a number of relevant marketing concepts. In summary, the chain of thought presented here argues that:

1. James Fenimore Cooper began the product life cycle of the cowboy story by depicting a strong, individualistic, moral force which was ultimately cast out of an amoral society. As time went on, the mythic elements of this product were embraced by others further down the diffusion of innovations cycle; late 19th century "dime novels," for example, brought it the lower classes. Cooper's product had a long life, although the target markets which embraced it changed over the years.

2. In the 1890s, historian Frederick Jackson Turner developed the frontier thesis of American history that asserted that American culture was superior to its European prototypes because exposure to a wild and raw frontier had honed the American spirit to a razor sharp edge. The frontier experience, the theory continued, made Americans and American culture inherently superior to their European counterparts. This theory led to an updating of the myth of American history. Owen Wister, although building on some key components of Cooper's work (such as Bumppo's character), changed the cowboy story by portraying the product of the frontier as successful in the modern world in ways which dovetail with the Turner thesis.

3. Although Wister's vision remained in vogue for a long period, certain authors transcended it; Zane Grey depicted the fatalistic hero while Walter Van Tilburg Clark portrays protagonists who suppress heroic potentials. The innovations of Grey and Clark had little impact upon the cowboy story because they conflicted with the prevailing worldview of the era.

4. By the 1960s, the American worldview evolved in ways which allowed the antiheroic and fatalistic Westerns to win popularity. A changing worldview transformed unacceptable variants of the cowboy story into major and lucrative innovations which symbolically portrayed the dilemmas of modern America.

This analysis blends the techniques of the myth and symbol method with relevant business theories of consumption such as the product life

Evolution of the Cowboy Story: A Generic Overview

Issue	Cooper's displaced hero	Wister's triumphant hero	Clark and Grey's mistimed innovations	Antiheroic and fatalistic plots successful
Plot	Noble hero cast out of society. Retreats of safe hinterland	Noble hero tempered on frontier. Returns to society as superior achiever.	*Clark:* Potential hero compromises himself to live. *Grey:* Noble hero dies	Clark's and Grey's innovations are successfully re-introduced at a later time.
Heroic persona	Strong, moral individualist, product of the frontier.	Same as Cooper.	*Clark:* Men become amoral to advance their agendas. *Grey:* Because he remains true to his ideals, the hero dies.	Same as Clark and Grey.
Fate of hero	Vestigial remain who must avoid society in order to survive.	Vital achiever who, having learned the lessons of the frontier, is able to surpass products of civilization.	*Clark:* By abandoning heroic mantle, survival is assured. *Grey:* By remaining true to ideals, hero brings on own death.	Same as Clark and Grey.
Worldview embraced	No place for individualism and the heritage of the frontier.	Frontier creates superior breed. Benefits survive closing of frontier.	Personality type represented by the cowboy hero cannot function in emerging world.	Same as Clark and Grey.
Evolution of genre	Genesis of frontier story as distinct genre.	Wister restarts the genre by responding to new worldview.	Society not ready for innovations. As a result they do not impact the genre.	When society ready to accept innovative product, they are successful.

Figure 1.

cycle and the diffusion of innovations model. By recognizing how these two research streams parallel and reinforce each other, scholars will be able to see how they can merge these research traditions in useful ways. In order to dramatize these correspondences, a series of point by point comparisons will be made. As a means of setting the stage for this analysis, a generic overview of the evolution of the cowboy story is presented in tabular form in Figure 1.

Having provided this generic overview, it becomes possible to focus upon more specific comparisons involving the myth and symbol method, on one hand, and the diffusion of innovations and the product life cycle models, on the other. In doing so, the compatibility of these different research streams is demonstrated. Figure 2 demonstrates the

Diffusion of Innovations and the Myth and Symbol Method Compared

Issue	Diffusion of Innovations Model	Myth and Symbol Method
Significance of social elites	Social elites wish to maintain status by demonstrating their distinctiveness. Products are used to portray superiority. This tendency is demonstrated by the plots of Cooper and Wister	The elites often provide literary innovations and present myths and symbols that become standardized. These motifs often depict the superiority of the elite. Both Cooper and Wister asserted the status of the American elite.
Not all innovators are elite	Rehabilitators of the trickledown theory point to other factors that are essential to a revised and updated theory. Since youth is one of these factors, the updated theory can account for the initial acceptance of the fatalistic and antiheroic westerns by youth.	The myth and symbol school often finds different groups (such as youth) may respond in ways that are (1.) different from the mainstream and (2.) prove to be avant garde. Since these critics often look beyond the myths and symbols of the elite, they have a broader vision.
Why innovation fails	Consumer researchers realize that most new products fail since they do not mesh with expectations, worldviews, and preferences. Producers and marketers must remember to consider products from the point of view of the consumer.	Scholars (such as the new critics) focus upon their own yardsticks of evaluation, not the readers. The myth and symbol method, in contrast, views literature from the reader's perspective in order to interpret society. As a result literature and popular culture become a lens with which society can be examined.
Overview	Both the expanded diffusion of innovations model and the myth and symbol method are designed to explore how and why certain products are successful or unsuccessful in the marketplace. Both models follow the behaviors of the elites when appropriate and center upon other phenomena as circumstances warrant. And both models can learn from failure in the marketplace.	

Figure 2.

similarities between the diffusion of innovations model and the myth and symbol method.

Clearly, the methods, goals, and orientations of the diffusion of innovations model and the myth and symbol method are largely parallel and can be pursued in concert with one another. A similar situation can be portrayed by a point by point comparison of the myth and symbol method and the product life cycle, as shown in Figure 3.

These two tabular comparisons demonstrate how the myth and symbol method parallels existing models from consumer research. As a result, consumer researchers can usefully augment their intellectual toolkit by incorporating the models, strategies, and tactics of the myth and symbol method in appropriate and useful ways.

Indeed, it is even possible to combine this myth and symbol analysis with the popular charting of the product life cycle as shown in Figure 4.

Product Life Cycle and Myth and Symbol Method Compared

Issue	Product Life Cycle	Myth and Symbol Method
Products analogous to living beings	Products, like living beings, go through a process of "birth", "growth", "maturity", "decline", and "death". By perceiving products in these terms, it becomes easier to understand their current status and what the future holds. There is no reason why this model cannot be expanded to deal with artistic products.	Myth and symbol critics are aware of the fact that certain literary genres go through cycles in which their popularity grows and wanes. These trends can prove useful as critics explore the evolution of society via an examination of the myths and symbols embedded in works of art. The metaphor of the product life cycle is a useful way of portraying these shifts in popularity through time.
Innovation can restart Product Life Cycle	Old products can be "restarted" on a new product life cycle. When this happens, the lifecycle process begins anew. The evolution of the cowboy story can be presented as an examples of this principle.	By focusing upon the myths and symbols present within various sub-genres and why they succeeded and/or failed over time, insights regarding literature, society, and product evolution can be gained.
Products must cater to consumer demands	Markets and their demands are constantly changing. Due to this fluid situation, the viability of certain products (and who will adopt them at certain periods) evolves. Products can cater to consumer demands by either (1.) catering to different markets as circumstances warrant or (2.) by evolving in order to satisfy the demands of specific targets. The history of the cowboy story is a textbook example of these processes.	The myth and symbol method seeks to understand the society via an examination of the motifs and plot elements inherent in works of art. It acknowledges that to be successful, artistic products must satisfy consumer demands. As society evolves, updated reworkings of existing myths and symbols are embraced by audiences.
Overview	Both the product life cycle and the myth and symbol method agree that products go through cycles that may be depicted as life cycles. Both techniques also link success in the marketplace to responding to the demands of a target market. And both recognize that an older, declining product can be returned to health by adjusting it to the marketplace.	

Figure 3.

Consumer researchers have long perceived the value of both (1) researching literature, film, and popular culture and (2) the appropriateness of borrowing/adapting specific concepts from the humanities. This book has taken this intellectual cross-fertilization one step further by systematically looking at a specific critical tool, the myth and symbol method, and showing how it fruitfully augments and supports important perspectives of marketing and consumer research. This book presents but one example of how consumer researchers and popular culture scholars can join forces in mutually beneficial ways.

The Product Life Cycle of the Cowboy Story

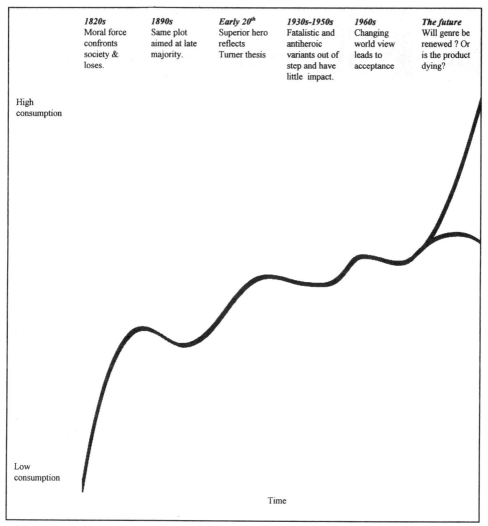

Figure 4.

Conclusion

The discussion has shown how the myth and symbol method can be employed in ways that usefully illustrate how consumers respond to popular culture. The value of this model is bolstered by the fact the myth and symbol method can be correlated with a number of well-known marketing/consumer behavior theories; as a result, this synthesis is more robust than if they were each employed in isolation.

The historic analysis of how products and their popularity evolve through time is very important to both consumer researchers and popular culture scholars. This chapter has demonstrated that by combining the myth and symbol method with models of consumer research, a robust and mutually beneficial cross-disciplinary analysis is possible. The resulting analysis, furthermore, is more productive and far-reaching than if the two disciplines were working independently of each other.

In recent years, consumer researchers have increasingly embraced humanistic research strategies. Most of the existing research, however, has concentrated upon what can be called "formalist" criticism that is linked to post World War II French philosophy. This research stream has been fruitful and is applauded. Nonetheless, other more macro cultural models, such as the myth and symbol method, are valuable and they have a significant role to play within this emerging cross-disciplinary endeavor. This discussion has provided a demonstration of this potential.

Notes

1. For my use of the terms "cowboy story," "Western," and "frontier fiction," see p. 52 above, note 2.

2. Ronald Fullerton, the marketing historian, has a professional interest in the cowboy story. He, however, has focused upon European variants of this literary tradition; for that reason, his work will be acknowledged, but not considered here.

Works Cited

Arac, Jonathan, Wlad Godzich, and Wallace Martin, eds. 1983. *The Yale Critics: Deconstruction in America*. Minneapolis: U of Minnesota P.

Belk, Russell. 1987. "A Child's Christmas in America: Santa Claus or Deity, Consumption or Religion." *Journal of American Culture* 10.1: 87-100.

Belk, Russell, and Richard Polley. 1985. "The Good Life in Twentieth Century Advertising." *Journal of Consumer Research* 11: 887-97.

Berkhofer, Robert F., Jr. 1978. *White Man's Indian: Images of the American Indian from Columbus to the Present*. New York: Vintage.

Bernstein, Richard J. 1978. *The Restructuring of Social and Political Theory*. New York: Harcourt Brace Jovanovich.

Boatwright, Moody. 1951. "The American Myth Rides the Range: Owen Wister's Man on Horseback." *Southwestern Review* 36 (Summer): 157-63.

Clark, Walter Van Tilburg. 1940. *The Ox Bow Incident*. New York: Random House.

Dhalla, Nariman K., and Sonia Yuspeh. 1976. "Forget the Product Life Cycle Concept." *Harvard Business Review* 54.1: 102-10.

Douglas, Kirk. 1976. Personal communication.

Drinnon, Richard. 1997. *Facing West: The Metaphysics of Indian-Hating and Empire Building.* Norman, OK: U of Oklahoma P.

Emerson, Ralph Waldo. 1837. "The American Scholar." *Ralph Waldo Emerson: Selected Prose and Poetry.* Ed. Reginald L. Cook. New York: Holt, Rinehart & Winston.

Fiedler, Leslie. 1969. *The Return of the Vanishing American.* New York: Stein & Day.

Flanagan, John T. 1941. "The Authority of Cooper's *The Prairie.*" *Modern Language Quarterly* 2: 99-104.

French, Phillip. 1973. *Westerns: Aspects of a Genre.* New York: Viking.

Grey, Zane. 1927. *The Vanishing American.* New York: Grosset & Dunlap.

Hartman, Geoffrey, Harold Bloom, Paul de Man, et al., eds. 1979. *Deconstruction and Criticism.* London: Routledge and Kegan Paul.

Hawkes, Terence. 1977. *Structuralism and Semiotics.* Berkeley: U of California P.

Holbrook, Morris, and Mark Grayson. 1986. "Cinematic Consumption: Symbolic Consumer Behavior in *Out of Africa.*" *Journal of Consumer Research* 13.3: 374-82.

Holbrook, Morris, and Robert Schindler. 1989. "Some Exploratory Findings on the Development of Musical Tastes." *Journal of Consumer Research* 16 (June): 119-25.

——. 1994. "Age Sex, and Attitude. . . ." *Journal of Consumer Research* 31.3: 412-23.

Jameson, Fredric. 1981. *The Political Unconscious.* Ithaca: Cornell UP.

Johnson, Barbara. 1980. *The Critical Difference.* Baltimore: Johns Hopkins UP.

Jones, Daryl. 1978. *The Dime Western Novel.* Bowling Green, OH: Bowling Green State University Popular Press.

Lears, T. J. Jackson. 1985. "The Concept of Cultural Hegemony: Problems and Possibilities." *American Historical Review* 90: 567-93.

Levitt, Theodore. 1965. "Exploit the Product Life Cycle." *Harvard Business Review* 43.6: 81-94.

Levy, Sidney. 1981. "Interpreting Consumer Mythology: A Structural Approach to Consumer Behavior." *Journal of Marketing* 45.3: 49-61.

Lipsky, David, and Alexander Abrams. 1995. *Late Bloomers: Coming of Age in Today's America: The Right Place at the Wrong Time.* New York: Random House.

Lounsbury, Thomas R. 1882. *James Fenimore Cooper.* Boston: Houghton & Mifflin.

McCracken, Grant. 1985. "The Trickledown Theory Rehabilitated." *The Psychology of Fashion*. Ed. Michael R. Solomon. Lexington, MA: Lexington Books.

——. 1986. "Culture and Consumption: A Theoretical Account of the Structure and Movement of the Cultural Meaning of Consumer Goods." *Journal of Consumer Research* 13: 71-84.

McDonald, Archie. 1987. *Shooting Stars: Heroes and Heroines of Western Film*. Ed. Archie McDonald. Bloomington: Indiana UP.

Michael, C. G. "Product Petrification: A New State in the Product Life Cycle." *California Management Review* 14.1 (Fall 1971): 88-91.

Parkman, Francis. 1929. *The Oregon Trail*. Boston: Little Brown. Originally published in 1846.

——. 1852. "The Works of James Fenimore Cooper." *North American Review* 74: 147-61.

Parks, Rita. 1982. *The Western Hero in Film and TV*. Ann Arbor, MI: UMI Research.

Rabinow, Paul, and William M. Sullivan, eds. 1979. *Interpretive Social Science: A Reader*. Berkeley: U of California P.

Riesman, David. 1950. *The Lonely Crowd: A Study of the Changing American Character*. New Haven, CT: Yale.

Rogers, Everett. 1983. *Diffusion of Innovations*. 3rd ed. New York: Free P. Originally published in 1962.

Sklar, Robert. 1975. "The Problem of American Studies 'Philosophy': A Bibliography of New Directions." *American Quarterly* 27: 245-62.

Slater, Philip Elliott. 1970. *The Pursuit of Loneliness: American Culture at the Breaking Point*. Boston: Beacon P.

Slotkin, Richard Sidney. 1973. *Regeneration through Violence: The Mythology of the American Frontier 1600-1800*. Middletown, CT: Wesleyan UP.

——. 1985. *The Fatal Environment: The Myth of the Frontier in the Age of Industrialization*. New York: Atheneum.

——. 1992. *Gunfighter Nation: The Myth of the Frontier in Twentieth Century america*. New York: Atheneum.

——. 1993. "Buffalo Bill's 'Wild West' and the Mythologization of the American Empire." *Cultures of United States Imperialism*. Ed. Amy Kaplan and Donald E. Pease. Durham, NC: Duke UP.

Smith, Henry Nash. 1950. *Virgin Land: The American West as Symbol and Myth*. Cambridge: Harvard UP.

Sproles, George B. 1981. "Analyzing Fashion Life-Cycles—Principles and Perspectives." *Journal of Marketing* 45.4: 116-24.

Stephen, Michell. 1994. "Jacques Derrida." *New York Times* 23 Jan.: 22.

Stern, Barbara B. 1994. "Classic and Vignette Television Advertising Dramas: Structural Models, Formal Analysis, and Consumer Effects." *Journal of Consumer Research* 20 (March): 601-15.

———. 1995. "Consumer Myths: Frye's Taxonomy and the Structural Analysis of Consumer Texts." *Journal of Consumer Research* 22 Sept.: 165-85.

———. 1996. "Deconstructive Strategy And Consumer Research: Concepts and Illustrative Exemplar." *Journal of Consumer Research* 23 Sept.: 136-48.

Turner, Frederick Jackson. 1894. "The Significance of the Frontier in American History." *Annual Report of the American Historical Society.* New York: American Historical Society.

Walle, Alf H. 1972. "The Western Hero: A Static Figure in an Evolving World." Presented at the Annual Meeting of the American Folklore Society, Nashville, TN.

———. 1973. "The Frontier Hero: A Static Figure in an Evolving World." *Keystone Folklore* 19: 207-24.

———. 1974. "Review of Richard Slotkin's *Regeneration through Violence: The Mythology of the American Frontier: 1600-1800.*" *Ethos* 25 (April): 24.

———. 1975. "Review of Phillip French's *Westerns: Aspects of a Genre.*" *Ethos* 26 (Feb.): 15.

———. 1976. *The Cowboy Hero: A Static Figure in an Evolving World.* Disseration written at the University at Buffalo, NY.

———. 1992. "High Noon and Its Analogues: Politics and the Western." Film, Individualism and Community Conference, Towson State University, MD.

———. 1994. "Walter Van Tilburg Clark's *Ox Bow Incident*: Prototype for the Antiheroic Western." *Platte Valley Review* 23.1: 50-67.

———. 1996. "Habits of Thought and Cultural Tourism: A Nineteenth Century Example." *Annals of Tourism Research* 23.4 (Oct.): 874-90.

Whyte, William. 1956. *The Organization Man.* Garden City: Doubleday.

Williams, Raymond. 1977. *Marxism and Literature.* Oxford: Oxford UP.

Wilson, Edmund. 1950. *Classics and Commercials.* New York: Farrar & Strauss.

Wister, Owen. 1902. *The Virginian.* New York: Macmillan.

Wright, Will. 1975. *Six Guns and Society.* Berkeley: U of California P.